THE 100 BEST Technology Stocks FOR THE LONG RUN

Investing in the New Economy and the Companies That Make It Click

SECOND EDITION

Gene Walden

Dearborn™
Trade Publishing
A Kaplan Professional Company

Editorial Director: Donald J. Hull
Senior Managing Editor: Jack Kiburz
Interior Design: Lucy Jenkins
Cover Design: Jody Billert, Billert Communications
Typesetting: the dotted i

Published by Dearborn Trade Publishing, a Kaplan Professional Company

Printed in the United States of America

01 02 10 9 8 7 6 5 4 3 2 1

Library of Congress Cataloging-in-Publication Data

Walden, Gene.
The 100 best technology stocks for the long run : investing in the new economy and the companies that make it click / Gene Walden.— 2nd ed.
p. cm.
Rev. ed. of: The 100 best internet stocks to own for the long run, 2000.
Includes index.
ISBN 0-7931-4437-X (paperback)
1. Internet industry—Finance—Directories. 2. High technology industries—Finance—Directories. 3. Online information services industry—Finance—Directories. 4. Investments—United States—Directories. 5. Stocks—United States—Directories. I. Title: One hundred best technology stocks for the long run. II. Title: Hundred best technology stocks for the long run. III. Walden, Gene. 100 best internet stocks to own for the long run. IV. Title.
HD9696.8.U62 W35 2003
332.63′2—dc21

2001003419

Dedication

To the memory of Clara and Walter Gingery

Contents

Alphabetical Listing of the 100 Best Technology Stocks

Acknowledgments

This book would not have been possible without key contributions from several people. Tom Shaughnessy, who was my coauthor on *The 100 Best Internet Stocks to Own for the Long Run,* offered additional technical advice and assistance for this book. Ed Lawler, who is an accomplished business book author, wrote a number of the company profiles in this book, as he has for several other *100 Best* books. Larry Nelson, who has helped on nearly every book I've written in the past decade, worked from start to finish on this project, assisting with the research and fact gathering, the graphs, the tables, and other key elements of the book.

I would also like to thank my editors at Dearborn Trade Publishing, including Cynthia Zigmund, vice president and publisher; Don Hull, editorial director; and Jack Kiburz, senior managing editor. Each helped develop and fine-tune the book into an attractive and professional format.

Acknowledgments

Introduction

Technology is slowly taking over our lives. From cell phones and home electronics to computers and the Internet, from genetically engineered drugs and implantable medical devices to the tiny microchips that control automotive functions and home appliances, the technology revolution has been following us through virtually every phase of our lives. And the end is nowhere in sight.

Despite the economic bump in the road that derailed many technology companies in 2000, the technology revolution continues to rumble along like a runaway freight train. Technology has been the driving force of the economy for the past quarter century, and it will continue to play an expanding role for decades to come, both in our daily lives and in the global economy.

This book features 100 companies that have been leading the technology revolution. The list is as diverse as technology itself, including microchip makers, computer makers, biotechs, software designers, and telecommunications, networking, and Internet companies, among others. The companies featured here are not only leaders in their particular niche, they also have a history of exceptional revenue growth, and—with few exceptions—a history of strong earnings growth. And all 100 are in industry sectors that appear to have the potential for solid growth for years to come.

Although technology stocks will continue to be volatile in the short term, technology remains a good bet for the long term because of the strong prospects for continuing innovation and advancement in every phase of the technology realm. There is no other area of the economy with the promise and possibilities of the technology sector.

WHAT HAPPENED?

Technology investors may never be the same after watching the recent tech crash that wiped out nearly $5 trillion in market capitalization and dropped tech stock prices to a fraction of their highs. The debate may rage for years on exactly what caused the biggest technology stock market crash in history. The most frequently offered explanation is simply that the speculative bubble burst, but that really explains very little. Let's briefly explore the causes of the crash—not for the purpose of reliving the misery that devastated many investors, but rather to identify some warning signs that might keep you from falling prey to the next market meltdown.

There were several elements that contributed to the crash. No question, part of the problem was the overexuberance of speculative investors who pushed Internet and technology stocks up to sky-high levels. Investors in search of the next home run were paying huge premiums for companies with short track histories and no earnings. A market correction was almost inevitable. But many economists have put part of the blame on some ill-advised policy decisions by the Federal Reserve.

Here are ten key events of the tech crash:

1. Quickly rising prices of tech stocks (particularly Internet stocks) attracted a horde of new investors to the tech sector who continued to push up prices.
2. Rapid revenue growth of tech stocks raised expectations of long-term hypergrowth, giving investors a reason to keep bidding up prices. Investors using margin accounts to borrow money and buy more stock pushed margin account levels to an all-time record.
3. Brokerage companies large and small jumped on the Internet bandwagon, offering nearly universal "buy" and "strong buy" recommendations on scores of unproven Internet stocks with little or no earnings. Striking while the iron was hot, brokerage firms also issued a record number of initial public stock offerings, often for shaky Internet retailers with little prospects for profitability. At their urging, the public continued to buy and drive up prices of the stocks to unreasonable levels.
4. Federal Reserve Chairman Greenspan and his board, fearing inflation and overexuberance in the stock market, started raising interest rates and tightening the money supply.
5. Internet and technology companies began to show some signs of weakening prospects. Reports from the industry indicated that the technology buying binge was beginning to soften. Ignoring the signs, the Fed continued to raise rates and tighten the money supply.
6. Internet companies, no longer able to get new financing to expand their businesses because of the tightened money supply, began to report financial difficulties. The Fed continued to ignore the signs and continued to tighten the money supply, citing their fear of inflationary pressures (although there was no evidence of mounting inflation).
7. The technology market began to slide as Wall Street traders began to anticipate a deep drop in tech company growth rates. Falling prices forced margin investors to sell out part of their portfolios, forcing a faster drop in the market, including a precipitous fall in prices in March and April 2000. The Fed continued to ignore the signs and, despite no signs of inflation, decided to raise rates yet again. The market contin-

ued to tank, and the technology sector continued to weaken. Wall Street stood behind their drooping picks. At one point, when the Nasdaq was down 60 percent, less than 1 percent of analysts' recommendations were to sell.

8. Once the market meltdown was underway and technology companies began reporting significant declines in sales, the Fed finally stopped raising rates and tightening the money supply, but took no action to move the economy in a positive direction.
9. The bankruptcies and closings of more than 1,000 Internet businesses, coupled with a steep decline in spending by telecommunications services companies, pushed more tech businesses to the verge of bankruptcy. The Fed finally began making moves to adjust the money supply and lower rates. Too little too late. The technology industry was in the middle of a recession, and investors had lost trillions of dollars in assets.
10. Once the Fed began to act decisively, it was too late to stem the tide, and the economic hardships and mass layoffs continued. Only after a series of aggressive Fed moves to boost the economy did the market finally begin to rebound on hopes that the slump in technology sales would end soon.

What are the repercussions of the tech crash? In addition to devastating losses in the retirement funds of millions of investors, the layoffs of tens of thousands of technology workers, and the bankruptcies of hundreds of young Internet and technology businesses, technological progress also took a hit. Advances in wireless and Internet services slowed considerably. DSL Internet access continued to be elusive in most parts of the country, and new generations of electronics and video products were put on hold or shelved altogether. Companies such as Copper Mountain that offered innovative new products for the telecommunications industry were forced to slash their staffs and cut their research budgets dramatically.

On the bright side, investors were able to buy into the technology revolution at a much lower price. Many stocks that once sold for $100 to $300 per share dropped to under $30. On the Internet, a new, more realistic business model has begun to take shape. Online retailers are striving to sell their goods at a profit (what a bold new concept!) and online services companies are finding that they can actually charge a reasonable fee for some services. Even America Online was able to raise its rates 10 percent without losing customers. The technology and Internet revolution remains alive and well with a few adjustments along the way.

What lessons can investors learn from the tech crash? Maintain a diversified portfolio, invest in what you know, and beware of stocks and entire sectors with excessive prices and price-earnings ratios (PEs). If the PEs climb over the 100 level, start looking for the next big opportunity and be ready to bail out of the overpriced sector. A correction is inevitable. Buying young, speculative companies with little or no earnings may be okay if you can get them at a bargain, but not at a premium. Many Internet and technology stocks were selling for 20 to 40 times sales—about 10 times typical levels. That's too much to pay for nearly any stock, let alone stocks with no earnings. One final lesson from the tech meltdown: Don't fight the Fed. When the Federal Reserve sets out to flatten a market, there's a good chance that sooner or later it will succeed.

THE FACE OF TECHNOLOGY

The technology revolution affects nearly every phase of our daily lives. Here is a brief look at the key technology sectors represented by the stocks in this book.

Computers. The engine of the technology revolution, the computer may finally have reached a temporary saturation point with American consumers. But newer, more power-hungry software and Internet applications should prompt consumers to keep buying upgraded PCs. Advances in graphics should also keep sales moving for the new generation of monitors and color printers. Corporations and organizations will also need to update and replace old computer equipment and peripherals to keep up with the increasingly sophisticated enterprise software and e-commerce applications. Dell and IBM are leaders in computer sales for both consumers and businesses. Advances in graphics, voice and video applications, and expanded use of e-mail and e-commerce have also created a rapidly growing demand for data storage systems. Companies that make data storage devices, such as EMC and Advanced Digital Information Corp. (ADIC), have seen their sales soar as organizations scramble to keep up with the increasing demand for data storage.

Semiconductors. Also referred to as "chips," "microchips," or "integrated circuits," semiconductors are the brains of the technology revolution. They are used to control a broad range of electronic devices, including computers, home appliances, machinery, automobiles, phones, remote control devices, and a growing legion of other products. Most chips are composed of a fingernail-sized sliver of silicon with layers of precise circuitry. The microchip market has been growing rapidly in recent years.

The real challenge in the semiconductor market is to continue to make the chips faster yet smaller. Traditionally, the number of transistors on an integrated circuit has been doubling about every 18 months. But now that some semiconductor components are as small as 1/500th the diameter of a human hair, reducing the size of the chips further is becoming increasingly difficult. Companies are turning to new materials to keep the shrinking process going. Some manufacturers are using copper in place of aluminum to connect the components, which improves conductivity. Others are replacing silicon with gallium arsenide, because its inherent physical properties allow its electrons to move up to five times faster than those of silicon.

There are many different types of chips:

- **Standard logic chips** are the traditional chips manufactured to exact specifications for a predetermined application.
- **Programmable logic chips** have become increasingly popular because they can be programmed to fit a particular application in computers, telephones, equipment, and industrial applications.
- **Flash memory chips** retain data even when the power is turned off. They are the primary memory devices for cellular telephones, set-top PC boxes, and many other electronic devices.
- **Static random access memory chips** are typically used for storage and retrieval of data in data communications, telecommunications, computers, and other electronic systems.
- **Linear circuits** are used primarily to monitor, condition, amplify, and transform continuous analog signals associated with physical properties, such as temperature, pressure, weight, light, sound, or speed.
- **Application specific standard products (ASSPs)** are designed to perform specific end-user applications, such as automotive remote keyless entry systems, automatic garage and gate openers, and smart cards.
- **Mixed signal devices** are used primarily in embedded control systems to convert or buffer input and output signals to or from a microcontroller. They are also used in disk drives, cell phones, and telephone line cards. Mixed signal is a mixture of analog and digital, usually for data conversion and signal processing.
- **Random access memory chips (RAM)** are sometimes referred to as the scratch pad of personal computers, because they temporarily store the instructions or data for software programs when they are being used by the computer. RAM is used in servers, workstations, computer games, telecommunications equipment, personal digital assistants, and other memory-intensive systems. DRAMs (dynamic random access memory chips) are similar but more powerful than RAMs.

- **Analog microchips** convert analog signals such as sound, light, temperature, and pressure into the digital language of numbers, which can be processed in real time by a digital signal processor. Analog integrated circuits also translate digital signals back to analog. They are used in electronic devices such as cellular phones, computers, printers, hard disk drives, modems, networking equipment, digital cameras, motor controls, automobiles, and home appliances.

Although the microchip market has been highly volatile, the long-term growth of the sector has been phenomenal and should continue its strong growth—with some occasional dips—well into the future. The number of chips manufactured worldwide in 1990 was 134 billion, and by 2004 that figure is expected to top 700 billion.

Software. Software serves as the operating system for computers and other types of electronic equipment and devices. Microsoft is the leader in the software market with its Windows operating software and its word processing, spreadsheet, financial, and other software applications. Oracle is the leader in business software, with a line of software for database and development, sales and service, manufacturing and supply chain, and finance and human resources applications. Other software companies offer software for a wide range of applications, including financial services and accounting, engineering and design, manufacturing and robotics, graphics, entertainment, and Web applications.

Telecommunications. Once one of the brightest spots of the technology industry, the telecom sector slipped into a severe slump as orders for new equipment dried up suddenly and dramatically. But with the growth in demand for cell phones, modem lines, faxes, and other telecommunications services, the telecommunications industry should rebound over time. Leading the way will be companies such as JDS Uniphase and Corning, who are leaders in high-speed fiber-optic equipment. Manufacturers of wireless equipment and high-speed routers and switches will also benefit from a rebound in the telecommunications industry.

Networking. Computer networking has become big business as large corporations and organizations add more applications and personnel to their already complex enterprise systems. Leaders in the networking sector, such as Foundry Networks and Brocade Communications, make products that tie together wide area networks (WANs) and local area networks (LANs).

Biotech. The mapping of the genetic code has opened up a new world of medical technology. Medical professionals and investors alike have been licking their chops at the enormous promise of biotechnology. While experts in the medical field have been pondering new cancer cures, cloned organ transplants, the prevention of birth defects, and a wide range of other medical advances that biotechnology could bring, investors have been betting on the profit potential of those miracle cures. Several of the stocks in the biotech sector, such as Genentech and Amgen, are already making money, and many of those that aren't have been posting exceptional revenue growth. One of the most promising areas of biotech is the quest for new and better cancer treatments. There are more than 120 forms of cancer, and traditional treatments such as chemotherapy have never been particularly successful. Not only is the cure rate for most forms of treatment unacceptably low, but the treatments also lead to a number of disturbing side effects, such as nausea, hair loss, removal of body parts, and the weakening of the body and its functions. But new advances in biotechnology could lead to cancer cures with a much higher success rate—without the side effects. One treatment now under development is *immunotherapy,* which relies on the body's natural healing mechanisms to find and destroy malignant cells without harming normal ones. Further development of cancer cures and other biotech therapies should lead to huge profits for the companies that get their products to market ahead of the pack.

THE INTERNET

With millions of computers sprouting on desktops across America and around the world in the 1980s, the computer revolution was in full force. But there was one missing ingredient—the ability of all of those computers to communicate with one another.

This critical shortcoming was not lost on two academics at Stanford University. In 1984, husband-wife team Len Bosack and Sandy Lerner noticed that students and researchers still had to physically exchange floppy disks in order to communicate. Lerner and Bosack saw this "sneaker net" arrangement as a gaping hole in the fabric of the computer age. They were aware of a networking technology called *local area networks* (LANs) that enabled users connected to the same cable to freely share data, printers, and messages. But there was still no easy way to share data between different LANs.

To solve the problem, the couple invented a device called the *router,* a combination of hardware and software designed to automatically move "packets" of data between LANs. Soon they had the Stanford campus wired with their routers, linking LANs into an "inter-network" that connected departments and labs. That was the birth of internetworking.

Bosack and Lerner went on to found Cisco Systems, which pioneered the development of the Internet and helped make the World Wide Web accessible to hundreds of millions of users around the world.

How the Internet Works

Put simply, the Internet is a decentralized collection of computers bound together by an intricate networking system called the Internet Protocol. The Internet Protocol, or IP, enables users to communicate with each other regardless of the make, model, or operating system of their computers. IP works its magic through two basic technologies:

1. A standardized "digital packet format" that can transport data across any local area network hooked to the Internet
2. An "addressing scheme" that directs packets of data anywhere on the Internet, with a minimum number of hops along the way

Internet Protocol was invented by the U.S. Department of Defense to enable its contractors in industry and academia to share research and development data more easily. But right away, people started using the fledgling IP network for such things as freewheeling discussion groups and e-mail. Word soon spread that IP was the unifying networking system for which the world had been waiting.

The Internet is anarchy by design. There is no central authority controlling Internet operations—in part because no central management team could possibly administer something of such size and dynamism. The closest thing to a central authority is a group called the Internet Society, based in Reston, Virginia. This not-for-profit organization coordinates such things as technical standards and the task of doling out IP addresses and domain names.

There is no dividing line between private organizations hooked to the Internet and the Internet itself. They are one and the same. The Internet is a "network of networks" through which traffic freely travels, but each network is independently owned and operated. Homes and small businesses link up to Internet service providers (ISPs) via dial-up connections, while larger companies have routers permanently connected to their ISPs, Larger companies operate private internetworks—called *intranets*—that are kept mostly inaccessible to Internet traffic. At the Internet's core is a "backbone" composed of Internet service providers freely exchanging traffic between themselves across very high-speed links. (A *backbone* is a network that only has other networks connected to it rather than user devices such as PCs or servers. This lets backbones operate at much higher speeds than regular LANs.)

This universe of home and small business users, corporate intranets, and Internet service providers adds up to the Internet as we know it.

Key Infrastructure Technologies

Computers on the Internet are connected by a global lattice of network devices and telecommunications links collectively called the *infrastructure.*

You've probably heard the term *bandwidth* used in connection with Internet speed. Bandwidth is the measure of how much raw data can be moved over a network link. The type of cable a network link uses can give it more bandwidth in much the same way that having eight lanes along a stretch of interstate highway will move traffic faster than four lanes.

The Internet is tied together through several key technologies:

Routers. The most important piece of Internet equipment is the router, the device that reads IP addresses in data packet headers to steer traffic to the correct destination. The router is the Internet's enabling technology.

You might think of the Internet as a global telephone system that handles data instead of sound waves. When you dial a phone, your call is switched between hard-wired circuits to find a path to the number you dialed. By contrast, when you send an Internet message, you turn your data packets over to a nearby router and leave it to that device to figure out how to get the packets to the destination.

While Web surfers generally use domain names, such as <www.allstarstocks.com> to move around, network devices translate them into numerical addresses, such as 209.22.234.19. Routers use the numerical IP address—not the domain name—to find the computer it represents. The development of the Internet Protocol system into a worldwide network made it possible for the first time for any computer user to communicate with virtually any other user.

Routers know the best routes to take at any given moment because they exchange updates on the status of nearby network links every few minutes. Send a message to the same IP address five minutes later, and your data packets may take a different route based on changing traffic patterns, a link gone down, a new link brought up, or some other factor. Physically, most routers look like VCRs, although the big ones resemble dormitory refrigerators or even full-sized ones. Like all network devices, routers are "black boxes" with no monitor, keyboard, or other peripherals. In fact, network devices don't even have disks for the simple reason that their sole mission is to move data to the "next hop" along the way, not to store it.

Switches. The switch is closely related to the router in that both are used to move data between LANs. Switches are dumber than routers, but they work a lot faster. Unlike routers, switches don't read IP addresses and don't exchange information on the best routes to take between locations. They simply keep a running list of what was recently sent from point A to point B. Demand for switches is booming. In fact, switching technology is now being integrated into routers to help speed things up by making it unnecessary to read IP addresses except for data packets headed to new or faraway destinations.

Firewalls. A *firewall* is a kind of router that specializes in security. It works by forming an intentional bottleneck in the flow of traffic between an intranet and the Internet. As traffic flows through the firewall, each data packet is inspected to enforce security rules programmed by the company's Network Manager.

Access servers. The most prevalent Internet technology is the access server, a device that answers calls from users logging in by phone. Internet service providers use banks of access servers to connect home subscribers, and companies use them to connect telecommuters. The trend in access servers is to build more intelligence into them, especially to provide better front-end security and do a better job of routing calls between the telephone network and the intranet.

Network media. Sometimes called "bandwidth" or "pipe" for short, this is the technology that moves data through physical space. Although simple twisted-pair copper is used in most office LANs, the future is in fiber optics. Fiber-optic technology passes data as light waves over glass or plastic strands instead of as electrical pulses over metal. All Internet backbones are now fiber, and all office LAN backbones soon will be. Thousands of times faster than metal cable, the only things holding fiber optics back are the electronic devices terminating the cables. Tens of billions of dollars are now being invested in fiber-optic plants.

Network appliances. "Network appliances" is a catchall name used to describe any specialized piece of network hardware dedicated to performing a single function. Examples include biometric devices that verify a user's fingerprint or retinal pattern before allowing log-in; so-called load-balancers, which shuffle traffic in and out of servers more efficiently; and credit card readers attached to home PCs.

E-COMMERCE

Although Amazon and other online retailers get most of the publicity, e-commerce between businesses is the bedrock of the Internet economy. It dwarfs e-tailing in size, accounting for about 80 percent of all electronic business.

Companies are flocking to business-to-business e-commerce—usually called B2B or *e-procurement* for short—because trading online saves money and eliminates paperwork. The benefits of B2B are so great that it's not a question of whether most companies will do their buying over the Internet, but *when*.

How fast is B2B growing? It accounted for only 2/10 percent of the trade between U.S. businesses in 1997. By 2003, it's expected to account for at least 10 percent—a 50-fold increase in just six years. Growth rates of this magnitude are unprecedented, but these startling projections seem reasonable in light of B2B's compelling benefits:

- **Lower transaction costs**. Processing a purchase over the Web can reduce administrative overhead by up to 70 percent.
- **Shorter purchasing cycles**. The average time between placing and filling an order is reduced from over seven days to less than two.
- **Improved inventory control**. Some early adopters of B2B report inventory carrying costs reduced by one-quarter to one-half.
- **Lower prices paid**. Increased bidding competition lowers the prices by as much as 10 percent.

Collectively, these operational benefits can reduce procurement costs by up to 15 percent. Some companies are reporting a 300 percent return on their investment in e-procurement in the first year alone.

Consumer spending on the Internet is not growing at quite the same pace. In fact, online sales account for no more than 1 percent of all retail sales. But that will change in the years ahead, particularly as mainstream brick-and-mortar stores such as Wal-Mart and Best Buy place increasing emphasis on their online marketing.

Online retail sales are already growing between 100 and 200 percent per year, but the growing dollar volume has not yet translated into profits for online retailers. Nevertheless, the online retail market still holds vast potential. Web efficiencies will become more of a factor as more households connect to the Internet and consumers grow more comfortable with the idea of using credit cards on the Web. As Internet sales climb beyond 1 percent of the $5 trillion retail market, and as e-tailers reach out to consumers in Asia and Europe, the growth of the e-tailing market could be substantial.

SELECTING THE 100 BEST TECHNOLOGY STOCKS

Narrowing the field of hundreds of technology stocks to an elite 100 was no small task. To assemble the list, I looked at the stock holdings of all of the top performing technology mutual funds, reviewed dozens of articles on technology stocks from magazines and newspapers, scanned the Web for news stories on technology stocks, talked to a few money managers and analysts, and ran a number of computerized screens to find the fastest growing stocks from every key sector of the technology industry.

In all, I compiled a list of several hundred prospects that appeared to have solid potential. I carefully analyzed all the companies on the list, looking at their products and services, their position within their sector, their revenue and earnings growth, their stock growth and stability, their management, their customers and strategic allies, and their leading investors. I checked their Web sites, read recent news reports about each company, viewed analysts' recommendations, and evaluated the industry niche of each of the stocks on the list.

Not every stock in our final 100 will achieve exceptional success, but many will be market leaders for years to come.

Ranking the Stocks

The stocks are ranked from number 1 through 100 based on a 16-point rating system, with four key factors—four-year earnings growth, four-year revenue growth, four-year stock growth, and four-year consistency of earnings and revenue growth. I also took some extenuating circumstances into consideration. For instance, a company whose earnings had weakened during the current year might lose a point. But for the most part, the stocks were rated based on a specific set of criteria.

As you can see in the chart below, the ranking system features these key points:

- Four categories
- 4 points maximum per category
- 16 points maximum total score

Earnings Progression	★★★★
Revenue Growth	★★★★
Stock Growth	★★★★
Consistency	★★★★
Total	16 Points

The Earnings Progression, Revenue Growth, and Stock Growth categories were rated based on the following point system (percentages are based on average annual growth rates over the past four years):

Avg. Annual Return	**Points Awarded**
10–14%	★
15–19%	★★
20–29%	★★★
30% and above	★★★★

In the Earnings Progression category, stocks that had no earnings but showed a positive progression from heavy losses to smaller losses (or from losses to positive earnings) could also earn 3 or 4 points. Lesser growth (or progress) meant fewer points. Companies with increasing losses received no points.

Consistency. A stock that has had four consecutive years of increased revenue and earnings per share would earn the maximum of four points. One point is deducted for every time the company did not post an increase in earnings or revenue. For instance, a company with earnings gains three of the past four years and revenue gains all four years would score a three out of four. A company with earnings gains three of the past four years and revenue gains three of the past four years would score just two out of four. A company with earnings gains and revenue gains just two of the past four years would have all four points deducted for a score of zero. However, a company with four consecutive years of revenue growth would receive at least one point for consistency, even if its earnings showed no consistent growth trend over the four-year period.

Breaking Ties

The higher the score, the higher the rank, but for stocks with the same score, I evaluated several factors to break the ties. First I looked at growth momentum. Companies whose revenue and earnings were still growing at a strong clip got the nod over companies that seemed to be losing steam. I also looked at the size of the company, the type of products or services it offered, its position within its sector, and its consistency in terms of revenue and earnings growth. The ones that looked to be the better bets for the long run got the higher ranking.

You should view these rankings strictly as a loose guideline. Make your choices based on your own knowledge, analysis, selection criteria, and gut feeling.

HOW TO INVEST IN TECHNOLOGY STOCKS

Because of the volatility of the technology sector, long-term investors will experience more than their fair share of emotional ups and downs. The best way to build a profitable tech portfolio is to make a series of small bets on a diverse group of stocks. By buying a few shares now, a few shares later, and still more down the road, you can accomplish your most important goal—to acquire a growing stake in the burgeoning technology sector.

However, even the most aggressive investors should be careful not to become overweighted in tech stocks. As the recent tech meltdown proved, putting all your assets in one narrow sector can lead to some devastating results. On the other hand, because the technology sector has been the fastest growing area of the economy over the past quarter-century, aggressive investors should certainly put a healthy share of their assets in tech stocks. For most investors, technology stocks should constitute about 20 to 60 percent of the total stock portfolio, depending on the individual's goals, needs, and threshold for risk.

Here are a few suggestions to help you build a winning technology portfolio:

1. **Buy quality.** Buy stocks that are either leaders in their sector or upstarts with strong growth momentum in a sector that has strong future prospects.
2. **Diversify**. Try to build a diversified portfolio by buying stocks of companies from several different technology sectors.
3. **Buy a few shares at a time**. Take a gradual accumulation approach through a series of small bets. By buying a few shares at a time, you

can spread your risks and minimize the effects of the market volatility. For the market-leading companies, start with a few shares and add more later—regardless of whether the stock price has climbed or dropped.

4. **Look for buying opportunities**. From time to time, tech stocks fall out of favor and may drop 10 to 30 percent. That can be a good time to snap up shares of the top companies.
5. **Accumulate—don't buy and sell**. Find good stocks and build a position in them. Don't sell out with the first quick run-up or the first time they take a dip. That's life in the stock market. Good stocks will continue to bounce back. Imagine the investor who bought Microsoft in 1988 and sold out shortly thereafter with a 25 percent gain. That may have been a great short-term success, but over the next ten years the stock climbed almost 10,000 percent. A $10,000 investment in Microsoft in 1989 would have grown to about $1 million by 2000. That's what you want with technology stocks—long-term home runs. A rapid buy-and-sell approach, in fact, is a poor strategy for investing in any type of stock. A recent study of consumer investing trends showed that the households that traded the most frequently over a recent five-year period had the lowest annual rate of return—about 13 percent—while households that traded the least had the highest rate of return—about 18.5 percent. And by holding for the long term, investors also avoid capital gains taxes and brokerage commissions.
6. **Never say never (when to sell).** You bought the stock because the company was growing quickly. Now you learn that revenue growth is flat and the company's fortunes are waning. Good time to sell the stock. The other time to sell is if you learn of another company in the same sector that is taking market share from a stock you hold. Go with the market leaders and the upstarts with momentum and dump the companies that lose their edge.
7. **Use this book to find prospects.** Think of this book as a catalog for investment shoppers. To select your portfolio of technology stocks, read through the 100 profiles and narrow your choices to 10 to 12 good prospects. The profiles will help you understand what the company does and how it's positioned within its niche. The financial tables and stock growth graphs will give you a snapshot of each company's past performance. Once you've selected 10 to 12 favorites from the book, use other sources, such as the Internet, the library, or recent publications, to find out more about how those companies are doing now. Follow their stock prices for a few days to get a feel for their trading range and then begin making relatively small investments in the stocks that you feel are the best bets at the time.

The world of technology awaits you. Do your best to select the top stocks for your portfolio, and give them time to grow. Add regularly to your holdings and keep the faith. Over the next few decades, technology will lead the growth of the global economy. Here's hoping you can cull from this list of 100 stocks some of the great technology companies of the 21st century.

1
Mercury Interactive Corporation

1325 Borregas Avenue
Sunnyvale, CA 94089
408-822-5200
Nasdaq: MERQ
www.mercuryinteractive.com

Chairman, President, and CEO: Amnon Landan

Earnings Progression	★ ★ ★ ★
Revenue Growth	★ ★ ★ ★
Stock Growth	★ ★ ★ ★
Consistency	★ ★ ★ ★
Total	**16 Points**

There seems to be no end to the number of problems an Internet company can encounter trying to keep its site up and running. Mercury Interactive makes software that enables Internet companies to test their Web functions and isolate bad links, slow applications, and a host of other potential problems.

The Sunnyvale, California operation got its start prior to the emergence of the Internet, making software used by companies to test normal computer functions under Unix or Windows. But in recent years, Mercury has focused increasingly on Internet testing.

In developing its software packages, Mercury collaborates with some of the leading Internet and computer technology companies in the world, including Oracle, BroadVision, Allaire, BEA, IBM, and Intel, to ensure that their products work effectively together.

The company offers a wide range of Web performance management software and services, including:

- **Functional Testing Products.** This software helps ensure that e-commerce applications work as expected.
- **Load Testing Products.** This software provides stress testing of e-commerce applications under real-world conditions to predict systems behavior and performance and to identify and isolate problems.
- **Test Process Management Products.** This software helps organize and manage the testing process to determine application readiness.
- **Web Performance Monitoring Products.** The company offers software that monitors Web applications in real time and alerts operations groups of performance problems before users experience them.
- **Hosted Web Performance Monitoring Service.** Mercury actively monitors sites in real time.
- **Hosted Load Testing Service.** The company can identify bottlenecks and capacity constraints before a site is actually opened for general use.

The company has provided software or services for more than 10,000 businesses worldwide, including major corporations across a wide range of industries, such as Anheuser-Busch, BMW, Charles Schwab, Citibank, DaimlerChrysler, Ford Motor, MCI WorldCom, Microsoft, Motorola, Sony, and Wal-Mart.

Mercury Interactive has about 850 employees and a market capitalization of about $3 billion.

EARNINGS PER SHARE PROGRESSION ★★★★

Past 4 years: 900 percent (77 percent per year)

REVENUE GROWTH ★★★★

Past 4 years: 463 percent (54 percent per year)

STOCK GROWTH ★★★★

Past 4 years: 1,746 percent (105 percent per year)
Dollar growth: $10,000 over 4 years would have grown to $184,600.

CONSISTENCY ★★★★

Increased earnings per share: 4 consecutive years
Increased sales: 4 consecutive years

MERCURY INTERACTIVE AT A GLANCE

Fiscal year ended: Dec. 31
Revenue and net income in $millions

	1996	1997	1998	1999	2000	4-Year Growth Avg. Annual (%)	4-Year Growth Total (%)
Revenue ($)	54.5	76.7	121	188	307	54	463
Net income ($)	4.63	5.73	19.5	33.1	64.7	92	1,298
Earnings/share ($)	0.07	0.08	0.25	0.39	0.70	77	900
PE range	33–85	28–83	21–63	26–141	57–230		

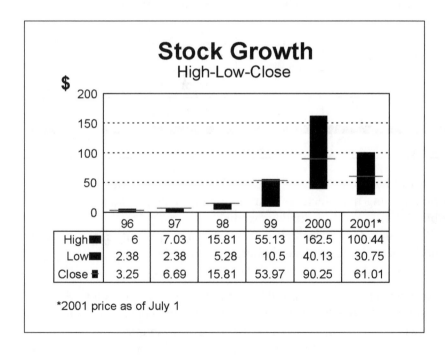

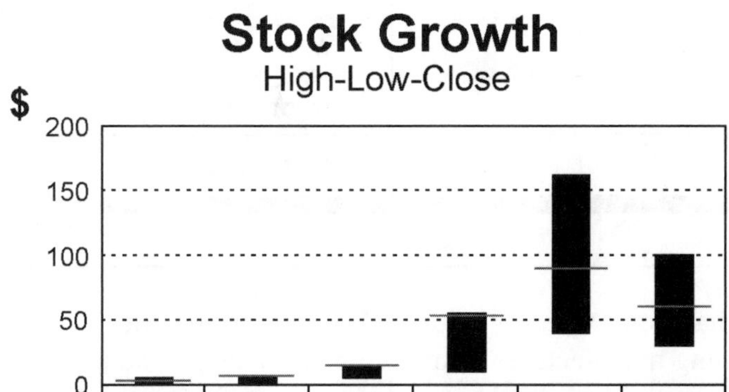

	96	97	98	99	2000	2001*
High	6	7.03	15.81	55.13	162.5	100.44
Low	2.38	2.38	5.28	10.5	40.13	30.75
Close	3.25	6.69	15.81	53.97	90.25	61.01

*2001 price as of July 1

2

Nokia Corporation

Keilalahdentie 4, FIN-02150
Espoo, Finland
(P.O. Box 226, FIN-00045 Nokia Group, Finland)
905-427-6654
NYSE: NOK
www.nokia.com

Chairman and CEO: Jorma Ollila
President: Pekka Ala-Pietila

Earnings Progression	★ ★ ★ ★
Revenue Growth	★ ★ ★ ★
Stock Growth	★ ★ ★ ★
Consistency	★ ★ ★ ★
Total	**16 Points**

The world has gone wireless with Nokia leading the way. Nokia is the world's leading manufacturer of mobile phones and a leading supplier of mobile Internet and broadband systems.

The Finland-based operation is global in scope, with manufacturing plants in 10 countries and sales operations in 130 countries.

Nokia divides its operations into two core groups:

- **Networks** (25 percent of total revenue). The company is a leading developer of mobile Internet applications, supplying data, video, and voice networks and related services for its telecommunications customers and Internet service providers. The division also provides service creation, network management, systems integration, and customer service. As part of its global system for mobile communications, Nokia provides systems for digital mobiles, network management, and professional services. The company has a customer base that includes more than 100 telecommunications operators in 46 countries. It also operates Nokia Broadband IP Access, which is an integrated end-to-end solution providing all the necessary components for network operators and service providers to offer "always-on" high bandwidth access and a variety of new services over DSL.

- **Mobile phones** (72 percent of revenue). The company manufactures a broad range of cellular phones for all major digital and analog standards worldwide. The firm introduces about 20 new phone models and other wireless products every year.

The company also has a "ventures" division that develops new products for consumers and businesses. Its ventures group accounts for about 3 percent of total revenue. The division includes Nokia Internet Communications, Nokia Home Communications, Nokia Mobile Display Appliances, and some related units.

Nokia was founded in 1865 as a paper producer. The firm began making cables for the telegraph industry in 1912 and has been manufacturing products for the telecommunications industry ever since.

Nokia has about 60,000 employees and a market capitalization of about $150 billion.

EARNINGS PER SHARE PROGRESSION ★★★★

Past 4 years: 567 percent (61 percent per year)

REVENUE GROWTH ★★★★

Past 4 years: 360 percent (46 percent per year)

STOCK GROWTH ★★★★

Past 4 years: 745 percent (71 percent per year)
Dollar growth: $10,000 over 4 years would have grown to $84,500.

CONSISTENCY ★★★★

Increased earnings per share: 4 consecutive years
Increased sales: 4 consecutive years

NOKIA AT A GLANCE

Fiscal year ended: Dec. 31
Revenue and net income in billions of Eurodollars
(0.89 Eurodollars = 1 U.S. dollar)

	1996	1997	1998	1999	2000	4-Year Growth Avg. Annual (%)	4-Year Growth Total (%)
Revenue ($)	6.61	8.85	13.3	19.8	30.4	46	360
Net income ($)	0.512	1.02	1.72	2.65	4.08	67	697
Earnings/share ($)	0.12	0.24	0.37	0.54	0.80	61	567
PE range	18–35	16–30	12–47	31–99	40–90		

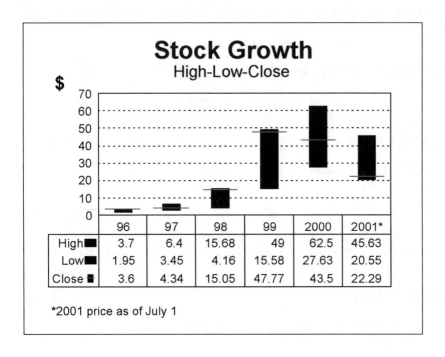

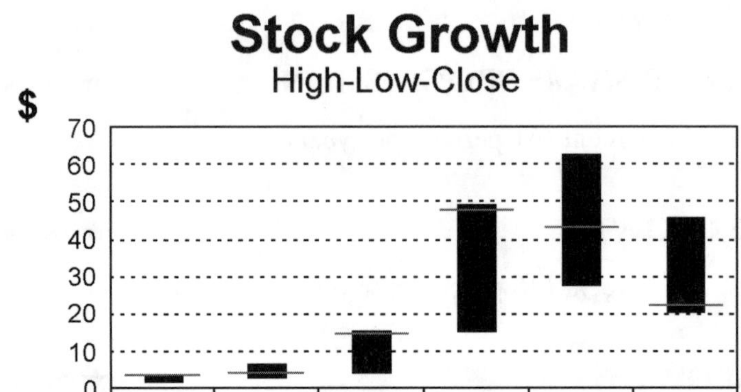

	96	97	98	99	2000	2001*
High	3.7	6.4	15.68	49	62.5	45.63
Low	1.95	3.45	4.16	15.58	27.63	20.55
Close	3.6	4.34	15.05	47.77	43.5	22.29

*2001 price as of July 1

3
Check Point Software Technology

3A Jabotinsky Street
Ramat-Gan
52520 94065
Israel
650-628-2000
Nasdaq: CHKP
www.checkpoint.com

Chairman, President, and CEO: Gil Shwed

Earnings Progression	★★★★
Revenue Growth	★★★★
Stock Growth	★★★★
Consistency	★★★★
Total	**16 Points**

Internet security has been a continuing threat for PC owners and network systems operators alike. That threat has been money in the bank for Check Point Software, which is a world leader in developing Internet security software.

Check Point founder and CEO Gil Shwed invented the firewall and is revered as one of the Internet's true pioneers. E-commerce wouldn't be possible without firewalls, which are security gateways that protect internal networks from hackers.

The operation, which was founded in Israel but also operates primarily out of its U.S. headquarters in Silicon Valley, dominates the Internet security market. It has more than 70,000 registered customers and nearly 200,000 installations. About 50 percent of sales come from the U.S., 35 percent from Europe, and the other 15 percent from elsewhere around the world.

Its leading products include:

- **Security software.** Firewall-1, its flagship product, integrates access control, authentication, encryption, network address translation, content security, and auditing.
- **Traffic control software.** The firm's IP Address Management line is used to boost network performance and reliability. In addition to software, Check Point manufactures PC boards to make certain network applications run faster.
- **IP Address Management.** Its Meta IP product provides centralized management and distributed administration of enterprise-scale IP network infrastructures.
- **Virtual private network (VPN) software.** Companies use VPNs to run their internal networks over the Internet with advanced security. Check Point is the early leader in the VPN market. VPNs can help companies save up to 60 percent on wide area networking costs. ISPs and corporations are turning to traffic control software to deliver the service levels IP telephony and video conferencing need to operate effectively.

Check Point has fortified its market position through its participation with the OPSEC alliance, a group of manufacturers that sets technical standards for integrating Check Point technology into their products. Partners include IBM, Hewlett-Packard, Sun, Microsoft, Netscape, Intel, MCI WorldCom, and others.

Check Point went public with its initial stock offering in 1996. The company has about 800 employees and a market capitalization of about $15 billion.

EARNINGS PER SHARE PROGRESSION ★ ★ ★ ★

Past 4 years: 1,100 percent (86 percent per year)

REVENUE GROWTH ★ ★ ★ ★

Past 4 years: 1,128 percent (88 percent per year)

STOCK GROWTH ★ ★ ★ ★

Past 4 years: 1,911 percent (110 percent per year)
Dollar growth: $10,000 over 4 years would have grown to $20,100.

CONSISTENCY ★ ★ ★ ★

Increased earnings per share: 4 consecutive years
Increased sales: 4 consecutive years

CHECK POINT SOFTWARE AT A GLANCE

Fiscal year ended: Dec. 31
Revenue and net income in $millions

						4-Year Growth	
	1996	1997	1998	1999	2000	Avg. Annual (%)	Total (%)
Revenue ($)	34.6	86.3	142	219	425	88	1,128
Net income ($)	15.1	40.3	69.9	95.8	221	94	1,363
Earnings/share ($)	0.07	0.17	0.30	0.39	0.84	86	1,100
PE range	31–86	15–48	6–26	9–95	34–140		

Stock Growth
High-Low-Close

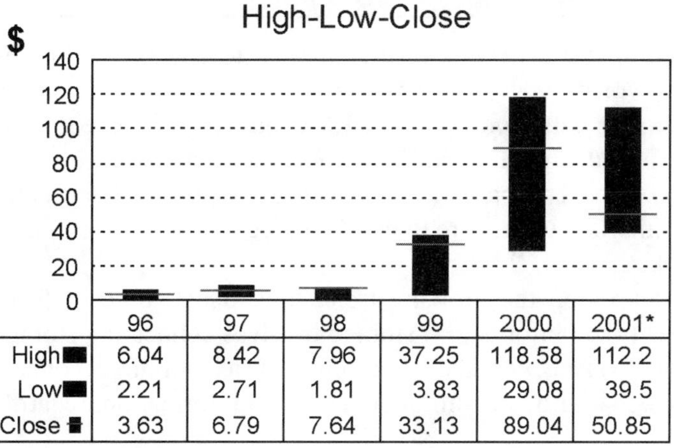

	96	97	98	99	2000	2001*
High	6.04	8.42	7.96	37.25	118.58	112.2
Low	2.21	2.71	1.81	3.83	29.08	39.5
Close	3.63	6.79	7.64	33.13	89.04	50.85

*2001 price as of July 1

4

EMC Corporation

35 Parkwood Drive
Hopkinton, MA 01748
508-435-1000
NYSE: EMC
www.emc.com

Chairman: Richard J. Egan
CEO: Michael C. Reuttgers
President: Joseph M. Tucci

Earnings Progression	★ ★ ★ ★
Revenue Growth	★ ★ ★ ★
Stock Growth	★ ★ ★ ★
Consistency	★ ★ ★ ★
Total	**16 Points**

Corporate computer networks have continued to expand, adding e-mail, e-commerce, voice, video, and graphics applications and creating an increasing need for data storage space. EMC has helped solve that storage shortage by introducing a line of high-capacity digital storage systems.

The Massachusetts operation is the market leader in the enterprise data storage market, with more than a 50 percent share of the main frame storage market.

EMC focuses on the growing trend toward networked information storage. Networked information storage involves connecting storage systems to servers via a networked environment instead of direct connections. The objective is to provide unlimited access to information, regardless of location.

Founded in 1979, EMC originally focused on selling add-on memory for the minicomputer market. But as corporate computer networks grew larger and more sophisticated, EMC shifted its focus to address the voracious data storage appetites of the large corporate networks.

The company introduced its Symmetrix 4200 storage system in 1990 and has been upgrading and expanding the Symmetrix systems ever since. In 1994, the firm added to its product mix by introducing a mirroring software for business continuity and disaster recovery called the Symmetrix Remote Data Facility. Since then, the company has introduced more than a dozen software products, including EMC ControlCenter, EMCE TimeFinder, EMCData Manager, and EMC PowerPath, that enable customers to manage, protect, and share information across the computer enterprise.

EMC's customers include 95 of the Fortune 100, all of the world's top telecommunications companies, all of the 25 largest banks in the U.S., 9 of the top 10 Internet service providers, and about 90 percent of the world's major reservation systems.

EMC has about 22,000 employees and a market capitalization of about $65 million.

EARNINGS PER SHARE PROGRESSION ★★★★

Past 4 years: 295 percent (43 percent per year)

REVENUE GROWTH ★★★★

Past 4 years: 290 percent (42 percent per year)

STOCK GROWTH ★★★★

Past 4 years: 914 percent (79 percent per year)
Dollar growth: $10,000 over 4 years would have grown to $101,000.

CONSISTENCY ★★★★

Increased earnings per share: 4 consecutive years
Increased sales: 4 consecutive years

EMC AT A GLANCE

Fiscal year ended: Dec. 31
Revenue and net income in $millions

	1996	1997	1998	1999	2000	4-Year Growth Avg. Annual (%)	4-Year Growth Total (%)
Revenue ($)	2,274	4,488	5,436	6,716	8,873	42	290
Net income ($)	386	587	654	1,010	1,782	47	362
Earnings/share ($)	0.20	0.28	0.30	0.46	0.79	43	295
PE range	9–23	14–29	19–71	45–120	59–132		

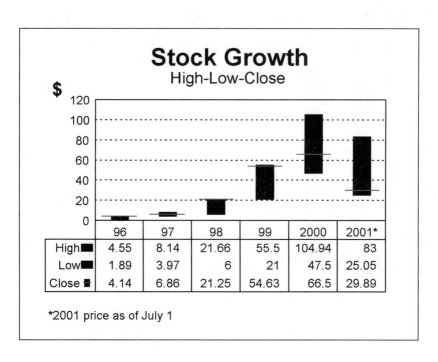

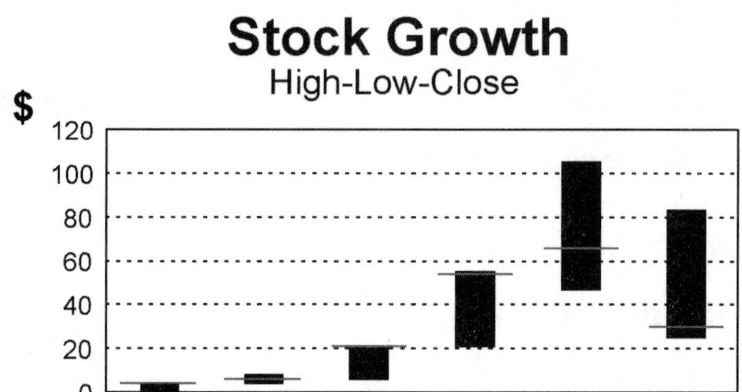

	96	97	98	99	2000	2001*
High	4.55	8.14	21.66	55.5	104.94	83
Low	1.89	3.97	6	21	47.5	25.05
Close	4.14	6.86	21.25	54.63	66.5	29.89

*2001 price as of July 1

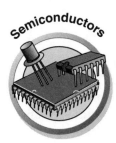

Semiconductors

5

Flextronics International

11 Ubi Road I #07-01/02
Meiban Industrial Building
Singapore 408723, Singapore
408-383-7722
Nasdaq: FLEX
www.flextronics.com

Chairman and CEO: Michael E. Marks

Earnings Progression	★ ★ ★ ★
Revenue Growth	★ ★ ★ ★
Stock Growth	★ ★ ★ ★
Consistency	★ ★ ★ ★
Total	**16 Points**

Want something done right? Get someone else to do it. That's what Flextronics has persuaded dozens of telecommunications, computer, networking, and electronics companies to do.

The Singapore-based operation is the world's third largest electronics manufacturing services operation. Flextronics does the manufacturing of hundreds of products for such leading technology companies as Cisco, Ericsson, Hewlett-Packard, Lucent, Microsoft, Motorola, and Nokia.

Companies have learned that by jobbing out some of their production to outside manufacturers like Flextronics, they can reduce production costs; accelerate time-to-market; take advantage of advanced manufacturing, design, and engineering capabilities; reduce capital investment; and improve inventory management.

Flextronics is more than just a manufacturing contractor. The company can provide its corporate customers with engineering, supply chain management, assembly, integration, testing, and logistics management. It provides complete product design services, including electrical and mechanical, circuit and layout, and radio frequency and test development engineering services.

Its manufacturing services include the fabrication and assembly of plastic and metal enclosures and related products. Flextronics specializes in advanced interconnect, miniaturization, and packaging technologies, as well as in the engineering and manufacturing of wireless communications products that use radio frequency technology.

The company breaks its services into several key areas, including:

- **Systems assembly.** The firm provides assembly and testing of systems and subsystems that incorporate complex electromechanical components.
- **Enclosures.** The company provides the design, manufacturing, and integration of electronics packaging systems, from custom enclosure systems, power and thermal subsystems, and interconnect subsystems to cabling and cases.
- **Semiconductor.** Flextronics can coordinate industrial design and tooling for semiconductor manufacturing, as well as production and assembly.
- **Plastics.** The firm provides tool fabrication, quick-turn prototyping, and full production of plastic parts.

About 43 percent of the company's manufacturing is performed in North and South America, 39 percent in Europe, and 18 percent in Asia.

Flextronics has about 37,000 employees and a market capitalization of about $13 billion.

EARNINGS PER SHARE PROGRESSION ★★★★

Past 4 years: 200 percent (31 percent per year)

REVENUE GROWTH ★★★★

Past 4 years: 708 percent (67 percent per year)

STOCK GROWTH ★★★★

Past 4 years: 592 percent (62 percent per year)
Dollar growth: $10,000 over 4 years would have grown to about $70,000.

CONSISTENCY ★★★★

Earnings progression: 4 consecutive years
Increased sales: 4 consecutive years

FLEXTRONICS AT A GLANCE

Fiscal year ended: March 31
Revenue and net income in $millions

	1997	1998	1999	2000	2001	4-Year Growth Avg. Annual (%)	4-Year Growth Total (%)
Revenue ($)	1,498	2,578	3,953	6,959	12,110	67	708
Net income ($)	71	116	131	211	416	56	486
Earnings/share ($)	0.29	0.40	0.41	0.55	0.87	31	200
PE range	25–73	19–79	26–78	NA	NA		

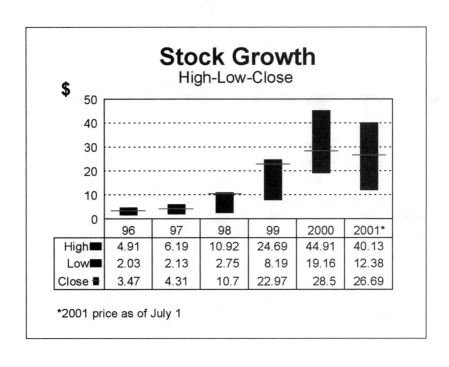

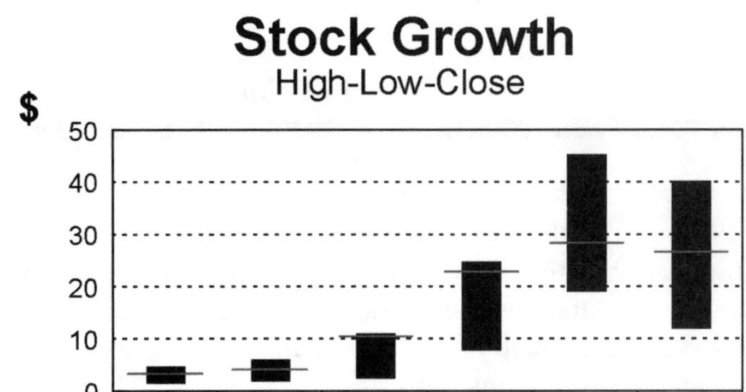

	96	97	98	99	2000	2001*
High	4.91	6.19	10.92	24.69	44.91	40.13
Low	2.03	2.13	2.75	8.19	19.16	12.38
Close	3.47	4.31	10.7	22.97	28.5	26.69

*2001 price as of July 1

6

Dell Computer Corporation

One Dell Way
Round Rock, TX 78682
512-338-4400
Nasdaq: DELL
www.dell.com

Chairman and CEO: Michael Dell

Earnings Progression	★ ★ ★ ★
Revenue Growth	★ ★ ★ ★
Stock Growth	★ ★ ★ ★
Consistency	★ ★ ★ ★
Total	**16 Points**

Founded in 1984, Dell is the world's largest direct seller of computer systems. The Round Rock, Texas operation sells a wide range of computer systems, including desktop computers, notebook computers, workstations and network server and storage products, and an extended selection of peripheral hardware and computing software.

Dell Computer founder Michael Dell built his business on the direct marketing approach. The Dell direct strategy cuts costs by eliminating the markups that would otherwise go to the wholesale and retail dealers. It also avoids the higher inventory costs associated with the traditional distribution channels and reduces the high risk of product obsolescence in the rapidly changing computer market. The direct sales strategy also gives the company a better opportunity to maintain, monitor, and update its customer database.

Dell offers two lines of desktop computers: the OptiPlex line for corporate and institutional customers using a network and the Dimension line for small businesses, workgroups, and individuals.

The company also offers a number of specialized services, including custom hardware and software integration, leasing and asset management, and network installation and support. Dell offers next-business-day delivery and extended training and support programs for many of its software offerings.

In addition to its own products, Dell also sells printers, scanners, digital cameras, monitors, and related products from other manufacturers.

Dell's customers range from large corporations, government agencies, and medical and educational institutions to small businesses and individuals. The company markets its products to the business sector through sales teams and to consumers through direct marketing advertising and the Internet.

The company sells its products worldwide. Sales outside of North America account for about 30 percent of total revenue.

The firm has manufacturing facilities in Texas, Tennessee, Brazil, Ireland, Malaysia, and China.

Dell has about 36,000 employees and a market capitalization of about $70 billion.

EARNINGS PER SHARE PROGRESSION ★★★★

Past 4 years: 365 percent (47 percent per year)

REVENUE GROWTH ★★★★

Past 4 years: 311 percent (41 percent per year)

STOCK GROWTH ★★★★

Past 4 years: 788 percent (73 percent per year)
Dollar growth: $10,000 over 4 years would have grown to about $89,000.

CONSISTENCY ★★★★

Increased earnings per share: 4 consecutive years
Increased sales: 4 consecutive years

DELL COMPUTER AT A GLANCE

Fiscal year ended: Jan. 31
Revenue and net income in $billions

	1996	1997	1998	1999	2000	4-Year Growth Avg. Annual (%)	4-Year Growth Total (%)
Revenue ($)	7.76	12.3	18.2	25.3	31.9	41	311
Net income ($)	0.531	0.944	1.46	1.67	2.24	43	322
Earnings/share ($)	0.17	0.32	0.53	0.61	0.79	47	365
PE range	8–49	18–76	31–118	59–104	26–97		

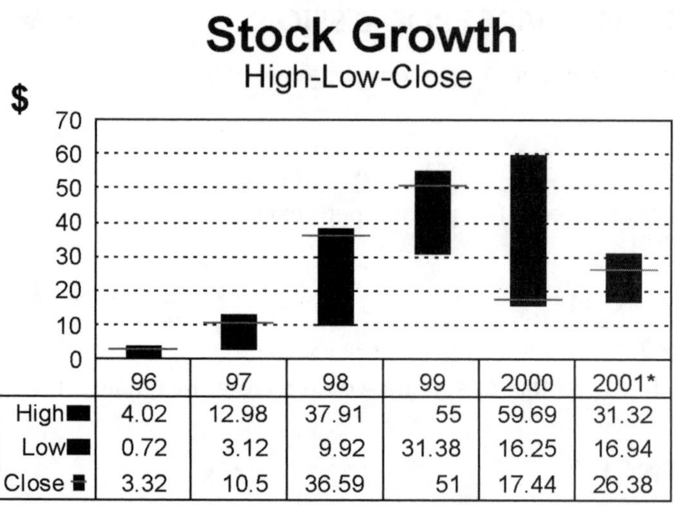

	96	97	98	99	2000	2001*
High	4.02	12.98	37.91	55	59.69	31.32
Low	0.72	3.12	9.92	31.38	16.25	16.94
Close	3.32	10.5	36.59	51	17.44	26.38

*2001 price as of July 1

7

Juniper Networks, Inc.

1194 N. Mathilda Avenue
Sunnyvale, CA 94089
408-745-2000
Nasdaq: JNPR
www.juniper.net

Chairman, President, and CEO: Scott Kriens

Earnings Progression	★ ★ ★ ★
Revenue Growth	★ ★ ★ ★
Stock Growth	★ ★ ★ ★
Consistency	★ ★ ★
Total	**15 Points**

Telecommunications companies looking for the best and fastest routers on the market once turned exclusively to Cisco Systems. Now Juniper Networks is capturing a growing share of the market, because its high-speed routers—used to transmit data across the Internet—operate about four times faster than Cisco's, according to some industries reports.

Although its growth was hampered by the recession in the telecommunications industry, Juniper has been arguably the fastest growing Internet infrastructure company in the world. The Silicon Valley operation has only been in business since 1995 but was projected to exceed $1 billion in revenue in 2001. Juniper's products have earned a reputation as the best backbone routers in the business, no small feat going up against Cisco.

Its line of M-series routers combine raw hardware with software-enabled routing intelligence, enabling Internet service providers (ISPs) to not only move data packets faster but also to engineer how traffic is handled. The company also makes optional boards that plug into its routers to let them work with different networking protocols or provide specialized network services.

All of Juniper's products work with the company's JUNOS operating system, which is the key to the firm's early success. ISP routers need to make lightning quick decisions on the best path to take to unknown Internet destinations, and industry insiders regard the JUNOS software the top of the line for this highly complex task.

The company sells its products to a wide range of end users, value-added resellers, and original equipment manufacturers in the telecommunications and Internet sectors worldwide, including MCI WorldCom, Ericsson, Cable and Wireless, and Qwest.

The company, which went public with its initial stock offering in 1999, has about 350 employees and a market capitalization of about $17 billion.

EARNINGS PER SHARE PROGRESSION ★★★★

The company has gone from losses to a gain in fiscal 2000.

REVENUE GROWTH ★★★★

Past 2 years: 17,591 percent

STOCK GROWTH ★★★★

Past 2 years: 300 percent (100 percent per year)
Dollar growth: $10,000 over 2 years would have grown to $40,000.

CONSISTENCY ★★★

Positive earnings progression: 2 consecutive years
Increased sales: 3 consecutive years

JUNIPER NETWORKS AT A GLANCE

Fiscal year ended: Dec. 30
Revenue and net income in $millions

	1996	1997	1998	1999	2000	2-Year Growth Avg. Annual (%)	2-Year Growth Total (%)
Revenue ($)	0	0	3.8	103	673.5	NA	17,591
Net income ($)	–1.8	–10.4	–30.1	117.2	479.4	309*	309*
Earnings/share ($)	–0.07	–0.20	–0.40	–0.05	0.42	NA	NA
PE range	NA	NA	NA	NA	114–575		

*Net income growth figures are based on 1-year performance.

Stock Growth
High-Low-Close

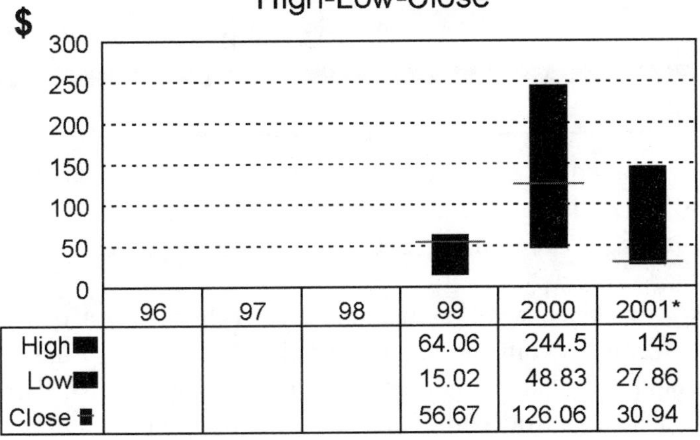

	96	97	98	99	2000	2001*
High				64.06	244.5	145
Low				15.02	48.83	27.86
Close				56.67	126.06	30.94

*2001 price as of July 1

8
Microsoft Corporation

One Microsoft Way
Redmond, WA 98052
425-882-8080
Nasdaq: MSFT
www.microsoft.com

Chairman: William H. Gates
CEO: Steven A. Ballmer
President: Richard Belluzzo

Earnings Progression	★ ★ ★ ★
Revenue Growth	★ ★ ★ ★
Stock Growth	★ ★ ★
Consistency	★ ★ ★ ★
Total	**15 Points**

Bruised and bloodied by the federal government's battle to break it into bits, Microsoft is still standing and as strong as ever. In fact, in the great tech meltdown, Microsoft held up better than most of the rest of the tech stock universe.

Founder Bill Gates, who has become the world's richest man, built Microsoft by turning a complex and powerful new technology into a useful, multifaceted tool that consumers the world over could use. Through Microsoft, Gates has introduced a long line of software products, such as Windows, DOS, Word, and Explorer, that have made computer technology user-friendly for the average consumer.

Founded in 1975, Microsoft is the worldwide leader in software for personal computers. The Redmond, Washington manufacturer helps maintain its edge in the market by spending generously on product development. It spends about $3 billion a year on research and development.

Microsoft has subsidiaries in about 60 countries around the world. Foreign sales have been growing quickly and currently account for about 54 percent of the company's total revenue.

Microsoft offers products in several key categories, including:

- **Platforms** (computer operating systems), including Windows 2000, Windows 2000 Professional, Windows 98, Windows NT Workstation, and Windows NT Server
- **Desktop applications,** including Microsoft Office (a software package that includes a wide range of business-related applications), Word (word processing), Excel (spreadsheet), PowerPoint (presentations), Access (database management), and Outlook (Internet e-mail)
- **Server applications,** including Windows NT Server for office networks, Microsoft Exchange Server, and SQL Server
- **Developer tools,** used by software developers to create new applications
- **Interactive media products,** including interactive entertainment and information products such as Microsoft Encarta encyclopedia, Microsoft Bookshelf, and other Internet and CD-ROM products

The company has also developed software for mobile devices, networks, and Web sites. Microsoft has about 39,000 employees and a market capitalization of about $300 billion.

EARNINGS PER SHARE PROGRESSION ★★★★

Past 4 years: 295 percent (41 percent per year)

REVENUE GROWTH ★★★★

Past 4 years: 153 percent (26 percent per year)

STOCK GROWTH ★★★

Past 4 years: 233 percent (35 percent per year)
Dollar growth: $10,000 over 4 years would have grown to $33,300.

CONSISTENCY ★★★★

Increased earnings per share: 4 consecutive years
Increased sales: 4 consecutive years

MICROSOFT AT A GLANCE

Fiscal year ended: June 30
Revenue and net income in $billions

	1996	1997	1998	1999	2000	4-Year Growth Avg. Annual (%)	4-Year Growth Total (%)
Revenue ($)	9.05	11.9	15.3	19.7	22.9	26	153
Net income ($)	2.19	3.45	4.49	7.78	9.42	44	330
Earnings/share ($)	0.43	0.66	0.83	1.41	1.70	41	295
PE range	25–50	30–57	37–86	48–84	23–69		

Stock Growth
High-Low-Close

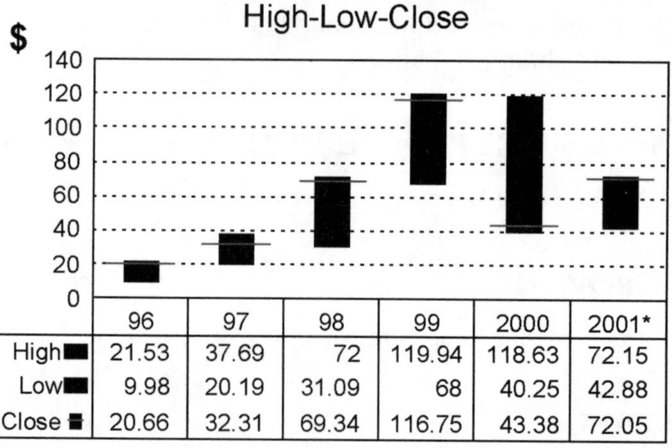

	96	97	98	99	2000	2001*
High	21.53	37.69	72	119.94	118.63	72.15
Low	9.98	20.19	31.09	68	40.25	42.88
Close	20.66	32.31	69.34	116.75	43.38	72.05

*2001 price as of July 1

9

Citrix Systems, Inc.

6400 Northwest Sixth Way
Ft. Lauderdale, FL 33309
954-267-3000
Nasdaq: CTXS
www.citrix.com

Chairman: Roger W. Roberts
President: Mark B. Templeton

Earnings Progression	★ ★ ★ ★
Revenue Growth	★ ★ ★ ★
Stock Growth	★ ★ ★ ★
Consistency	★ ★ ★
Total	**15 Points**

Citrix Systems brings uniformity to the complex and divergent world of computer technology. The company's application server software gives companies the ability to run any application on any device over any connection from wireless to the Web. With Citrix software, companies can manage their applications without regard to location, network connection, or type of hardware platform.

The company's software has become universally popular with corporations. Citrix boasts 100,000 corporate customers, including 90 percent of the Fortune 500 companies.

The firm's products allow customers to use Windows or UNIX applications in a variety of environments, including the Internet, wireless devices, computer networks, wide area networks, UNIX workstations, Java applications, X-Terminals, and Macintosh systems.

In addition to its application server software (known as MetaFrame), Citrix offers a line of management products that provide certain enhancements to its application servers product line, including:

- **Load balancing system.** This system allows application-based load balancing and enterprise scalability.
- **Resource management system.** This software provides the means to monitor and manage critical system resources.
- **Installation management services.** This enables companies to easily package applications for installation on MetaFrame servers across the enterprise.
- **Extranet products.** Citrix offers software that helps companies create secure, encrypted, and authenticated virtual private networks capable of ensuring secure application delivery via the Internet.
- **Nfuse.** This application portal product enables applications running on a Citrix MetaFrame server farm to be published onto a Web page. It also allows end users to access and subscribe to interactive applications and content through a standard Web browser.

The company markets its products worldwide.

Citrix was incorporated in 1989 and shipped its first products in 1991. It went public with its initial stock offering in 1995. The company has about 1,400 employees and a market capitalization of about $5 billion.

EARNINGS PER SHARE PROGRESSION ★★★★

Past 4 years: 327 percent (44 percent per year)

REVENUE GROWTH ★★★★

Past 4 years: 956 percent (80 percent per year)

STOCK GROWTH ★★★★

Past 4 years: 319 percent (42 percent per year)
Dollar growth: $10,000 over 4 years would have grown to $41,900.

CONSISTENCY ★★★

Increased earnings per share: 3 of the past 4 years
Increased sales: 4 consecutive years

CITRIX SYSTEMS AT A GLANCE

Fiscal year ended: Dec. 31
Revenue and net income in $millions

	1996	1997	1998	1999	2000	4-Year Growth	
						Avg. Annual (%)	Total (%)
Revenue ($)	44.5	124	249	403	470	80	956
Net income ($)	18.7	41.3	61.1	117.0	94.5	50	405
Earnings/share ($)	0.11	0.24	0.33	0.61	0.47	44	327
PE range	17–82	6–59	27–72	21–107	30–258		

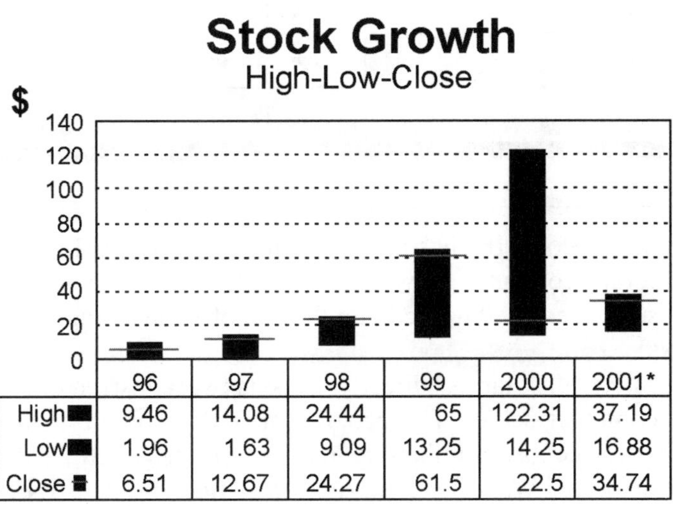

	96	97	98	99	2000	2001*
High	9.46	14.08	24.44	65	122.31	37.19
Low	1.96	1.63	9.09	13.25	14.25	16.88
Close	6.51	12.67	24.27	61.5	22.5	34.74

*2001 price as of July 1

10

Brocade Communications

1745 Technology Drive
San Jose, CA 95110
408-487-8000
Nasdaq: BRCD
www.brocade.com

Chairman: Seth D. Neiman
President and CEO: Gregory L. Reyes

Earnings Progression	★ ★ ★
Revenue Growth	★ ★ ★ ★
Stock Growth	★ ★ ★ ★
Consistency	★ ★ ★ ★
Total	**15 Points**

Data storage has become big business with the advent of the Internet and massive corporate computer networks. Brocade is a leading maker of switching systems designed to facilitate the use of large storage area networks (SANs).

SANs connect "disk farms" directly to the network instead of through a dedicated computer server. The benefits of SANs are substantial, including faster service, better reliability, more room for growth, and lower operating costs. Large Web sites are expected to flock to the SANS technology over the next few years.

Storage area networks are based on an industry standard called "fiber channel" that any company can use. As a result, Brocade is getting plenty of competition, but it has become one of the leaders of the pack in this fast-growth area. Its strong product line has helped it differentiate its products from the competition. Its leading products include:

- **SilkWorm Fiber Channel Switches.** The company's controller devices have been rated the best performing and easiest to manage in product comparison studies.

- **Fabric OS.** This is Brocade's proprietary management software used to configure and operate interconnected "fabrics" containing up to thousands of disks.
- **Brocade SES.** Allows Brocade switches to be managed in large computer rooms that are still largely based on non-SAN disk technology.

Brocade outsources its manufacturing (primarily to Solectron Corp.) and most of its supply chain management operations. Most of its sales are made through leading storage systems and server manufacturers who incorporate Brocade's hardware into their systems.

The San Jose operation's primary target market is disk product manufacturers. The company's equipment is used in products manufactured by IBM, Dell, Compaq, StorageTek, Hitachi, and other market leaders.

The company, which has about 600 employees, made its initial public stock offering in 1999. It has a market capitalization of about $5 billion.

EARNINGS PER SHARE PROGRESSION ★ ★ ★

The company went from large losses in past years to a substantial gain in 2000.

REVENUE GROWTH ★ ★ ★ ★

Past 3 years: 3,780 percent (256 percent per year)

STOCK GROWTH ★ ★ ★ ★

Past 2 years: 750 percent
Dollar growth: $10,000 over the past 2 years would have grown to about $85,000.

CONSISTENCY ★ ★ ★ ★

Positive earnings progression: 4 consecutive years
Increased sales: 4 consecutive years

BROCADE COMMUNICATIONS AT A GLANCE

Fiscal year ended: Oct. 31
Revenue and net income in $millions

	1996	1997	1998	1999	2000	3-Year Growth Avg. Annual (%)	3-Year Growth Total (%)
Revenue ($)	0	8.48	24.2	68.7	329	256	3,780
Net income ($)	–3.93	–9.62	–15.1	2.48	67.9	NA	NA
Earnings/share ($)	–1.19	–0.60	–0.56	0.01	0.28	NA	NA
PE range	NA	NA	NA	343–3687	118–477		

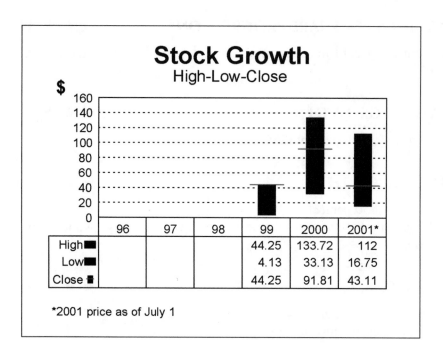

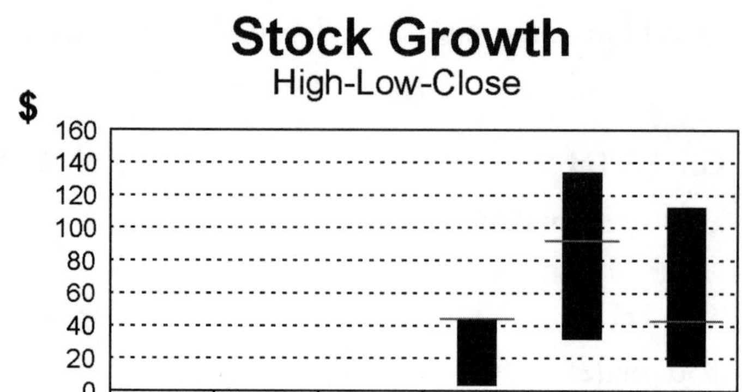

	96	97	98	99	2000	2001*
High				44.25	133.72	112
Low				4.13	33.13	16.75
Close				44.25	91.81	43.11

*2001 price as of July 1

11

Mercury Computer Systems, Inc.

199 Riverneck Road
Chelmsford, MA 01824
978-256-1300
Nasdaq: MRCY
www.mc.com

President and CEO: James R. Bertelli

Earnings Progression	★ ★ ★ ★
Revenue Growth	★ ★ ★
Stock Growth	★ ★ ★ ★
Consistency	★ ★ ★ ★
Total	**15 Points**

Superman was known to use his X-ray vision to see through walls and behind closed doors. Mercury Computer Systems has honed its own see-through technology to help doctors see inside the human body and help military commanders see behind enemy lines.

The Chelmsford, Massachusetts operation manufactures digital signal processing computer systems that transform sensor generated data into information that can be displayed as images for human interpretation or subjected to additional computer analysis.

The company markets its embedded computer systems to three key markets:

- **Military.** In the defense field, Mercury's systems process the stream of data from sensors attached to radar or sonar equipment to enable military commanders to "see" the battle through natural barriers such as clouds, darkness, water, or foliage, so that the position and strength of the enemy can be analyzed. Mercury is the dominant player in the military segment of its industry, supplying technology to many of the leading defense contractors, such as Lockheed Martin, Northrup, Ericsson, Israel Ministry of Defense, and Raytheon.

- **Medical.** Mercury's computer systems are embedded in magnetic resonance imaging (MRI), computed tomography (CT), and digital X-ray machines. The systems process the continuous stream of data provided by the machines to create an image a physician may use to diagnose a patient's ailment. The company supplies technology for some of the MRIs and similar machines developed by General Electric Medical Systems, Siemens, and Marconi Medical Systems.
- **Wireless communications.** The company recently formed a wireless communications group to produce products that will increase bandwidth and signal processing capabilities for wireless base stations.

Military electronics sales account for about three-quarters of the company's $140 million in annual revenue.

Mercury went public in 1998 with its initial stock offering. The company has about 500 employees and a market capitalization of about $1 billion.

EARNINGS PER SHARE PROGRESSION ★★★★

Past 4 years: 293 percent (41 percent per year)

REVENUE GROWTH ★★★

Past 4 years: 142 percent (25 percent per year)

STOCK GROWTH ★★★★

Past 2 years: 227 percent (34 percent per year)
Dollar growth: $10,000 over 2 years would have grown to $32,700.

CONSISTENCY ★★★★

Increased earnings per share: 4 consecutive years
Increased sales: 4 consecutive years

MERCURY COMPUTER SYSTEMS AT A GLANCE

Fiscal year ended: June 30
Revenue and net income in $millions

	1996	1997	1998	1999	2000	4-Year Growth Avg. Annual (%)	4-Year Growth Total (%)
Revenue ($)	58.3	64.6	85.5	106	141	25	142
Net income ($)	4.43	4.61	8.73	13.5	24.9	53	462
Earnings/share ($)	0.28	0.29	0.47	0.62	1.10	41	293
PE range	NA	NA	9–30	12–56	15–62		

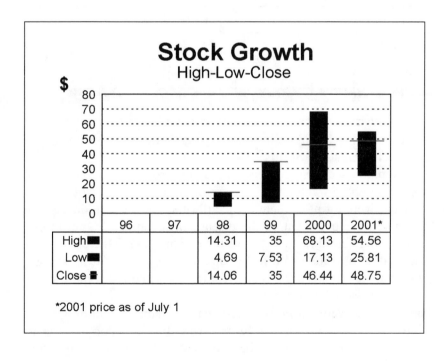

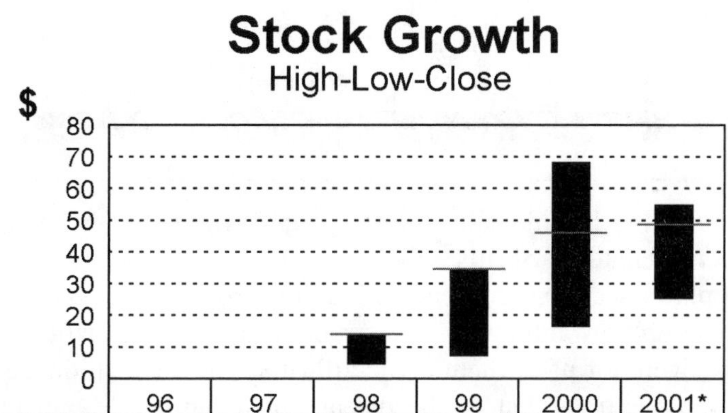

	96	97	98	99	2000	2001*
High			14.31	35	68.13	54.56
Low			4.69	7.53	17.13	25.81
Close			14.06	35	46.44	48.75

*2001 price as of July 1

12

Immunex Corporation

51 University Street
Seattle, WA 98101
206-587-0430
Nasdaq: IMNX
www.immunex.com

Chairman, President, and CEO: Edward V. Fritzky

Earnings Progression	★ ★ ★
Revenue Growth	★ ★ ★ ★
Stock Growth	★ ★ ★ ★
Consistency	★ ★ ★ ★
Total	**15 Points**

Immunex is making life more livable for people who suffer from cancer, asthma, and rheumatoid arthritis.

The biopharmaceutical company's leading product is Enbrel, which reduces the symptoms and delays the structural damage in patients with moderate to severe forms of rheumatoid arthritis. The medication has also been approved for treatment of the disease in juveniles. Enbrel arrests joint erosion in about three-quarters of the patients taking the drug.

Rheumatoid arthritis can affect people of any age, but it most commonly afflicts people aged 25 to 50. Women are three times more likely than men to develop the disease.

Patients who were formerly bedridden or unable to climb a set of stairs have praised the medication for restoring them to a normal or near-normal lifestyle. Medical studies have indicated that it works for about two out of three people who have used it.

Immunex markets a half dozen cancer-fighting medications including Leukine, which stimulates infection-resistant white blood cells. It has been approved for treatment of people older than 55 undergoing chemotherapy for an acute form of leukemia. It has also been approved for patients who have undergone bone marrow transplants.

Another leading medication in its product stable is Novantrone, which is designed to kill cancer cells and reduce inflammation that contributes to worsening forms of multiple sclerosis. It is also marketed for the treatment of pain for people suffering from a form of prostate cancer.

Immunex is developing other cancer drugs as well as drugs to treat asthma and osteoporosis.

Immunex, founded in 1981, has spent more than $1 billion on research. The company believes that it is well positioned with a diverse product pipeline to capitalize on future opportunities to combat disease. It has about 1,400 employees and a market capitalization of about $17 billion. (American Home Products owns a majority interest in Immunex. The company also provides Immunex marketing assistance for some of its products.)

EARNINGS PER SHARE PROGRESSION ★★★

The company has moved steadily the past few years from large losses to solid profits.

REVENUE GROWTH ★★★★

Past 4 years: 471 percent (55 percent per year)

STOCK GROWTH ★★★★

Past 4 years: 789 percent (74 percent per year)
Dollar growth: $10,000 over 4 years would have grown to about $90,000.

CONSISTENCY ★★★★

Positive earnings progression: 4 consecutive years
Increased sales: 4 consecutive years

IMMUNEX AT A GLANCE

Fiscal year ended: Dec. 31
Revenue and net income in $millions

	1996	1997	1998	1999	2000	4-Year Growth Avg. Annual (%)	4-Year Growth Total (%)
Revenue ($)	151	185	243	542	862	55	471
Net income ($)	–53.6	–15.8	.986	44.3	154	NA	NA
Earnings/share ($)	–0.11	–0.03	0.00	0.09	0.28	NA	NA
PE range	NA	NA	NA	114–478	86–297		

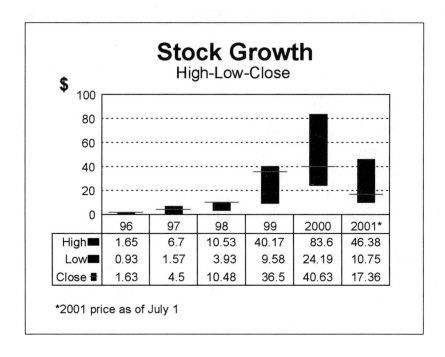

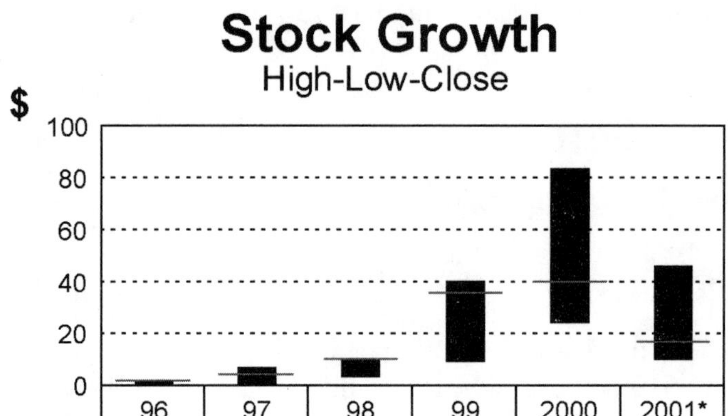

	96	97	98	99	2000	2001*
High	1.65	6.7	10.53	40.17	83.6	46.38
Low	0.93	1.57	3.93	9.58	24.19	10.75
Close	1.63	4.5	10.48	36.5	40.63	17.36

*2001 price as of July 1

13

ViaSat, Inc.

6155 El Camino Real
Carlsbad, CA 92009
760-476-2200
Nasdaq: VSAT
www.viasat.com

Chairman, President, and CEO: Mark D. Dankberg

Earnings Progression	★ ★ ★
Revenue Growth	★ ★ ★ ★
Stock Growth	★ ★ ★ ★
Consistency	★ ★ ★ ★
Total	**15 Points**

Once the play toys of NASA, satellites have become an important part of the communications network. ViaSat is a leading manufacturer of digital satellite telecommunications and wireless signal processing equipment.

The firm utilizes Demand Assigned Multiple Access (DAMA) technology, which allows large numbers of satellite subscribers to share common satellite transponders for high-performance voice, fax, or data communications.

ViaSat's DAMA products include satellite modems, networking processors, and network control systems for managing large numbers of network subscribers. The company's DAMA technology consists of proprietary software designed to run on industry-standard digital signal processors. Its technology operates on satellites in the military UHF and SHF frequency bands and commercial C and K bands.

The Carlsbad, California operation also provides network information security products, communications simulation and test equipment, and spread spectrum digital radios for satellite and terrestrial data networks.

One of its newer offerings is the Skylinx terminal, which provides inexpensive, toll-quality telephone service for voice and fax communication for small businesses and cities in areas lacking adequate telephone infrastructure.

ViaSat also offers an advanced line of communications and tracking systems. The systems provide gateway infrastructure, remote sensing ground stations, and tracking, telemetry, and command ground stations. The systems include a large satellite antenna dish, a high-powered radio transmitter and receiver, and an ultra-high-speed satellite modem.

Although the majority of ViaSat revenue has comes from the U.S. government through military-related projects, the company has made significant investments in commercial satellite networking operations. For instance, it recently acquired the Satellite Networks Business from Scientific-Atlanta, which is focused exclusively on the development of commercial products and services.

Founded in 1986, ViaSat went public with its initial stock offering in 1996. The company has about 350 employees and a market capitalization of about $400 million.

EARNINGS PER SHARE PROGRESSION ★ ★ ★

Past 4 years: 175 percent (28 percent per year)

REVENUE GROWTH ★ ★ ★ ★

Past 4 years: 244 percent (36 percent per year)

STOCK GROWTH ★ ★ ★ ★

Past 4 years: 287 percent (40 percent per year)
Dollar growth: $10,000 over 4 years would have grown to about $39,000.

CONSISTENCY ★ ★ ★ ★

Increased earnings per share: 4 consecutive years
Increased sales: 4 consecutive years

VIASAT AT A GLANCE

Fiscal year ended: March 31
Revenue and net income in $millions

	1997	1998	1999	2000	2001	4-Year Growth Avg. Annual (%)	4-Year Growth Total (%)
Revenue ($)	47.7	64.2	71.5	75.9	164	36	244
Net income ($)	3.17	5.29	6.3	7.91	14.9	47	370
Earnings/share ($)	0.24	0.32	0.38	0.45	0.66	28	175
PE range	18–50	10–31	10–72	26–115	NA		

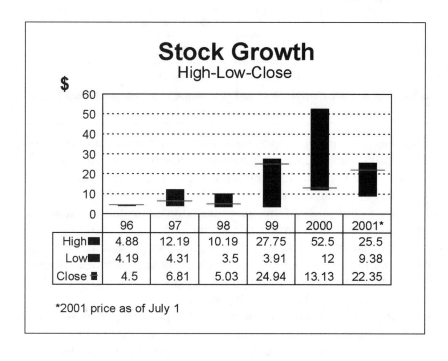

Stock Growth
High-Low-Close

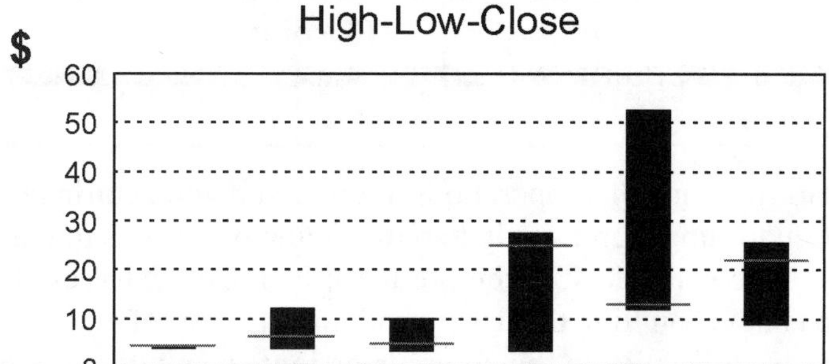

	96	97	98	99	2000	2001*
High	4.88	12.19	10.19	27.75	52.5	25.5
Low	4.19	4.31	3.5	3.91	12	9.38
Close	4.5	6.81	5.03	24.94	13.13	22.35

*2001 price as of July 1

14

Jabil Circuit, Inc.

10560 Ninth Street North
St. Petersburg, FL 33716
727-577-9749
NYSE: JBL
www.jabil.com

Chairman and CEO: William D. Morean

Earnings Progression	★ ★ ★ ★
Revenue Growth	★ ★ ★ ★
Stock Growth	★ ★ ★ ★
Consistency	★ ★ ★
Total	**15 Points**

In an effort to fine-tune their operations, high-tech manufacturing companies have been turning increasingly to outsourcing operations to manufacture many of the components in their products. Jabil Circuit has established a growing business handling the design and manufacture of electronic circuit boards for companies in the communications, computer peripherals, personal computer, automotive, and consumer electronics markets.

Jabil does contract work for many of the world's leading high-tech companies, including Cisco Systems (which accounts for about 20 percent of Jabil's annual revenue), Dell Computer (16 percent of revenue), Hewlett-Packard (14 percent), and Lucent (10 percent).

Jabil offers several core services, including integrated design and engineering service, component selection, sourcing and procurement, automated assembly, product testing, parallel global production, systems assembly, and direct order fulfillment services.

By using Jabil's manufacturing services, manufacturing companies can reduce product manufacturing costs and time-to-market, improve inventory management, and reduce capital investment in manufacturing while still getting access to the most advanced manufacturing technologies available.

Jabil breaks its operations into three core segments:

- **Design services.** The company designs integrated circuits for cell phones, computers, video set-top boxes, and automotive and consumer appliance controls. It also designs printed circuit boards as well as the plastic-and-metal enclosures that house printed circuit board assemblies.
- **System assembly, test, and direct order fulfillment services.** The company assembles and tests its circuit boards and related products. It also offers direct order fulfillment of final products that it assembles for its customers.
- **Repair and warranty services.** The company offers its customers the additional option of product warranties and a repair service.

The St. Petersburg, Florida operation has manufacturing plants worldwide, including four plants in China, three in Mexico, three in Europe, and five in the U.S.

Founded in 1966, Jabil has about 20,000 employees and a market capitalization of about $6 billion.

EARNINGS PER SHARE PROGRESSION ★ ★ ★ ★

Past 4 years: 310 percent (42 percent per year)

REVENUE GROWTH ★ ★ ★ ★

Past 4 years: 238 percent (36 percent per year)

STOCK GROWTH ★ ★ ★ ★

Past 4 years: 555 percent (60 percent per year)
Dollar growth: $10,000 over 4 years would have grown to about $66,000.

CONSISTENCY ★ ★ ★

Increased earnings per share: 3 of the past 4 years
Increased sales: 4 consecutive years

JABIL CIRCUIT AT A GLANCE

Fiscal year ended: August 31
Revenue and net income in $millions

	1996	1997	1998	1999	2000	4-Year Growth Avg. Annual (%)	4-Year Growth Total (%)
Revenue ($)	1,051	1,179	1,484	2,238	3,558	36	238
Net income ($)	30.4	59.3	57.5	84.8	146	48	380
Earnings/share ($)	0.19	0.36	0.35	0.49	0.78	42	310
PE range	3–27	10–49	16–53	29–80	23–87		

Stock Growth
High-Low-Close

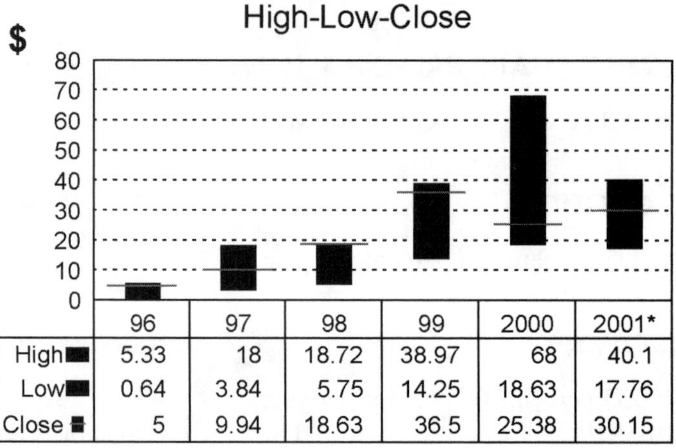

	96	97	98	99	2000	2001*
High	5.33	18	18.72	38.97	68	40.1
Low	0.64	3.84	5.75	14.25	18.63	17.76
Close	5	9.94	18.63	36.5	25.38	30.15

*2001 price as of July 1

15

Sanmina Corporation

2700 North First Street
San Jose, CA 95134
408-964-3500

Nasdaq: SANM

www.sanmina.com

Chairman and CEO: Jure Sola
President: Randy W. Furr

Earnings Progression	★★★★
Revenue Growth	★★★★
Stock Growth	★★★★
Consistency	★★★
Total	**15 Points**

In the fast-paced world of high technology, time to market has become increasingly important. That's one reason why electronics manufacturers are turning increasingly to high-tech specialty firms such as Sanmina to manufacture the sophisticated components inside their products.

Sanmina specializes in custom-manufacturing printed circuit boards and related items used in a variety of electronic devices such as computers, telephones, and medical equipment. The company can offer its corporate customers a total manufacturing service, including engineering design, fabrication of bare boards, cable assemblies, enclosures, complete system integration, and testing, as well as global order fulfillment.

In addition to printed circuit boards, the firm specializes in the design and manufacture of backplane assemblies, custom cables and wire harness assemblies, and electronic enclosure systems.

The San Jose, California company offers manufacturers several advantages, including:

- **Shorter time to market.** Sanmina helps companies reduce the time to market for new products by turning out custom-designed circuit boards faster than the manufacturer could make them itself.
- **Reduced capital investment.** The technology manufacturing process has become increasingly automated, requiring a greater level of capital investment in equipment. By using specialty manufacturers, original manufacturers have access to the leading technologies without continually investing in costly new equipment.
- **Improved inventory management.** Manufacturers, faced with short product life cycles, can use specialty manufacturers to keep them at the leading edge of technology without overmanufacturing products that will soon be obsolete.

Sanmina's primary customers include Alcatel, Cisco Systems, Lucent Technologies, Motorola, Nokia, Nortel Networks, and Tellabs. About 72 percent of the company's revenue comes from telecommunications manufacturers, 16 percent from medical and industrial instrument manufacturers, and 16 percent from high-speed computer makers.

Founded in 1980, the company went public with its initial stock offering in 1993. It has about 24,000 employees and a market capitalization of about $9 billion.

EARNINGS PER SHARE PROGRESSION ★★★★

Past 4 years: 195 percent (32 percent per year)

REVENUE GROWTH ★★★★

Past 4 years: 898 percent (78 percent per year)

STOCK GROWTH ★★★★

Past 4 years: 289 percent (42 percent per year)
Dollar growth: $10,000 over 4 years would have grown to $38,900.

CONSISTENCY ★★★

Increased earnings per share: 3 of the past 4 years
Increased sales: 4 consecutive years

SANMINA AT A GLANCE

Fiscal year ended: Sept. 30
Revenue and net income in $millions

	1996	1997	1998	1999	2000	4-Year Growth Avg. Annual (%)	4-Year Growth Total (%)
Revenue ($)	392	803	1,941	2,394	3,911	78	898
Net income ($)	36.5	49.3	33.2	118	197	53	440
Earnings/share ($)	0.21	0.23	0.13	0.41	0.62	32	195
PE range	12–33	20–49	37–119	30–66	33–94		

Stock Growth
High-Low-Close

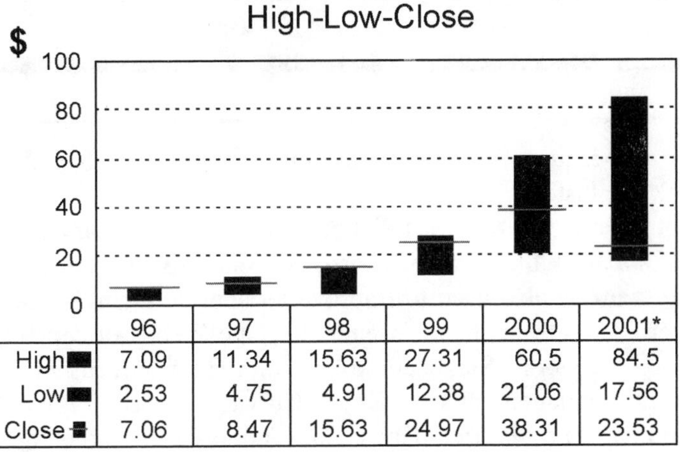

	96	97	98	99	2000	2001*
High	7.09	11.34	15.63	27.31	60.5	84.5
Low	2.53	4.75	4.91	12.38	21.06	17.56
Close	7.06	8.47	15.63	24.97	38.31	23.53

*2001 price as of July 1

16

Siebel Systems, Inc.

2207 Bridgepoint Parkway
San Mateo, CA 94404
650-295-5000
Nasdaq: SEBL
www.siebel.com

Chairman and CEO: Thomas M. Siebel

Earnings Progression	★★★★
Revenue Growth	★★★★
Stock Growth	★★★★
Consistency	★★★
Total	**15 Points**

It's time for a pop quiz. Which software maker topped the $1 billion in revenue mark the fastest?

Microsoft? Oracle? No, it was Siebel Systems, a well-managed, low-key maker of software that manages customer relations. Its eBusiness applications software is also used to improve a client company's sales and marketing across multiple channels, including the Web, call centers, and dealer and retail networks. Siebel commands more than a third of the market for customer management software, or CRM.

Founded in 1993 by Patricia House and Thomas Siebel, the company quickly found a niche and watched its sales reach $1.8 billion by the end of 2000. Its roster of clients includes such corporate giants as Charles Schwab, Lockheed Martin, and Ford—all intent on striking closer relationships with customers.

One of Siebel's largest growth areas has been the federal government, whose agencies have never been particularly well known for their customer service. But the agencies have recognized the need to be more attentive and have turned to Siebel for some high-tech help.

The company believes it has just scratched the surface. Only a small percentage of corporations and government agencies have begun to address their sales and customer service needs with software solutions. Siebel Systems believes that for companies to succeed, they must create and maintain the highest possible level of customer satisfaction.

Conventional wisdom holds that it's five to ten times more costly to prospect a new customer than to keep an existing one. Siebel helps boost customer loyalty through software solutions designed to keep customers satisfied.

Siebel practices what it preaches. It bases its sales reps' compensation program on regular, third-party audits designed to determine a customer's level of satisfaction. Nearly half of a rep's pay is based on customer evaluations rather than traditional commissions. A Siebel rep can only succeed if his or her company does.

The company has about 7,000 employees and a market capitalization of about $21 billion.

EARNINGS PER SHARE PROGRESSION ★★★★

Past 4 years: 500 percent (58 percent per year)

REVENUE GROWTH ★★★★

Past 4 years: 1,677 percent (103 percent per year)

STOCK GROWTH ★★★★

Past 4 years: 1,202 percent (90 percent per year)
Dollar growth: $10,000 over 4 years would have grown to about $130,000.

CONSISTENCY ★★★

Increased earnings per share: 3 of the past 4 years
Increased sales: 4 consecutive years

SIEBEL SYSTEMS AT A GLANCE

Fiscal year ended: Dec. 31
Revenue and net income in $millions

	1996	1997	1998	1999	2000	4-Year Growth Avg. Annual (%)	4-Year Growth Total (%)
Revenue ($)	101	222	417	813	1,795	103	1,677
Net income ($)	12.9	0.643	42.3	110	222	102	1,621
Earnings/share ($)	0.04	0.00	0.10	0.12	0.24	58	500
PE range	33–92	828–3085	34–84	29–170	138–507		

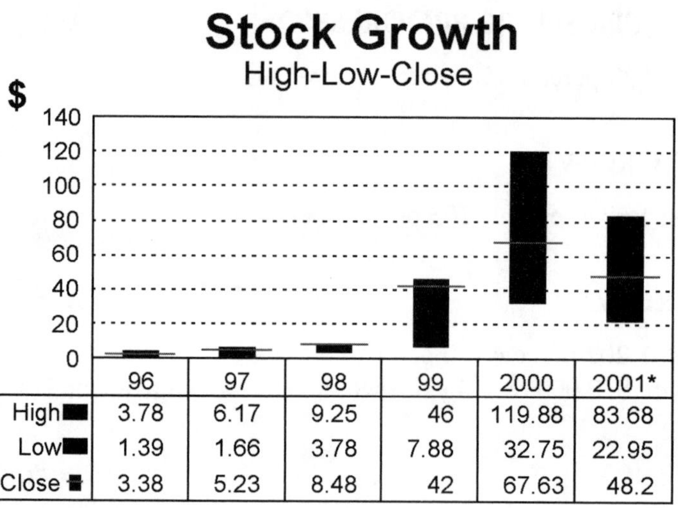

	96	97	98	99	2000	2001*
High	3.78	6.17	9.25	46	119.88	83.68
Low	1.39	1.66	3.78	7.88	32.75	22.95
Close	3.38	5.23	8.48	42	67.63	48.2

*2001 price as of July 1

17

Advanced Digital Information Corporation

11431 Willows Road N.E.
P.O. Box 97057
Redmond, WA 98073
425-881-8004
Nasdaq: ADIC
www.adic.com

Chairman and CEO: Peter van Oppen
President: Charles Stonecipher

Earnings Progression	★ ★ ★ ★
Revenue Growth	★ ★ ★ ★
Stock Growth	★ ★ ★ ★
Consistency	★ ★ ★
Total	**15 Points**

The ongoing quest for bigger computer systems, more complex software, and larger Web sites has cranked up the need for computer data storage space. Advanced Digital Information Corporation (ADIC) has developed a line of high-capacity data storage devices to cash in on that growing demand.

ADIC makes hardware and software-based data storage systems for the open systems marketplace. Its storage systems are used to capture, protect, manage, and archive the increasingly complex stream of computer data. Most of its storage devices are used as part of a computer network operated by a business or organization.

Disk storage sales have been growing by more than 80 percent per year, according to International Data Corp., an industry research company. Storage space sales went from 10,000 terabytes (a trillion bytes) in 1994 to 116,000 terabytes in 1998—a 1,000 percent rise—and is projected to reach 1.4 million terabytes (1.4 million-trillion bytes) of disk space in 2002.

The Redmond, Washington operation incorporates its hardware, software, and connectivity products with hardware and software from other manufacturers to tailor its systems to the requirements of each customer.

ADIC offers a broad range of automated storage "libraries" priced from about $5,000 to nearly $2 million, depending on the size and speed of the storage systems. Its largest mixed media systems hold up to 70,000 data tape cartridges. At the low end, it sells stand-alone tape drives for about $2,000 to $10,000.

The core component of ADIC's storage system is its automated tape library. The system can be programmed to automatically back up a network's data, using specific tapes at predetermined times. The company is also developing libraries that use optical technology.

ADIC sells its products through a worldwide network of independent distributors and original manufacturers, such as Dell Computer, IBM, and Fujitsu.

Founded in 1983, ADIC has about 800 employees and a market capitalization of about $800 million.

EARNINGS PER SHARE PROGRESSION ★ ★ ★ ★

Past 4 years: 364 percent (46 percent per year)

REVENUE GROWTH ★ ★ ★ ★

Past 4 years: 360 percent (46 percent per year)

STOCK GROWTH ★ ★ ★ ★

Past 4 years: 383 percent (48 percent per year)
Dollar growth: $10,000 over 4 years would have grown to $48,300.

CONSISTENCY ★ ★ ★

Increased earnings per share: 3 of the past 4 years
Increased sales: 4 consecutive years

ADVANCED DIGITAL INFORMATION AT A GLANCE

Fiscal year ended: Oct. 31
Revenue and net income in $millions

						4-Year Growth	
	1996	1997	1998	1999	2000	Avg. Annual (%)	Total (%)
Revenue ($)	58.9	93.2	114	223	271	46	360
Net income ($)	3.43	8.5	1.55	15.5	27.2	68	693
Earnings/share ($)	0.11	0.23	0.04	0.36	0.51	46	364
PE range	23–41	13–25	39–131	9–80	6–30		

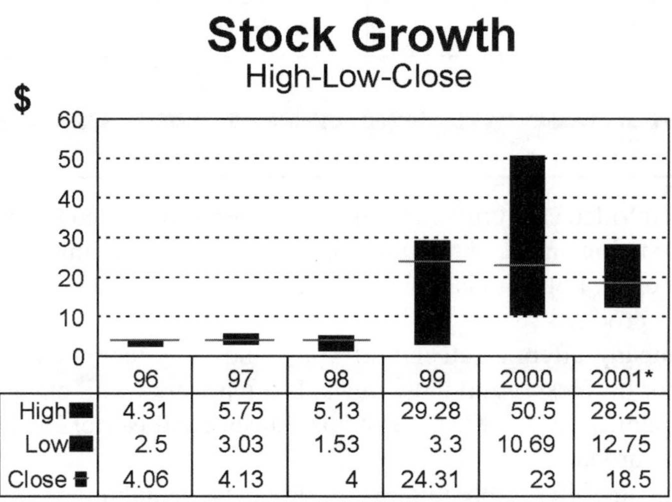

	96	97	98	99	2000	2001*
High	4.31	5.75	5.13	29.28	50.5	28.25
Low	2.5	3.03	1.53	3.3	10.69	12.75
Close	4.06	4.13	4	24.31	23	18.5

*2001 price as of July 1

18

Polycom, Inc.

1565 Barber Lane
Milpitas, CA 95035
408-474-2000
Nasdaq: PLCM
www.polycom.com

Chairman, President, and CEO: Robert C. Hagerty

Earnings Progression	★ ★ ★ ★
Revenue Growth	★ ★ ★ ★
Stock Growth	★ ★ ★ ★
Consistency	★ ★ ★
Total	**15 Points**

Polycom's ViaVideo can turn your home computer into a video telephone, and its ViewStation units can turn any room in your business into a videoconference center. Polycom is the world market leader in video and voice conferencing products.

The company offers a full line of voice and video communications equipment for businesses and individuals. It often works with other technology companies, such as Cisco Systems, Lucent, and Nortel Networks, to create new products.

The company offers a broad range of products, including:

- **Network access products.** Polycom makes integrated access devices and DSL routers that provide DSL and VoDSL (voice-over DSL) service, which makes it possible to send both data and voice over a single DSL connection. In addition to its own NetEngine product line, the company also produces some cobranded and private label versions for leading communications companies, such as Lucent and Nortel.
- **Video communications products.** The company makes video communications products for home and office. For the home computer, its

ViaVideo unit (which costs $599) is a tiny camera with a microphone that can be plugged into the back of a PC and used to conduct video phone conversations through the computer. Its ViewStation video conferencing units for businesses come in several styles and sizes ranging in price from $3,999 to $18,999.

- **Voice communications products.** The company's flagship SoundStation products are designed specifically for voice conferencing, with a microphone and speaker technology that minimizes background echoes, word clipping, and distortion. The units range in cost from $249 to $2,799.

The Milpitas, California operation sells its products worldwide, with regional offices in Europe, Asia, and Latin America. Its video-conferencing products are now used by most Fortune 100 companies, and Polycom is expanding its marketing efforts to smaller businesses, schools, and home offices.

Founded in 1990, Polycom has about 550 employees and a market capitalization of about $2 billion.

EARNINGS PER SHARE PROGRESSION ★★★★

Past 4 years: 2,000 percent (112 percent per year)

REVENUE GROWTH ★★★★

Past 4 years: 749 percent (70 percent per year)

STOCK GROWTH ★★★★

Past 4 years: 859 percent (76 percent per year)
Dollar growth: $10,000 over 4 years would have grown to about $96,000.

CONSISTENCY ★★★

Positive earnings progression: 3 of the past 4 years
Increased sales: 4 consecutive years

POLYCOM AT A GLANCE

Fiscal year ended: Dec. 31
Revenue and net income in $millions

	1996	1997	1998	1999	2000	4-Year Growth Avg. Annual (%)	4-Year Growth Total (%)
Revenue ($)	39	50.4	117	200	331	70	749
Net income ($)	1.43	–14.1	15.6	29.3	49.2	140	3,340
Earnings/share ($)	0.03	–0.33	0.23	0.40	0.63	112	2,000
PE range	55–158	NA	10–50	14–83	40–113		

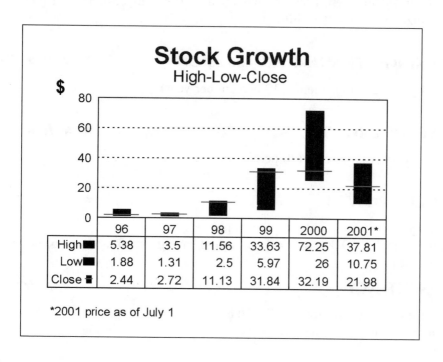

Stock Growth
High-Low-Close

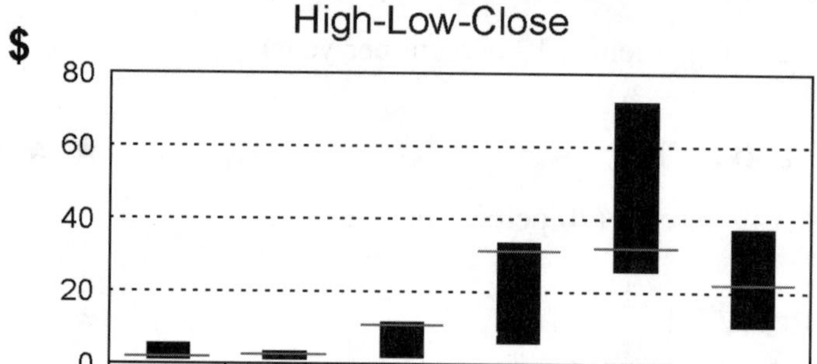

	96	97	98	99	2000	2001*
High	5.38	3.5	11.56	33.63	72.25	37.81
Low	1.88	1.31	2.5	5.97	26	10.75
Close	2.44	2.72	11.13	31.84	32.19	21.98

*2001 price as of July 1

19

TriQuint Semiconductor

2300 N.E. Brookwood Parkway
Hillsboro, OR 97124
503-615-9000
Nasdaq: TQNT
www.triquint.com

Chairman, President, and CEO: Steven J. Sharp

Earnings Progression	★ ★ ★ ★
Revenue Growth	★ ★ ★ ★
Stock Growth	★ ★ ★ ★
Consistency	★ ★ ★
Total	**15 Points**

Silicon microchips may be well known for their high speeds, but compared with gallium arsenide chips, silicon chips move at a snail's pace. Gallium arsenide has inherent physical properties that allow its electrons to move up to five times faster than those of silicon. That enables the chips to operate at much faster rates—or at a similar rate with reduced power consumption.

TriQuint Semiconductor specializes in manufacturing high-speed gallium arsenide microchips for the wireless communications, telecommunications, data communications, and aerospace markets. The firm provides its specialty chips for many of the largest telecommunications companies in the world, including Ericsson, Alcatel, Hughes Electronics, Lucent, Motorola, Nokia, Nortel, and Raytheon.

TriQuint was founded in 1985 by a group of researchers who had been working with gallium arsenide since 1978. The company merged with two other companies involved in making gallium arsenide chips in 1991. The company went public with its initial stock offering in 1993.

The Hillsboro, Oregon operation focuses on four key markets for its specialized chips:

- **Wireless communications.** Its chips are used in satellites, satellite receivers, wireless transceivers for data networks, wireless local area networks, cellular phones, and pagers.
- **Telecommunications.** TriQuint's gallium arsenide chips are used in multiplexers, data transmission systems, and transceivers.
- **Data communications.** Its chips are used to speed up data transmission in computer networks. They are also used in other applications that required the transmission of large amounts of data at high speeds, such as multimedia computing, supercomputing, multiprocessor systems, interactive computer aided design, medical imaging, and high resolution printing.
- **Millimeter wave communications.** Its integrated chips are used in a variety of applications for the digital radio market.

The company sells its microchips to manufacturers worldwide. International sales account for about 44 percent of the company's total revenue.

TriQuint has about 1,100 employees and a market capitalization of about $2 billion.

EARNINGS PER SHARE PROGRESSION ★★★★

Past 4 years: 592 percent (63 percent per year)

REVENUE GROWTH ★★★★

Past 4 years: 405 percent (50 percent per year)

STOCK GROWTH ★★★★

Past 4 years: 508 percent (57 percent per year)
Dollar growth: $10,000 over 4 years would have grown to $61,000.

CONSISTENCY ★★★

Increased earnings per share: 3 of the past 4 years
Increased sales: 4 consecutive years

TRIQUINT SEMICONDUCTOR AT A GLANCE

Fiscal year ended: Dec. 31
Revenue and net income in $millions

	1996	1997	1998	1999	2000	4-Year Growth Avg. Annual (%)	4-Year Growth Total (%)
Revenue ($)	59.5	71.4	112	164	301	50	405
Net income ($)	6.3	6.9	–3.9	24.9	71.4	84	1,033
Earnings/share ($)	0.12	0.13	–0.07	0.34	0.83	63	592
PE range	12–42	22–60	NA	7–84	25–81		

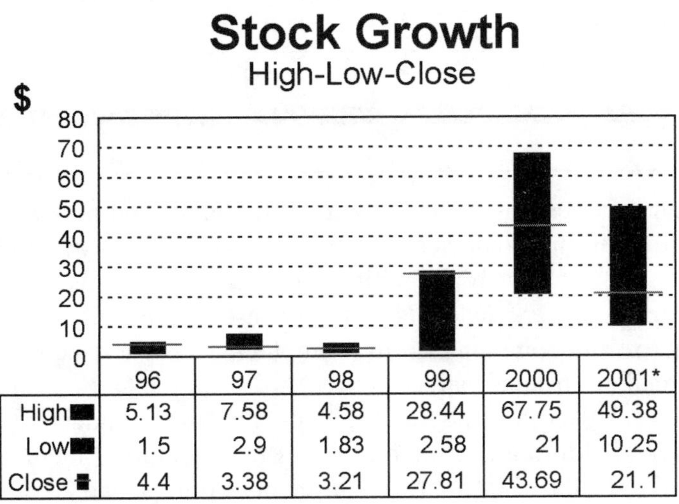

	96	97	98	99	2000	2001*
High	5.13	7.58	4.58	28.44	67.75	49.38
Low	1.5	2.9	1.83	2.58	21	10.25
Close	4.4	3.38	3.21	27.81	43.69	21.1

*2001 price as of July 1

20

Semtech Corporation

652 Mitchell Road
Newbury Park, CA 91320
805-498-2111
Nasdaq: SMTC
www.semtech.com

Chairman, President, and CEO: John D. Poe

Earnings Progression	★★★★
Revenue Growth	★★★★
Stock Growth	★★★★
Consistency	★★★
Total	**15 Points**

Semtech manufactures semiconductors used to control and protect computers and other electronic devices. At one time, the company's products were used almost exclusively for military applications, but over the past six years, Semtech has expanded its customer base dramatically, with corporate clients in the communications, computer, video, test equipment, and commercial electronics markets.

Semtech makes both analog and mixed-signal semiconductors. The Newbury Park, California operation also has manufacturing facilities in Mexico and Scotland and sales offices throughout Europe and Asia.

The company produces products for five core markets:

- **Power management circuits.** Its semiconductors are used to control and regulate the electric pulses in PCs, servers, workstations, notebook computers, cell phones, routers, hubs, and industrial power supplies.
- **Protection.** Semtech chips are used to protect against voltage spikes and other electrical damage in notebook computers, network cards, cell phones, base stations, routers, hubs, and industrial test instruments.

- **High performance circuits.** The firm makes pin electronics, timing, clock distribution, and parametric measurement products for use in automated test equipment, workstations, cellular base stations, routers, hubs, and networks.
- **Advanced communications circuits.** The company's newest line of integrated circuits is designed to transmit and receive signals over fiber-optic lines and provide timing and synchronization and other communications functions. The chips are used for computer networks, cell phone base stations, routers, hubs, switches, and fiber-optic modems.
- **Human interface devices and system management.** Semtech makes touch-screen and touch-pad controllers, pointing stick devices, and battery management circuits for notebook computers, cell phones, and handheld digital devices.

The company also makes rectifiers (used to convert alternating current to direct current) primarily for the military and aerospace market, and it makes customized integrated circuits for the industrial, consumer electronics, and automotive manufacturing markets.

Semtech has about 800 employees and a market capitalization of about $2 billion.

EARNINGS PER SHARE PROGRESSION ★★★★

Past 4 years: 427 percent (52 percent per year)

REVENUE GROWTH ★★★★

Past 4 years: 259 percent (37 percent per year)

STOCK GROWTH ★★★★

Past 4 years: 1,255 percent (91 percent per year)
Dollar growth: $10,000 over 4 years would have grown to $135,500.

CONSISTENCY ★★★

Positive earnings progression: 3 of the past 4 years
Increased sales: 4 consecutive years

SEMTECH AT A GLANCE

Fiscal year ended: Jan. 31
Revenue and net income in $millions

	1997	1998	1999	2000	2001	4-Year Growth Avg. Annual (%)	4-Year Growth Total (%)
Revenue ($)	71.6	103	114	174	257	37	259
Net income ($)	8.49	14.8	12.9	29.4	60.2	63	609
Earnings/share ($)	0.15	0.24	0.20	0.42	0.79	52	427
PE range	4–21	13–60	9–36	30–141	36–144		

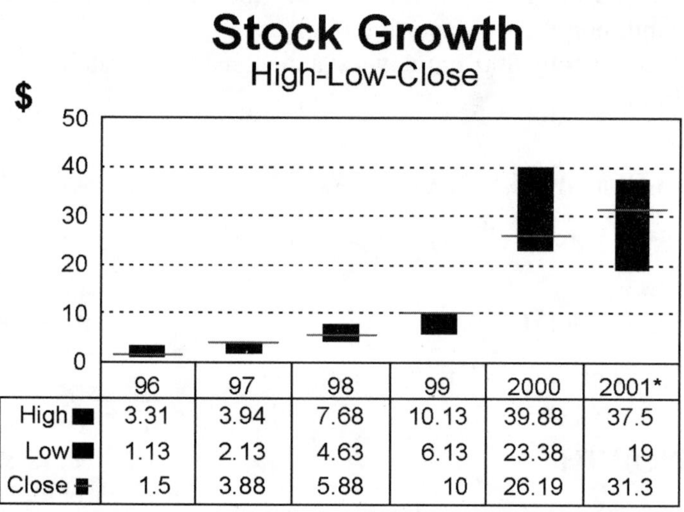

	96	97	98	99	2000	2001*
High	3.31	3.94	7.68	10.13	39.88	37.5
Low	1.13	2.13	4.63	6.13	23.38	19
Close	1.5	3.88	5.88	10	26.19	31.3

*2001 price as of July 1

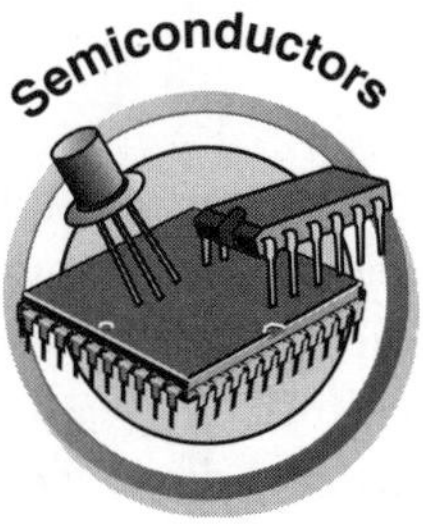

21
Altera Corporation

101 Innovation Drive
San Jose, CA 95134
408-544-7000
Nasdaq: ALTR
www.altera.com

Chairman: Rodney Smith
President and CEO: John Daane

Earnings Progression	★ ★ ★ ★
Revenue Growth	★ ★ ★
Stock Growth	★ ★ ★ ★
Consistency	★ ★ ★ ★
Total	**15 Points**

Electronics companies are able to design and market their products faster these days thanks to a semiconductor chip technology developed by Altera in the 1980s. Altera's leading product is the "programmable logic chip," which is used to set up many of the standard functions in computers, telephones, data communications equipment, and industrial applications. The magic of Altera's chips is that they can be programmed by engineers quickly and easily with software that runs on personal computers or engineering workstations.

Altera also offers a line of software tools for logic development. The company's primary markets include communications equipment (67 percent of sales), electronic data processing (17 percent), industrial equipment (11 percent), consumer products (2 percent), and other applications such as military and aerospace systems (3 percent). Altera chips are used in the electronic systems of high-speed trains, high definition television sets, professional videorecording systems, complex medical equipment, traffic lights, printers, and a wide variety of other high-end, high-tech products.

In all, the company has more than 13,000 corporate customers around the world. International sales account for about 43 percent of total revenue. The company sells more than 500 different products and product combinations.

The first logic chip, introduced by Altera in 1984, boasted a density of 300 gates (a unit of measurement for logic). Now the densities reach as high as 1.5 million gates on a single chip, allowing dramatically faster and more complex programmable performance. Altera also produces specialized software packages for engineering functions and provides application assistance, design services, and customer training.

The programmable chip market has been growing rapidly in recent years. Altera's programmable chips can be purchased "off the shelf" and configured by customers to their specific requirements.

Founded in 1983, Altera Corporation has about 2,000 employees and a market capitalization of about $9 billion.

EARNINGS PER SHARE PROGRESSION ★★★★

Past 4 years: 310 percent (43 percent per year)

REVENUE GROWTH ★★★

Past 4 years: 177 percent (29 percent per year)

STOCK GROWTH ★★★★

Past 4 years: 230 percent (32 percent per year)
Dollar growth: $10,000 over 4 years would have grown to $33,000.

CONSISTENCY ★★★★

Increased earnings per share: 4 consecutive years
Increased sales: 4 consecutive years

ALTERA AT A GLANCE

Fiscal year ended: Dec. 31
Revenue and net income in $millions

	1996	1997	1998	1999	2000	4-Year Growth	
						Avg. Annual (%)	Total (%)
Revenue ($)	497	631	654	837	1,377	29	177
Net income ($)	109	151	165	232	498	46	357
Earnings/share ($)	0.29	0.34	0.39	0.54	1.19	43	310
PE range	11–34	19–42	18–39	22–63	16–56		

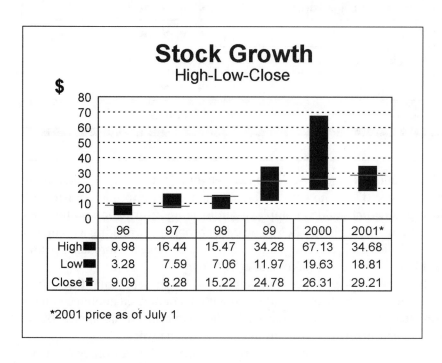

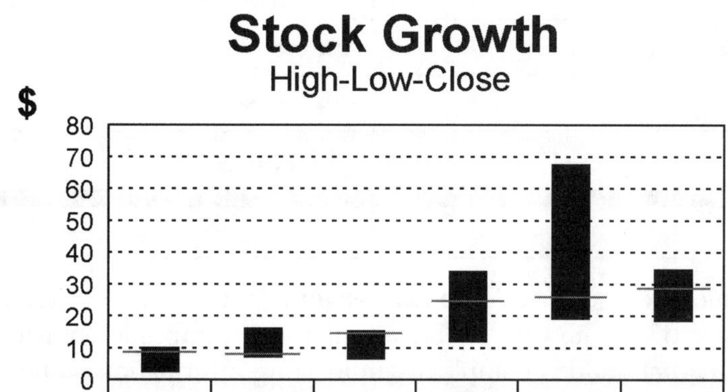

	96	97	98	99	2000	2001*
High	9.98	16.44	15.47	34.28	67.13	34.68
Low	3.28	7.59	7.06	11.97	19.63	18.81
Close	9.09	8.28	15.22	24.78	26.31	29.21

*2001 price as of July 1

22
Network Appliance, Inc.

495 East Java Drive
Sunnyvale, CA 94089
408-822-6000
Nasdaq: NTAP
www.networkappliance.com

Chairman: Donald T. Valentine
President: Thomas F. Mendoza
CEO: Daniel J. Warmenhoven

Earnings Progression	★ ★ ★ ★
Revenue Growth	★ ★ ★ ★
Stock Growth	★ ★ ★ ★
Consistency	★ ★ ★
Total	**15 Points**

As companies expand their computer networks, they also must add more storage disks to keep up with the increasing flow of information. But with added disks comes added complexity in locating information on that network. Network Appliance helps solve that problem by making a computer storage device called a "filer" that companies can use to store and retrieve data on their network quickly and efficiently.

The Network Appliance filer concept works by separating the storage system from the application and placing it on a dedicated appliance that is optimized to serve data. Attached to the network, the appliance offers quicker centralized access to all the data in the network.

The filers give organizations virtually unlimited data storage capacity. And because they are attached to the organization's network, all the computer users in the organization have easy access to store and retrieve data. The filers are built with a software system that optimizes file service task performance, providing faster and more dependable access than the general-purpose computers traditionally used to store data. They also guarantee data and system availability even after a disk failure.

The Sunnyvale, California operation markets its data storage devices worldwide. The company's products are used by 10 of the 15 most popular Web sites.

Network Appliance offers a variety of storage devices and related products, including:

- **SnapMirror and SnapRestore.** These products provide data backup and disaster recovery, allowing companies to minimize downtime and eliminate unnecessary storage investment and time-consuming backup routines.
- **Caching appliance.** The company's NetCache appliances are used to make it quicker and easier for users to retrieve data from computer networks and data centers.
- **SecureAdmin.** This network security device allows administrators to conduct encrypted sessions over the Internet and corporate intranets.

Network Appliance went public with its initial stock offering in 1995. It has about 1,500 employees and a market capitalization of about $7 billion.

EARNINGS PER SHARE PROGRESSION ★ ★ ★ ★

Past 3 years: 200 percent (45 percent per year)

REVENUE GROWTH ★ ★ ★ ★

Past 4 years: 978 percent (82 percent per year)

STOCK GROWTH ★ ★ ★ ★

Past 4 years: 568 percent (61 percent per year)
Dollar growth: $10,000 over 4 years would have grown to $66,800.

CONSISTENCY ★ ★ ★

Increased earnings per share: 3 of the past 4 years
Increased sales: 4 consecutive years

NETWORK APPLIANCE AT A GLANCE

Fiscal year ended: April 30
Revenue and net income in $millions

	1997	1998	1999	2000	2001	4-Year Growth Avg. Annual (%)	4-Year Growth Total (%)
Revenue ($)	93.3	166	289	579	1,006	82	978
Net income ($)	0.250	20.9	35.6	73.8	74.9	135	29,860
Earnings/share ($)	0.00	0.07	0.11	0.21	0.21	45*	200*
PE ratio range	1328–4500	44–164	83–402	158–713	NA		

* Earnings per share growth figures are based on 3-year growth.

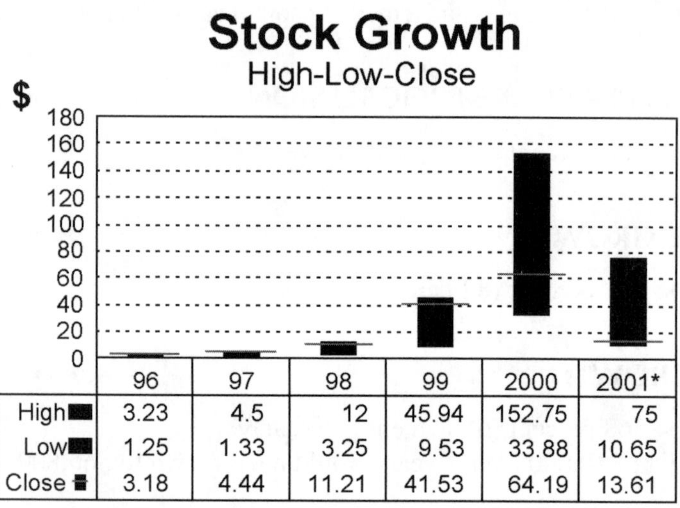

	96	97	98	99	2000	2001*
High	3.23	4.5	12	45.94	152.75	75
Low	1.25	1.33	3.25	9.53	33.88	10.65
Close	3.18	4.44	11.21	41.53	64.19	13.61

*2001 price as of July 1

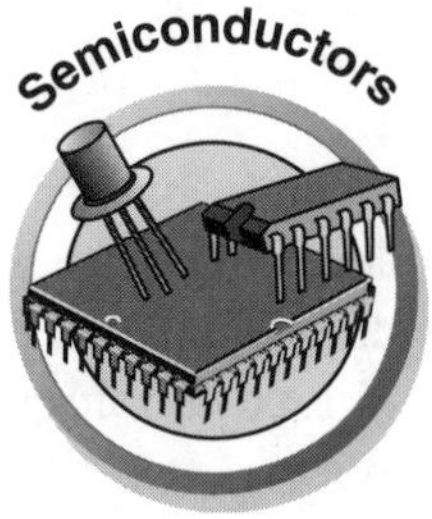

23

Broadcom Corporation

16215 Alton Parkway
Irvine, CA 92618
949-450-8700
Nasdaq: BRCM
www.broadcom.com

Co-Chairman, President, and CEO: Henry T. Nicholas, III
Co-Chairman: Henry Samueli

Earnings Progression	★★★★
Revenue Growth	★★★★
Stock Growth	★★★★
Consistency	★★★
Total	**15 Points**

Broadcom's high bandwidth microchips have helped bring "convergence" to the Internet. The company's innovative microchips are designed to enable high-speed communications devices to merge voice, video, and data into a single common Internet medium.

But Broadcom offers more than just microchips. In fact, the Irvine, California operation provides a broad range of sophisticated products designed to facilitate the convergence process, including cable set-top boxes and cable modems, digital broadcast satellites and terrestrial digital broadcast stations, digital subscriber line (DSL) modems, and central phone office switches. It also makes broadband interface cards that connect PCs and larger computers to office networks, communications processors, 10-Gigabit switching devices, and high-performance software for server and storage platforms, network appliances, and workstations.

Competing in such a wide range of markets is very uncommon in the chip business, especially with a small company. But Broadcom has found that serving diverse markets can be a real advantage, because it can transfer know-how learned in one broadband chip market to the others.

Broadcom's strategy seems to be right on target. Not only have its flagship cable products captured an 80 percent market share, but its other products are compiling impressive results as well. Broadcom is the first manufacturer to develop single chip products for three distinct technology applications. Its chips are used for Internet connection devices, local networks, and cable modems.

Broadcom's secret seems to be in its rigorous design and development methods. The company's strategy also spreads risk across the various media competing for the Internet convergence marketplace—especially in the battle between DSL modems and cable for the "last mile" of wire linking the home to the Internet.

Founded in 1991, Broadcom positioned itself at the ground floor of the convergence arena. The company went public with its initial stock offering in 1998. Broadcom has about 1,100 employees and a market capitalization of about $8 billion.

EARNINGS PER SHARE PROGRESSION ★ ★ ★ ★

Past 4 years: 5,100 percent (170 percent per year)

REVENUE GROWTH ★ ★ ★ ★

Past 4 years: 4,486 percent (164 percent per year)

STOCK GROWTH ★ ★ ★ ★

Past 3 years: 150 percent (36 percent per year)
Dollar growth: $10,000 over 3 years would have grown to about $25,000.

CONSISTENCY ★ ★ ★

Positive earnings progression: 3 of the past 4 years
Increased sales: 4 consecutive years

BROADCOM AT A GLANCE

Fiscal year ended: Dec. 31
Revenue and net income in $millions

	1996	1997	1998	1999	2000	4-Year Growth Avg. Annual (%)	4-Year Growth Total (%)
Revenue ($)	23.9	42.3	217	521	1,096	164	4,486
Net income ($)	2.44	–6.97	21.4	99.8	271	380	11,006
Earnings/share ($)	0.02	–0.06	0.10	0.31	1.04	170	5,100
PE range	NA	NA	112–324	75–469	NA	NA	

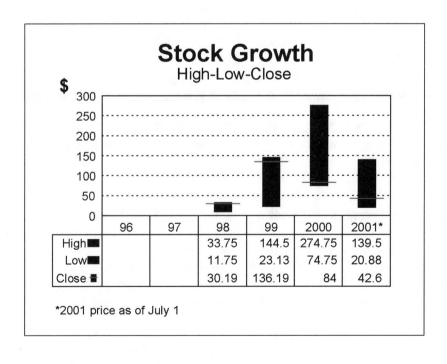

Stock Growth
High-Low-Close

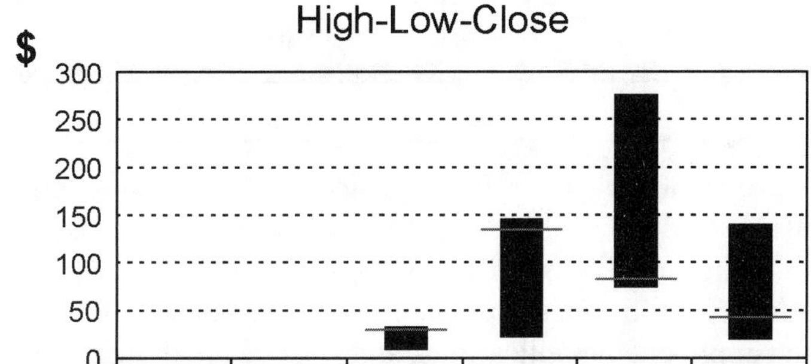

	96	97	98	99	2000	2001*
High			33.75	144.5	274.75	139.5
Low			11.75	23.13	74.75	20.88
Close			30.19	136.19	84	42.6

*2001 price as of July 1

24

Oracle Corporation

500 Oracle Parkway
Redwood Shores, CA 94065
650-506-7000
Nasdaq: ORCL
www.oracle.com

Chairman and CEO: Lawrence Ellison

Earnings Progression	★ ★ ★ ★
Revenue Growth	★ ★ ★
Stock Growth	★ ★ ★ ★
Consistency	★ ★ ★
Total	**14 Points**

Oracle software is not as pervasive as Microsoft's Windows operating software, but the Redwood Shores, California operation has become the world's second largest software maker. Oracle specializes in database and development software, business applications for sales and service, manufacturing and supply chain applications, and finance and human resources software.

With Oracle software, computer users can tap into computer resources anywhere, anytime. The Oracle relational database management systems enable users to define, retrieve, manipulate, and control data stored on multiple computers, and to manage video, audio, text, messaging, and spatial data.

Oracle's e-business software suite is designed to put a company's entire business on the Internet, including marketing, sales, service, procurement, supply chain, manufacturing, accounting, and human resources. "All the applications in our suite are designed and engineered to work together," says Oracle founder and CEO Larry Ellison. "So customers buying the entire suite don't need to do any systems integration."

Oracle makes software products that fit into three different categories: server technologies, application development and business intelligence tools, and business applications.

The company's server technology products include database servers, connectivity products, and gateways. Its application development tools consist of a set of software products used to build database applications for both client server and Web environments. Oracle's business application products consist of more than 45 integrated software modules for financial management, supply chain management, manufacturing, project systems, human resources, and front office applications.

The company's principal products run on a broad range of computers, including mainframes, minicomputers, workstations, personal computers, and laptops. Oracle software can function on 85 different operating systems, including UNIX, Windows, and Windows NT.

Oracle markets its products in 145 countries around the world. International sales account for about half of its total revenue.

Founded in 1977, Oracle has about 41,000 employees and a market capitalization of $110 billion.

EARNINGS PER SHARE PROGRESSION ★ ★ ★ ★

Past 4 years: 590 percent (62 percent per year)

REVENUE GROWTH ★ ★ ★

Past 4 years: 139 percent (24 percent per year)

STOCK GROWTH ★ ★ ★ ★

Past 4 years: 288 percent (41 percent per year)
Dollar growth: $10,000 over 4 years would have grown to $38,800.

CONSISTENCY ★ ★ ★

Increased earnings per share: 3 of the past 4 years
Increased sales: 4 consecutive years

ORACLE AT A GLANCE

Fiscal year ended: May 31
Revenue and net income in $billions

	1996	1997	1998	1999	2000	4-Year Growth Avg. Annual (%)	4-Year Growth Total (%)
Revenue ($)	4.22	5.68	7.14	8.83	10.1	24	139
Net income ($)	0.603	0.821	0.814	1.29	2.1	37	250
Earnings/share ($)	0.10	0.14	0.14	0.22	0.69	62	590
PE range	29–56	25–51	21–54	24–130	20–44		

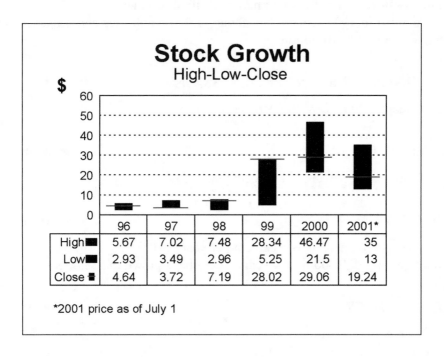

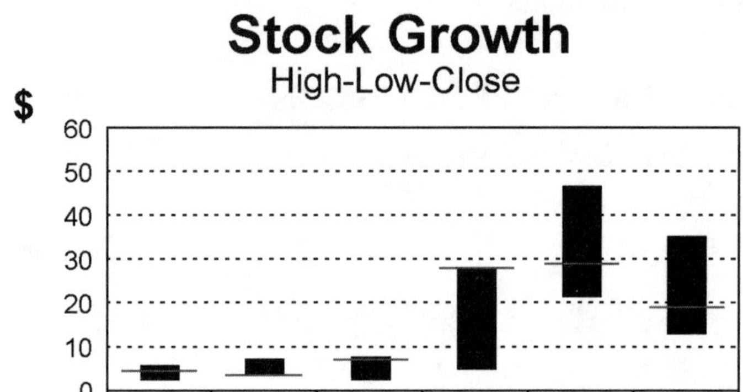

	96	97	98	99	2000	2001*
High	5.67	7.02	7.48	28.34	46.47	35
Low	2.93	3.49	2.96	5.25	21.5	13
Close	4.64	3.72	7.19	28.02	29.06	19.24

*2001 price as of July 1

25

Sun Microsystems, Inc.

901 San Antonio Road
Palo Alto, CA 94303
650-960-1300
Nasdaq: SUNW
www.sun.com

Chairman and CEO: Scottt G. McNealy
President: Edward J. Zander

Earnings Progression	★★★★
Revenue Growth	★★★
Stock Growth	★★★★
Consistency	★★★
Total	**14 Points**

One of the brightest lights in the high-technology galaxy is Sun Microsystems, a maker of sophisticated workstations, storage devices, and servers.

In 2001, Sun introduced high-end servers using its own well-regarded SPARC microprocessors and Solaris operating system to power big B2B e-commerce sites and service provider networks.

Sun management believes e-commerce has a sunny future despite the meltdown of many dot-coms in 2000. However, Sun, which had been billing itself as the company that put "the dot in .com," changed its tune in a new $100 million ad campaign. The new campaign puts the spotlight on Sun's server products as tools to help information technology managers take their businesses to the next level of e-commerce.

The new tagline "Take it to the nth" is engineer-speak that suggests Sun can help technology managers expand their business to an exponential degree. The company, which has always been well thought of in Fortune 500 circles, plans to focus its energies on serving that market while distancing itself from the dying-breed dot-coms.

Another leading product is Java, a programming language Sun invented in 1991 that can help create software to run on any type of computer without being modified. Many companies have chosen Java to develop server-based Internet commerce applications.

Sun's iPlanet, the e-commerce arm of the Sun-Netscape alliance, sees great potential for extending office communications and workgroup management functions into wireless devices through the Java programming language. Companies such as Motorola, Nokia, Sprint PCS, Japan's NTT DoCoMo, and other handset builders and wireless Internet providers are using Java. Sun's Jini technology allows electronic devices to communicate with each other and over networks.

CEO Scott McNealy, who founded the company in 1982, maintains a high profile in the technology world. He has been one of the most outspoken critics of Bill Gates and Microsoft. Sun has about 38,000 employees and a market capitalization of about $70 billion.

EARNINGS PER SHARE PROGRESSION ★★★★

Past 4 years: 267 percent (37 percent per year)

REVENUE GROWTH ★★★

Past 4 years: 121 percent (22 percent per year)

STOCK GROWTH ★★★★

Past 4 years: 414 percent (51 percent per year)
Dollar growth: $10,000 over 4 years would have grown to about $51,000.

CONSISTENCY ★★★

Increased earnings per share: 3 of the past 4 years
Increased sales: 4 consecutive years

SUN MICROSYSTEMS AT A GLANCE

Fiscal year ended: June 30
Revenue and net income in $billions

						4-Year Growth	
	1996	1997	1998	1999	2000	Avg. Annual (%)	Total (%)
Revenue ($)	7.09	8.6	9.86	11.8	15.7	22	121
Net income ($)	0.476	0.762	0.755	1.03	1.85	40	289
Earnings/share ($)	0.15	0.24	0.24	0.31	0.55	37	267
PE range	14–29	13–27	19–46	34–132	45–117		

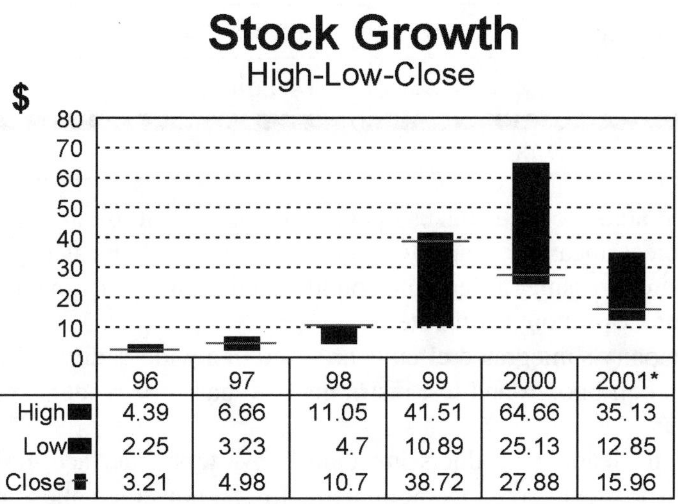

	96	97	98	99	2000	2001*
High	4.39	6.66	11.05	41.51	64.66	35.13
Low	2.25	3.23	4.7	10.89	25.13	12.85
Close	3.21	4.98	10.7	38.72	27.88	15.96

*2001 price as of July 1

26
Maxim Integrated Products

120 San Gabriel Drive
Sunnyvale, CA 94086
408-737-7600
Nasdaq: MXIM
www.maxim-ic.com

Chairman, President, and CEO: John Gifford

Earnings Progression	★ ★ ★
Revenue Growth	★ ★ ★
Stock Growth	★ ★ ★ ★
Consistency	★ ★ ★ ★
Total	**14 Points**

Maxim Integrated Products makes integrated circuits that use digital technology to detect, measure, amplify, and convert real world measures, such as temperature, pressure, speed, and sound into digital signals that can be stored and processed on a computer.

The company's integrated circuits are used in a wide variety of applications from cell phones and test instruments to bar-code readers and cable TV.

Among its leading products are data converters, interface circuits, microprocessor supervisors, operational amplifiers, power supplies, multiplexers, switches, battery chargers, battery management circuits, fiber-optic transceivers, and voltage references.

In all, the Sunnyvale, California operation markets more than 2,000 products. Many of its products are used on microprocessor-based electronics equipment, such as personal computers and peripherals, test equipment, handheld devices, wireless phones and pagers, and video displays.

The company produces products for four key industries:

- **Communications.** It makes products for broadband networks, cable systems, central office switches, direct broadcast TV, fiber optics, pagers, cellular phones, satellite communications, and video communications.
- **Industrial control industry.** Its products are used to control temperature, velocity, flow, pressure, and position.
- **Instrumentation.** Maxim circuits are used for automatic test equipment, analyzers, data recorders, and instruments used to measure electricity, light, pressure, sound, speed, and temperature.
- **Data processing.** The firm's circuits are used for handheld computers, bar-code readers, disk drives, mainframes, minicomputers, personal computers, printers, point-of-sale terminals, tape drives, servers, and workstations.

The company also produces products for military, video, and medical equipment applications.

Maxim markets its products worldwide. International sales account for about 57 percent of its annual revenue.

The company spends more than $140 million a year on research and development and introduces about 250 new products a year.

Founded in 1983, Maxim has about 4,200 employees and 1,000 shareholders. It has a market capitalization of about $15 billion.

EARNINGS PER SHARE PROGRESSION ★ ★ ★

Past 4 years: 105 percent (20 percent per year)

REVENUE GROWTH ★ ★ ★

Past 4 years: 105 percent (20 percent per year)

STOCK GROWTH ★ ★ ★ ★

Past 4 years: 344 percent (45 percent per year)
Dollar growth: $10,000 over 4 years would have grown to $44,400.

CONSISTENCY ★ ★ ★ ★

Increased earnings per share: 4 consecutive years
Increased sales: 4 consecutive years

MAXIM INTEGRATED PRODUCTS AT A GLANCE

Fiscal year ended: June 30
Revenue and net income in $millions

	1996	1997	1998	1999	2000	4-Year Growth Avg. Annual (%)	4-Year Growth Total (%)
Revenue ($)	422	434	560	607	865	20	105
Net income ($)	123	137	178	196	281	23	127
Earnings/share ($)	0.43	0.47	0.59	0.64	0.88	20	105
PE range	11–27	22–40	18–38	30–74	47–102		

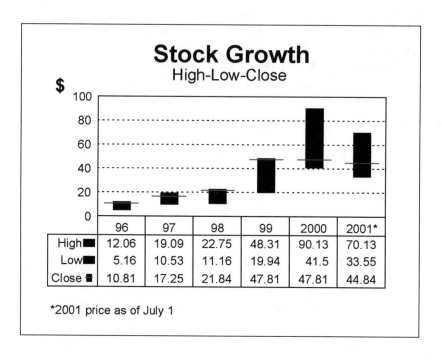

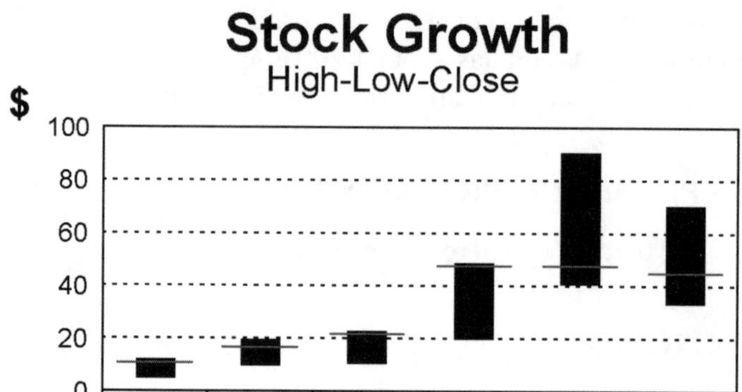

	96	97	98	99	2000	2001*
High	12.06	19.09	22.75	48.31	90.13	70.13
Low	5.16	10.53	11.16	19.94	41.5	33.55
Close	10.81	17.25	21.84	47.81	47.81	44.84

*2001 price as of July 1

27

Cisco Systems, Inc.

170 West Tasman Drive
San Jose, CA 95134
408-526-4000
Nasdaq: CSCO
www.cisco.com

Chairman: John Morgridge
President and CEO: John T. Chambers

Earnings Progression	★ ★ ★
Revenue Growth	★ ★ ★ ★
Stock Growth	★ ★ ★
Consistency	★ ★ ★ ★
Total	**14 Points**

The World Wide Web is held together by Cisco routers, switches, and access servers. The company supplies more than 80 percent of all routers used on the Internet backbone. Nearly all the information on the Internet travels through Cisco Systems products.

Cisco is also the world's leading supplier of networking products for corporate intranets in addition to the global Internet. The San Jose, California operation markets its products to four types of buyers, including:

- Large organizations with complex networking needs, such as corporations, government agencies, and universities
- Major network operators, such as telecommunications carriers, cable companies, and Internet service providers (ISPs)
- Volume markets, such as small businesses and home office users
- Other suppliers who license features of Cisco software for inclusion in their products or services

Under Cisco's corporate growth strategy, dubbed "technical agnosticism," the company adopts competing technologies instead of fighting them. It pursues this strategy mostly by acquiring the most promising startup technology companies (about a half dozen each year). This keeps Cisco at the cutting edge of technology and prevents the management team from becoming inbred and stale.

One of Cisco's most notable strengths is its product architecture. Its entire product line runs the company's IOS operating system, which is perhaps second only to Microsoft Windows in importance. Customers like the fact that its technicians need learn only a single computing environment to do almost any task—which helps lock in Cisco's market position.

Cisco's management track record is unrivaled over the last decade. The company has been able to seamlessly absorb new technologies and corporate acquisitions, while still maintaining a high level of customer satisfaction.

Cisco sells its products through a direct sales force of about 15,000 representatives and technical support personnel. Internationally, the company sells its products in 115 countries through about 120 distributors. Foreign sales account for about 40 percent of the revenue.

Cisco was founded in 1984 by a husband-wife team working at Stanford University who set out to develop a way to tie the world's local networks together. The company brought its first product to market in 1986, and sales have been soaring ever since.

The company has about 34,000 employees and a market capitalization of about $150 billion.

EARNINGS PER SHARE PROGRESSION ★ ★ ★

Past 4 years: 140 percent (25 percent per year)

REVENUE GROWTH ★ ★ ★ ★

Past 4 years: 362 percent (48 percent per year)

STOCK GROWTH ★ ★ ★

Past 4 years: 154 percent (26 percent per year)
Dollar growth: $10,000 over 4 years would have grown to about $25,000.

CONSISTENCY ★ ★ ★ ★

Increased earnings per share: 4 consecutive years
Increased sales: 4 consecutive years

CISCO SYSTEMS AT A GLANCE

Fiscal year ended: July 31
Revenue and net income in $billions

						4-Year Growth	
	1996	1997	1998	1999	2000	Avg. Annual (%)	Total (%)
Revenue ($)	4.09	6.45	8.49	12.2	18.9	48	362
Net income ($)	0.913	1.05	1.33	2.02	2.67	32	192
Earnings/share ($)	0.15	0.17	0.20	0.29	0.36	25	140
PE range	23–50	29–60	42–122	78–186	97–228		

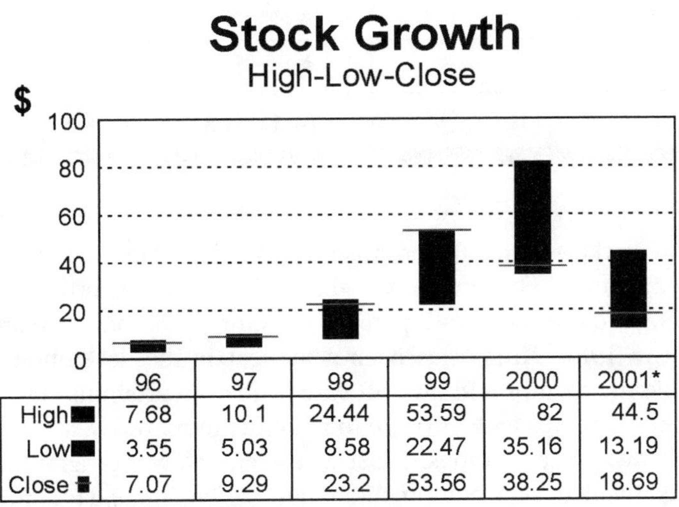

	96	97	98	99	2000	2001*
High	7.68	10.1	24.44	53.59	82	44.5
Low	3.55	5.03	8.58	22.47	35.16	13.19
Close	7.07	9.29	23.2	53.56	38.25	18.69

*2001 price as of July 1

28
Xilinx, Inc.

2100 Logic Drive
San Jose, CA 95124
408-559-7778
Nasdaq: XLNX
www.xilinx.com

Chairman: Bernard V. Vonderschmitt
President and CEO: Willem P. Roelandts

Earnings Progression	★★★★
Revenue Growth	★★★★
Stock Growth	★★★★
Consistency	★★
Total	**14 Points**

Faster time to market—that's the promise Xilinx microchips offer for electronics manufacturers. The company is the leading manufacturing of programmable logic chips, with a 42 percent share of the $4 billion market.

Founded in 1984, Xilinx has been a pioneer in the development of programmable microchips and the software needed to program them.

Xilinx sells its chips and software to manufacturers who can program them to their own specifications. Most of the company's programmable chips are used by electronic equipment manufacturers in the data processing, telecommunications, networking, industrial control, instrumentation, and military markets. The chips are used in computer peripherals, high-speed servers, medical equipment, routers, cellular base stations, industrial instruments, and other electronics equipment and devices.

Among the company's leading customers are IBM, EMC, Cisco Systems, Nortel Networks, Sun Microsystems, and NEC. In all, Xilinx has more than 15,000 clients around the world.

The San Jose operation has offices throughout North America, Europe, and Asia. About 44 percent of the company's revenue comes from customers outside the U.S., including 23 percent from Europe and 12 percent from Japan.

The real competitive edge Xilinx brings to the market is speed. Standard logic chips can require weeks or months of design time before they are ready for the manufacturing stage. Xilinx's "field programmable gate array" chips enable customers to accelerate the programming and development stage to just a few days, allowing them to bring their products to market much faster. Xilinx chips can also be changed in just a few hours, whereas other chips can require several weeks for the same type of adjustments.

Xilinx does not own or operate its own silicon wafer production facilities. Rather, it forms strategic alliances with chip manufacturers who produce chips to Xilinx's specifications at their foundries. That strategy allows Xilinx to focus its resources on research and development, technical support, and marketing.

The company has about 2,000 employees and a market capitalization of about $15 billion.

EARNINGS PER SHARE PROGRESSION ★ ★ ★ ★

Past 4 years: 208 percent (32 percent per year)

REVENUE GROWTH ★ ★ ★ ★

Past 4 years: 192 percent (31 percent per year)

STOCK GROWTH ★ ★ ★ ★

Past 4 years: 433 percent (52 percent per year)
Dollar growth: $10,000 over 4 years would have grown to about $53,000.

CONSISTENCY ★ ★

Increased earnings per share: 2 of the past 4 years
Increased sales: 4 consecutive years

XILINX AT A GLANCE

Fiscal year ended: March 31
Revenue and net income in $millions

	1997	1998	1999	2000	2001	4-Year Growth Avg. Annual (%)	4-Year Growth Total (%)
Revenue ($)	568	613	662	1,021	1,659	31	192
Net income ($)	110	124	134	646	383	36	248
Earnings/share ($)	0.35	0.40	0.33	1.90	1.08	32	208
PE range	20–42	18–42	36–115	18–51	NA		

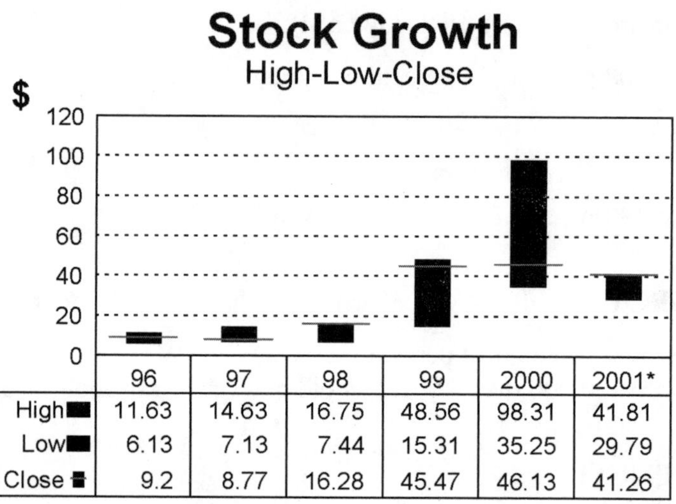

	96	97	98	99	2000	2001*
High	11.63	14.63	16.75	48.56	98.31	41.81
Low	6.13	7.13	7.44	15.31	35.25	29.79
Close	9.2	8.77	16.28	45.47	46.13	41.26

*2001 price as of July 1

29

VeriSign, Inc.

1350 Charleston Road
Mountain View, CA 94043
650-961-7500
Nasdaq: VRSN
www.verisign.com

Chairman: D. James Bidzos
President and CEO: Stratton D. Sclavos

Earnings Progression	★ ★ ★
Revenue Growth	★ ★ ★ ★
Stock Growth	★ ★ ★ ★
Consistency	★ ★ ★
Total	**14 Points**

VeriSign helps businesses get up and running on the World Wide Web. The company offers domain name registration, digital security certificates, and global registry and payment services, which provide the critical Web identity, authentication, and transaction infrastructure online businesses need to establish a Web presence.

The Mountain View, California operation built its business initially by issuing and managing digital certificates, which make it possible to safely pay for goods on the Internet. Its digital certificates are computer files encrypted with virtually unbreakable codes. The tamper-proof certificates are essentially electronic ID cards used by computers to verify the identity of individuals, and even other computers, and are known only to the identified party and the e-commerce site.

In 2000, VeriSign acquired Network Solutions, which is the world leader in domain name registration services. As a result of that acquisition, VeriSign now operates a database of more than 30 million Web addresses in .com, .net, and .org and continues to assign new domain names every day.

The company offers three major service lines through its VeriSign Trust Network:

- **Web site certificate services.** E-merchants use VeriSign not only to protect themselves, but also to give consumers a feeling of security as they expose their credit cards and other personal assets over the Internet.
- **Enterprise certificate services.** VeriSign helps guarantee security within its internal networks and in private "extranet" connections to trading partners.
- **VeriSign affiliate certificate services.** VeriSign outfits affiliates with the software, data centers, and expertise to operate trust services for closed e-commerce and communications networks running over the Internet.

VeriSign is well on its way to becoming the standard for online certificates. Microsoft and Netscape have embedded VeriSign software into their browsers and Web server packages, and Cisco Systems has incorporated VeriSign software into its routers.

The company has about 2,300 employees and a market capitalization of about $11 billion.

EARNINGS PER SHARE PROGRESSION ★★★

The company has gone from losses to gains the past 4 years.

REVENUE GROWTH ★★★★

Past 4 years: 35,085 percent (146 percent per year)

STOCK GROWTH ★★★★

Past 3 years: 445 percent (75 percent per year)
Dollar growth: $10,000 over 3 years would have grown to about $54,000.

CONSISTENCY ★★★

Positive earnings progression: 3 of the past 4 years
Increased sales: 4 consecutive years

VERISIGN AT A GLANCE

Fiscal year ended: Dec. 31
Revenue and net income in $millions

	1996	1997	1998	1999	2000	4-Year Growth Avg. Annual (%)	4-Year Growth Total (%)
Revenue ($)	1.35	13.3	38.9	84.8	475	146	35,085
Net income ($)	–11.1	–20.1	–21	3.12	129	NA	NA
Earnings/share ($)	–0.19	–0.27	–0.24	0.03	0.72	NA	NA
PE range	NA	NA	NA	385–6057	80–400		

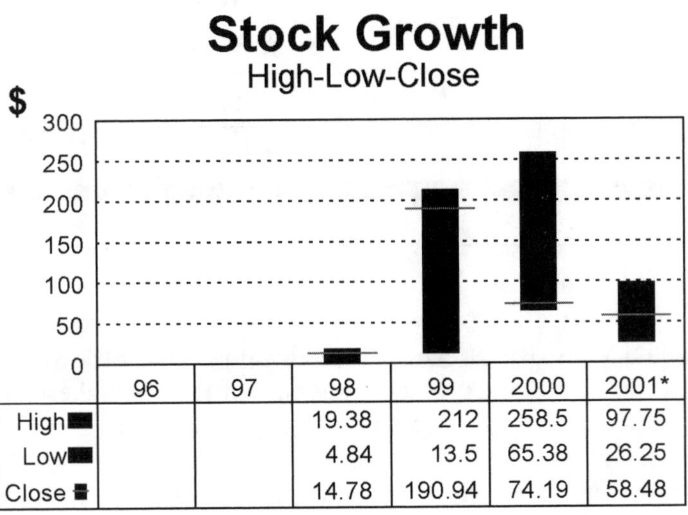

	96	97	98	99	2000	2001*
High			19.38	212	258.5	97.75
Low			4.84	13.5	65.38	26.25
Close			14.78	190.94	74.19	58.48

*2001 price as of July 1

30

MedImmune, Inc.

35 West Watkins Mill Road
Gaithersburg, MD 20878
301-417-0770
Nasdaq: MEDI
www.medimmune.com

Chairman: Wayne Hockmeyer
President: Melvin Booth
CEO: David Mott

Earnings Progression	★★★
Revenue Growth	★★★★
Stock Growth	★★★★
Consistency	★★★
Total	**14 Points**

MedImmune helps children—and their parents—breathe easier.

The company's flagship product, Synagis, is designed to combat respiratory synctial virus (RSV), which is the leading cause of lower respiratory illness in children. Risk for a serious case of RSV is highest among premature infants as well as those with congenital heart disease, chronic lung problems, and immune deficiencies.

The disease, which also affects older people, is responsible for 120,000 pediatric hospitalizations and 4,500 deaths annually. MedImmune, a biotechnology company, launched Synagis in the United States in 1998. The medication has been preventing RSV, the leading cause of viral pneumonia and bronchiolitis in infants and children. The disease most commonly strikes during the cold and flu season of November through March.

Synagis produces about 90 percent of the company's sales. MedImmune took a big step toward broadening its product line in 1999 when it acquired U.S. Bioscience, which gave it access to three drugs already on the market. One of the products, Ethyol, is used in the treatment of ovarian cancer.

One of MedImmune's homegrown products is CytoGam, which prevents and treats disease in people who have undergone kidney, lung, liver, pancreas, or heart transplants. Due to the highly weakened immune systems of the transplant patients, they are vulnerable to infections that can cause pneumonia and other complications that can lead to organ failure and death. The product is marketed through MedImmune's hospital-based sales force.

To keep its new-product pipeline stoked, the company is developing a portfolio of new drugs including those that promise to treat urinary tract infections, genital warts, cocaine addiction, and lyme disease. The company continues to work on feasibility studies in a number of other areas, any one of which it believes can become a significant contributor to the company's profits and revenues.

Founded in 1987, the company has about 800 employees and a market capitalization of about $9 billion.

EARNINGS PER SHARE PROGRESSION ★ ★ ★

The company has gone from large losses to positive earnings over the past 4 years.

REVENUE GROWTH ★ ★ ★ ★

Past 4 years: 1,214 percent (91 percent per year)

STOCK GROWTH ★ ★ ★ ★

Past 4 years: 1,137 percent (87 percent per year)
Dollar growth: $10,000 over 4 years would have grown to $124,000.

CONSISTENCY ★ ★ ★

Increased earnings per share: 3 of the past 4 years
Increased sales: 4 consecutive years

MEDIMMUNE AT A GLANCE

Fiscal year ended: Dec. 31
Revenue and net income in $millions

	1996	1997	1998	1999	2000	4-Year Growth Avg. Annual (%)	4-Year Growth Total (%)
Revenue ($)	41.1	106	227	383	540	91	1,214
Net income ($)	–29.5	–44.8	47.2	93.4	145	75*	207*
Earnings/share ($)	–0.23	–0.30	0.28	0.49	0.66	53*	136*
PE range	NA	NA	26–69	32–132	68–141		

*Net income and earnings per share growth figures are based on 2-year growth.

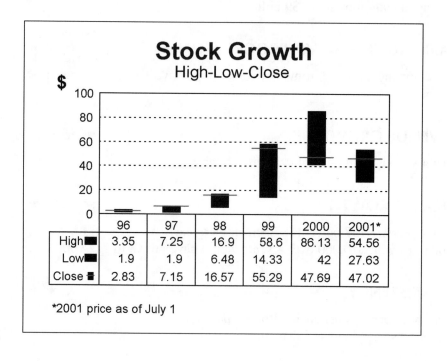

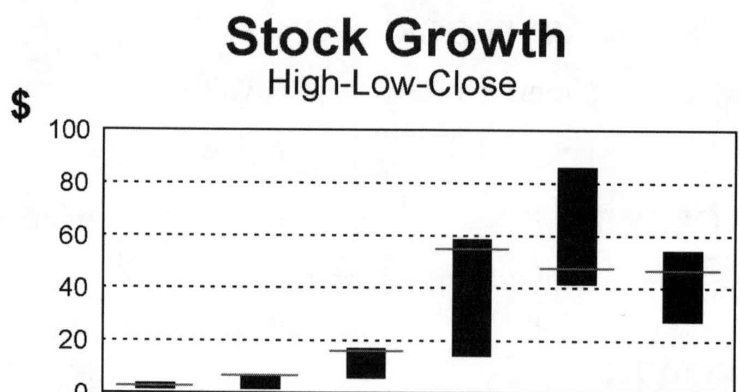

	96	97	98	99	2000	2001*
High	3.35	7.25	16.9	58.6	86.13	54.56
Low	1.9	1.9	6.48	14.33	42	27.63
Close	2.83	7.15	16.57	55.29	47.69	47.02

*2001 price as of July 1

31

AstroPower, Inc.

Solar Park
Newark, DE 19716
302-366-0400
Nasdaq: APWR
www.astropower.com

President and CEO: Allen M. Barnett

Earnings Progression	★ ★ ★ ★
Revenue Growth	★ ★ ★ ★
Stock Growth	★ ★ ★ ★
Consistency	★ ★
Total	**14 Points**

Rising oil prices continue to fuel the growth of AstroPower, which is a leading manufacturer of solar electric power products. The Delaware-based operation makes solar cells, modules, and panels.

AstroPower's solar sells are semiconductor devices that convert sunlight into electricity and form the building block for all solar electric power products.

Although solar power still has limited energy capacity, AstroPower is making progress. Its products are used in three types of applications. The fastest growing is on-grid, in which solar power is used as a supplemental source for customers already connected to a power grid. It is also used for minimal electrification applications in rural areas of underdeveloped countries where standard electric service is not available.

The company's solar cells are also used for a wide range of applications related to the telecommunications and transportation industries, such as cellular phone base stations, fiber-optic and radio repeaters, traffic information, and warning displays.

The company sells several categories of products, including:

- **Solar cells.** These semiconductor devices convert sunlight directly into electricity through a process known as the photovoltaic effect.
- **Modules.** These assemblies of solar cells are connected together and encapsulated in a weatherproof package.
- **Panels.** These are made of several modules wired together at the factory and mounted on a common support structure.
- **Systems.** These groups of panels and system controls are designed primarily for residential rooftops.

AstroPower supplies products worldwide, with regional offices in South Africa and Singapore. It also has a joint venture headquartered in Spain called AstraSolar that helps solar entrepreneurs and distributors enter into the solar module manufacturing business.

Business continues to grow for the company. It recently opened a new manufacturing facility designed to triple the company's manufacturing capacity.

Founded in 1983, AstroPower has about 350 employees and a market capitalization of about $350 million.

EARNINGS PER SHARE PROGRESSION ★ ★ ★ ★

Past 4 years: 1,000 percent (83 percent per year)

REVENUE GROWTH ★ ★ ★ ★

Past 4 years: 248 percent (37 percent per year)

STOCK GROWTH ★ ★ ★ ★

Past 3 years: 305 percent (43 percent per year)
Dollar growth: $10,000 over 3 years would have grown to about $40,000.

CONSISTENCY ★ ★

Increased earnings per share: 2 of the past 4 years
Increased sales: 4 consecutive years

ASTROPOWER AT A GLANCE

Fiscal year ended: Dec. 31
Revenue and net income in $millions

	1996	1997	1998	1999	2000	4-Year Growth Avg. Annual (%)	4-Year Growth Total (%)
Revenue ($)	9.94	10.6	16.6	23.2	34.6	37	248
Net income ($)	0.098	–2.4	0.653	2.41	2.27	119	2,216
Earnings/share ($)	0.02	–0.40	0.10	0.28	0.22	83	1,000
PE range	NA	NA	21–39	37–82	47–235		

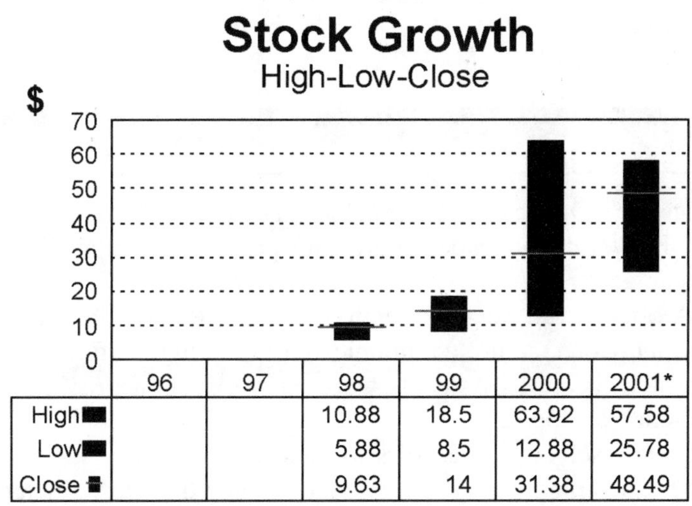

*2001 price as of July 1

32
NVIDIA Corporation

3535 Monroe Street
Santa Clara, CA 95051
408-615-2500
Nasdaq: NVDA
www.nvidia.com

President and CEO: Jen-Hsun Huang

Earnings Progression	★ ★ ★
Revenue Growth	★ ★ ★ ★
Stock Growth	★ ★ ★ ★
Consistency	★ ★ ★
Total	**14 Points**

NVIDIA puts the 3D in computer graphics. The Santa Clara, California operation is the worldwide leader in graphics processors and media communications devices.

NVIDIA offers a full range of semiconductor-based graphics processors for 3D, 2D, video, audio, communications, and high definition digital video and television. Its products work on workstations, mobile PCs, and Internet-enabled appliances.

The company sells its processors to most of the leading electronics manufacturers and computer system builders around the world, including Apple, Compaq, Dell, Gateway, Hewlett-Packard, IBM, NEC, Packard Bell, and Sony.

Its processors are used mostly for video games, although they are also used for manufacturing, e-business, science, entertainment, and education. The company's leading products include:

- **Quadro family of workstation graphics processing units** (GPUs). The company's first graphics boards for the workstation market offer design professionals a complete system for both development and deployment of leading-edge content.

- **GeForce 3.** This GPU adds life to computer-generated graphics. It is the core architecture for the Microsoft Xbox game console.
- **GeForce family of desktop GPUs.** These processing units provide per-pixel operations, such as per-pixel shading, which allow software to present finer detail and enhanced effects.
- **GeForce2 mobile GPU.** This is the first graphics processor available for mobile PCs.
- **TNT2 family of 3D graphics processors.** This high-end GPU offers crisp visuals, higher resolutions, 32-bit color, and outstanding 3D effects.
- **Media communications processors.** This new generation of processors performs demanding multimedia processing for broadband connectivity, communications, and audio functions. It is capable of executing up to 4 billion operations per second.

The company sells its products worldwide, with offices in Australia, Europe, Asia, Japan, and throughout the U.S.

First incorporated in 1993, NVIDIA has about 800 employees and a market capitalization of about $6 billion.

EARNINGS PER SHARE PROGRESSION ★ ★ ★

The company has gone from losses to gains the past 3 years.

REVENUE GROWTH ★ ★ ★ ★

Past 3 years: 1,633 percent (155 percent per year)

STOCK GROWTH ★ ★ ★ ★

Past 2 years: 690 percent
Dollar growth: $10,000 over 2 years would have grown to $79,000.

CONSISTENCY ★ ★ ★

Positive earnings progression: 3 consecutive years
Increased sales: 3 consecutive years

NVIDIA AT A GLANCE

Fiscal year ended: Jan. 31
Revenue and net income in $millions

	1997	1998	1999	2000	2001	3-Year Growth Avg. Annual (%)	3-Year Growth Total (%)
Revenue ($)	NA	42.4	158	374	735	155	1,633
Net income ($)	NA	–2.24	4.13	38.1	99.9	NA	NA
Earnings/share ($)	NA	–0.12	0.07	0.53	1.25	NA	NA
PE range	NA	NA	106–316	33–166	NA		

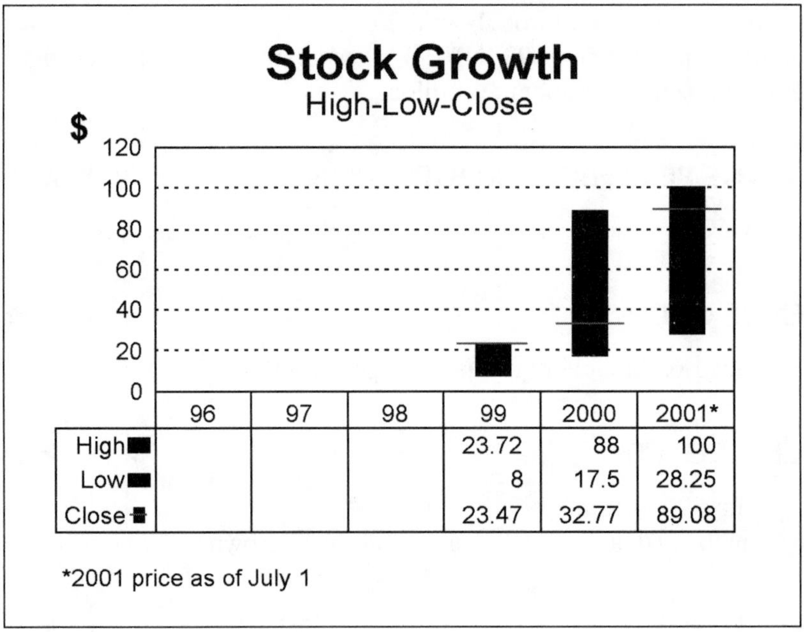

33

Clear Channel Communications

200 East Basse Road
San Antonio, TX 78209
210-822-2828
NYSE: CCU
www.clearchannel.com

Chairman and CEO: Lowry Mays
President: Mark P. Mays

Earnings Progression	★ ★ ★
Revenue Growth	★ ★ ★ ★
Stock Growth	★ ★ ★ ★
Consistency	★ ★ ★
Total	**14 Points**

Clear Channel Communications has become a major player in the electronic media market through an aggressive series of acquisitions. In all, the company owns or operates about 1,200 radio stations and 19 television stations in the United States, and an additional 240 radio stations outside the U.S.

The company also owns more than 700,000 outdoor advertising displays around the world, including billboards, benches, and mass transit panels.

Radio broadcasting accounts for about 45 percent of the company's total revenue, outdoor advertising accounts for 32 percent, live entertainment events account for about 17 percent, and television broadcasting and other sources make up about 6 percent.

Clear Channel's rapid growth began in 1996 after the passage of the Telecommunications Act, which removed the cap on radio station owner restrictions. At the time, Clear Channel owned just 36 radio stations and

10 television stations. It also operated 7 other radio stations and 6 TV stations under time sales, time brokerage, or local marketing agreements.

But the San Antonio operation quickly went into an aggressive acquisition mode, buying out entire groups of stations whenever possible. In addition to its 1,200 radio stations, the company also operates some leading radio network shows, such as Dr. Laura Schlessinger, Jim Rome, Casey Kasem, Rush Limbaugh, and Rick Dees. In all, the network draws about 180 million listeners each week.

In addition to its broadcasting and outdoor advertising businesses, Clear Channel also operates several other divisions. The largest is its live entertainment division, which produces touring and original Broadway shows as well as other entertainment ventures. The firm also owns Katz Media Group, a full-service media representation agency that sells national advertising for radio and TV. Clear Channel also merged with SFX, a sports representation business with such noted athletes as Kobe Bryant, Michael Jordan, Roger Clemens, and Greg Norman.

Clear Channel was founded in 1972 and went public in 1984. The company has about 18,000 employees and a market capitalization of about $34 billion.

EARNINGS PER SHARE PROGRESSION ★ ★ ★

Past 4 years: 128 percent (23 percent per year)

REVENUE GROWTH ★ ★ ★ ★

Past 4 years: 1,418 percent (97 percent per year)

STOCK GROWTH ★ ★ ★ ★

Past 4 years: 243 percent (36 percent per year)
Dollar growth: $10,000 over 4 years would have grown to about $34,000.

CONSISTENCY ★ ★ ★

Increased earnings per share: 3 of the past 4 years
Increased sales: 4 consecutive years

CLEAR CHANNEL AT A GLANCE

Fiscal year ended: Dec. 31
Revenue and net income in $millions

						4-Year Growth	
	1996	**1997**	**1998**	**1999**	**2000**	**Avg. Annual (%)**	**Total (%)**
Revenue ($)	352	697	1,351	2,678	5,345	97	1,418
Net income ($)	42.8	57.0	45.6	69.6	249	55	482
Earnings/share ($)	0.25	0.33	0.22	0.25	0.57	23	128
PE range	50–119	142–287	203–357	72–158	77–168		

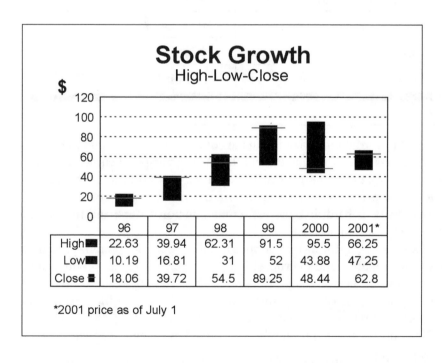

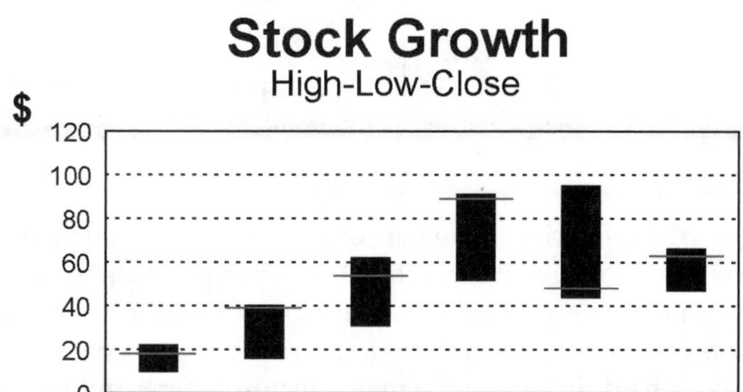

	96	97	98	99	2000	2001*
High	22.63	39.94	62.31	91.5	95.5	66.25
Low	10.19	16.81	31	52	43.88	47.25
Close	18.06	39.72	54.5	89.25	48.44	62.8

*2001 price as of July 1

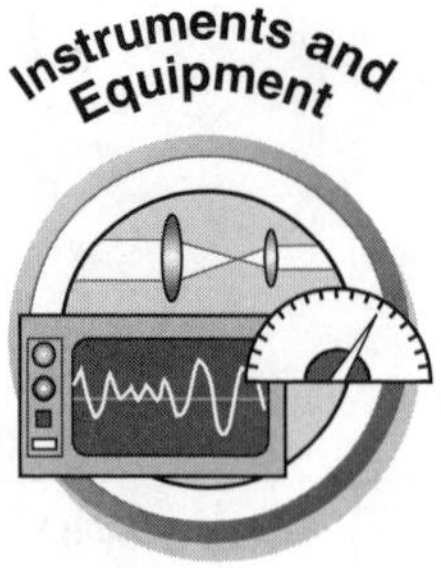

34

Newport Corporation

1791 Deere Avenue
Irvine, CA 92606
949-863-3144
Nasdaq: NEWP
www.newport.com

Chairman, President, and CEO: Robert G. Deuster

Earnings Progression	★ ★ ★ ★
Revenue Growth	★ ★ ★
Stock Growth	★ ★ ★ ★
Consistency	★ ★ ★
Total	**14 Points**

The trend toward miniaturization in the computer and telecommunications industries has forced manufacturers to design their products with greater precision within extremely narrow tolerances. Newport makes test equipment that helps manufacturers make and test reduced-size components of such products as hard disk drives, semiconductor wafers, and fiber-optic communications equipment.

The Irvine, California operation is a leading supplier of high-precision optics, instruments, and micropositioning and measurement products and systems. In all, the company offers more than 10,000 standard products, including a full line of compatible optics, fiber optics, positioners, instruments, and vibration control systems.

Newport breaks its product line into five key categories, including:

- **Positioning equipment.** Newport makes a line of manually operated and motorized positioning equipment for motion control and precision automation applications. Its positioning systems include drives, linear and rotary stages, motion controllers, and related hardware.

- **Optics.** Targeted toward laser users and those working with collimated light, Newport's optics product line includes opto-mechanical devices such as collimators, beam expanders, and spatial filters, as well as optical components such as mirrors, beam splitters, prisms, polarized filters, and lenses.
- **Vibration control.** Newport offers precision product manufacturers a wide selection of tables, workstations, breadboards, accessories, legs, and isolators. It boasts an installed base of over 30,000 systems worldwide.
- **Photonics.** The company makes laser diode instrumentation, optical power and energy meters, optical detectors, optical fibers and fiber-optic components, precision fiber alignment components and systems, as well as lasers and other light sources.
- **Automated photonics packaging.** The firm makes high-precision automated solutions for performing fiber alignment, device characterization, and pigtailing/connectorizing of opto-electronic and integrated optic devices.

Newport sells its products worldwide. International sales account for about one-third of the company's total revenue.

Founded in 1967, Newport has about 1,800 employees and a market capitalization of about $1.3 billion.

EARNINGS PER SHARE PROGRESSION ★★★★

Past 4 years: 406 percent (50 percent per year)

REVENUE GROWTH ★★★

Past 4 years: 111 percent (21 percent per year)

STOCK GROWTH ★★★★

Past 4 years: 1,200 percent (90 percent per year)
Dollar growth: $10,000 over 4 years would have grown to $130,000.

CONSISTENCY ★★★

Increased earnings per share: 3 of the past 4 years
Increased sales: 4 consecutive years

NEWPORT AT A GLANCE

Fiscal year ended: Dec. 31
Revenue and net income in $millions

	1996	1997	1998	1999	2000	4-Year Growth Avg. Annual (%)	4-Year Growth Total (%)
Revenue ($)	120	133	143	144	253	21	111
Net income ($)	4.7	7.1	11.2	7.9	27.8	56	491
Earnings/share ($)	0.17	0.26	0.32	0.29	0.86	50	406
PE range	14–20	10–22	9–23	13–52	15–223		

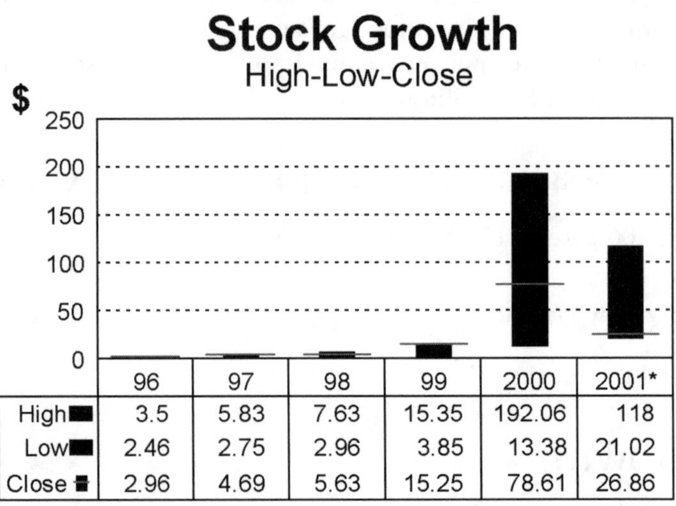

	96	97	98	99	2000	2001*
High	3.5	5.83	7.63	15.35	192.06	118
Low	2.46	2.75	2.96	3.85	13.38	21.02
Close	2.96	4.69	5.63	15.25	78.61	26.86

*2001 price as of July 1

35

Yahoo! Inc.

3420 Central Expressway
Santa Clara, CA 95051
408-731-3300
Nasdaq: YHOO
www.yahoo.com

Chairman and CEO: Timothy Koogle
President: Jeff Mallett

Earnings Progression	★ ★ ★
Revenue Growth	★ ★ ★ ★
Stock Growth	★ ★ ★ ★
Consistency	★ ★ ★
Total	**14 Points**

Yahoo may well be the world's most popular spot. Nearly 200 million Web surfers use the Internet portal service each month for news, online shopping, and search engine services. On average, Yahoo logs nearly a billion page views per day!

Yahoo is the leading Internet portal in terms of traffic, advertising, and household and business user reach. The company, which offers its site free to users, generates revenue primarily through the sale of advertisements, promotions, sponsorships, merchandising, and direct marketing. In all, the company has about 3,700 advertising customers, including more than half of the Fortune 100 companies.

The Santa Clara, California operation offers a comprehensive online navigational guide to the Web utilizing a subject-based directory of Web sites. The Yahoo online directory includes more than a million Web sites organized under a broad range of categories, such as arts and humanities, business and economy, computers and Internet, education, entertainment, government, health, news and media, sports, reference, science, and culture. Each category is broken down further by scores of subcategories to make it easier for users to pinpoint the exact type of site they need.

Users can also search the Web by entering key words that direct them to a variety of Web site choices.

The Yahoo site also includes current information and reference material from such leading content providers as Reuters, Associated Press, Deutsche Presse, ESPN, The Sporting News, the Weather Channel, and the Wall Street Journal. The site includes printed and audio news, sports, business, stock quotes, entertainment news, and weather. It also has auctions, Yellow Pages, maps, driving directions, classified listings, online shopping, chats, message boards, and personal calendars and address book options.

Yahoo has established a prominent global presence on the Web, with 24 international online properties in 13 languages, including localized versions of Yahoo in Argentina, Asia, Australia and New Zealand, Brazil, Canada, China, Denmark, France, Germany, Hong Kong, India, Italy, Japan, Korea, Mexico, Norway, Singapore, Spain, Sweden, the United Kingdom and Ireland, and Taiwan.

Founded in 1994, the company went public with its initial stock offering in 1996. It has about 3,300 employees and a market capitalization of about $11 billion.

EARNINGS PER SHARE PROGRESSION ★ ★ ★

The company has gone from losses to gains the past 4 years.

REVENUE GROWTH ★ ★ ★ ★

Past 4 years: 5,063 percent (167 percent per year)

STOCK GROWTH ★ ★ ★ ★

Past 4 years: 1,349 percent (93 percent per year)
Dollar growth: $10,000 over 4 years would have grown to about $145,000.

CONSISTENCY ★ ★ ★

Positive earnings progression: 3 of the past 4 years
Increased sales: 4 consecutive years

YAHOO! AT A GLANCE

Fiscal year ended: Dec. 31
Revenue and net income in $millions

						4-Year Growth	
	1996	1997	1998	1999	2000	Avg. Annual (%)	Total (%)
Revenue ($)	21.5	84.1	245	592	1,110	167	5,063
Net income ($)	–6.43	–43.4	–12.7	47.8	70.8	NA	NA
Earnings/share ($)	–0.02	–0.11	–0.03	0.08	0.12	NA	NA
PE range	NA	NA	NA	539–2196	216–2155		

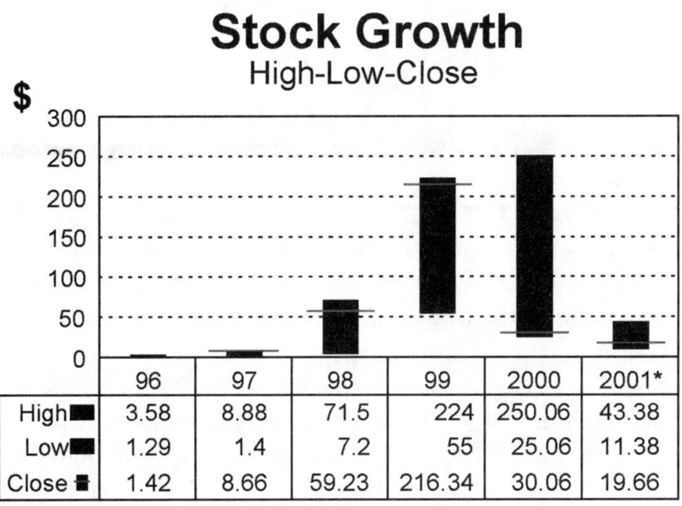

	96	97	98	99	2000	2001*
High	3.58	8.88	71.5	224	250.06	43.38
Low	1.29	1.4	7.2	55	25.06	11.38
Close	1.42	8.66	59.23	216.34	30.06	19.66

*2001 price as of July 1

36

eBay, Inc.

2145 Hamilton Avenue
San Jose, CA 95125
408-558-7400
Nasdaq: EBAY
www.ebay.com

Chairman: Pierre Omidyar
President and CEO: Margaret Whitman

Earnings Progression	★★★★
Revenue Growth	★★★★
Stock Growth	★★★
Consistency	★★
Total	**13 Points**

In the great e-commerce meltdown, more than 2,000 e-tailers gave up the ghost, and scores of others were left gasping for breath. But eBay held tough, standing alone as the one online economic business model that actually works.

Founded in 1995, eBay is the flea market to the world. As the world's biggest online auction, eBay moves one of humanity's most primordial urges—bargain hunting—off the fairgrounds parking lot and onto the Web.

eBay's business model works because it has built-in margins, big growth potential, even natural barriers to would-be competitors. But that's not all—it has no inventory to carry, no warehouse to operate, no order fulfillment to worry about, and can even rely, in large part, on word-of-mouth advertising (that's the only kind its customers listen to anyway). And the company has natural staying power given that its constituency is best served by having a single place to meet and trade. Having dozens of venue options would only dilute the action.

The company's *SafeHarbor* program goes to great lengths to make its Web auction as fraud-proof as possible. Measures include independent verification of user identities, a *Feedback Forum* to check on reputations, an escrow money transfer service, and even free insurance up to $200.

The company charges a nominal item listing fee and collects a 5 percent commission on most sales (somewhat less on high ticket items).

eBay's approach is working. Its site creates more economic activity than any other e-commerce site. The site auctions off well over 100 million items a year and is used by well over 10 million consumers. The company is steadily adding new goods categories.

eBay went public with its initial stock offering in 1998. It has about 140 employees and a market capitalization of about $10 billion.

EARNINGS PER SHARE PROGRESSION ★ ★ ★ ★

Past 4 years: 1,800 percent (106 percent per year)

REVENUE GROWTH ★ ★ ★ ★

Past 4 years: 115,760 percent (480 percent per year)

STOCK GROWTH ★ ★ ★

Past 2 years: 105 percent (43 percent per year)
Dollar growth: $10,000 over 2 years would have grown to about $21,000.

CONSISTENCY ★ ★

Increased earnings per share: 2 of the past 4 years
Increased sales: 4 consecutive years

EBAY AT A GLANCE

Fiscal year ended: Dec. 31
Revenue and net income in $millions

						4-Year Growth	
	1996	1997	1998	1999	2000	Avg. Annual (%)	Total (%)
Revenue ($)	0.372	41.4	86.1	225	431	480	115,760
Net income ($)	0.148	7.7	7.6	9.67	45.2	319	30,441
Earnings/share ($)	0.01	0.14	0.07	0.05	0.19	106	1,800
PE range	NA	NA	135–1673	691–2925	155–741		

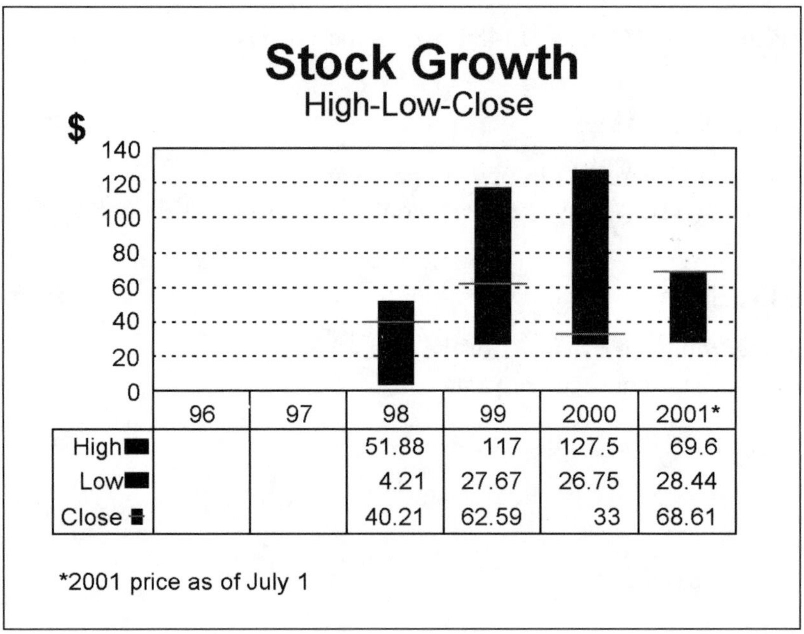

37

AOL Time Warner Inc.

22000 AOL Way
Dulles, VA 20166
703-265-1000
NYSE: AOL
www.aoltimewarner.com

Chairman: Steve Case
CEO: Gerald Levin

Earnings Progression	★★
Revenue Growth	★★★★
Stock Growth	★★★★
Consistency	★★★
Total	**13 Points**

With its acquisition of Time Warner, America Online became the world's leading media conglomerate. In addition to its own online presence, AOL Time Warner now commands a diversified array of magazines, television stations, and other media assets.

AOL is the world's leading Internet portal with more than 23 million subscribers.

Time Warner operates the world's largest media empire, including such popular magazines as *Time, Sports Illustrated, People,* and *Fortune.* It also operates some leading cable television networks, such as CNN, TBS, and TNT, and two of the world's leading music recording operations, Warner Music Group and EMI Group.

AOL operates two Internet services, America Online and CompuServe (which has nearly 3 million subscribers). The company also owns Netscape, which is one of the leading Internet browsers.

AOL was launched in 1989 as an outgrowth of a much smaller service called Q-Link that was started in 1985. Shortly after the name change, the company began aggressively marketing to computer users throughout the U.S.

AOL members pay a monthly fee ranging from about $10 to $22 (depending on the hourly package) that provides them with a wide range of online information and services, including breaking news, business and financial news, stock quotes, investment research, sports, e-mail, and Internet access. Other features include electronic magazines and newspapers, travel features and weather reports, online classes and conferences, an online encyclopedia, and a variety of children's games and information features. The company also offers online shopping through its site, a service that is growing rapidly.

AOL is expanding worldwide, with similar services in Europe and Asia. It also owns about a 25 percent share of Hong Kong-based China.com.

The Virginia-based operation went public with its initial stock offering in 1992. With the Time Warner acquisition, AOL jumps from about 15,000 employees to about 80,000. It has a market capitalization of about $215 billion.

EARNINGS PER SHARE PROGRESSION ★★

The company has had strong growth the past two years after two years of losses.

REVENUE GROWTH ★★★★

Past 4 years: 606 percent (63 percent per year)

STOCK GROWTH ★★★★

Past 4 years: 2,256 percent (118 percent per year)
Dollar growth: $10,000 over 4 years would have grown to about $235,000.

CONSISTENCY ★★★

Positive earnings progression: 3 consecutive years
Increased sales: 4 consecutive years

AOL TIME WARNER AT A GLANCE

Fiscal year ended: June 30
Revenue and net income in $billions

	1996	1997	1998	1999	2000*	4-Year Growth Avg. Annual (%)	4-Year Growth Total (%)
Revenue ($)	1.09	2.19	3.11	4.80	7.70	63	606
Net income ($)	0.30	–0.485	–0.080	0.754	1.15	40	283
Earnings/share ($)	0.02	–0.29	–0.04	0.30	0.45	NA	NA
PE range	82–261	NA	NA	37–321	68–175		

*AOL changed fiscal year end to Dec. 31 in 2000.

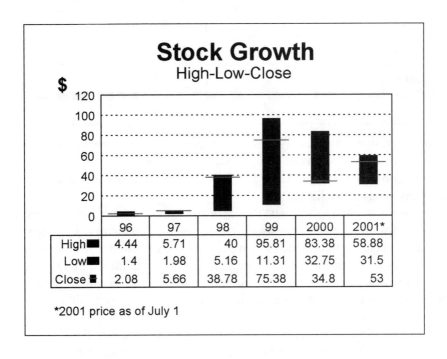

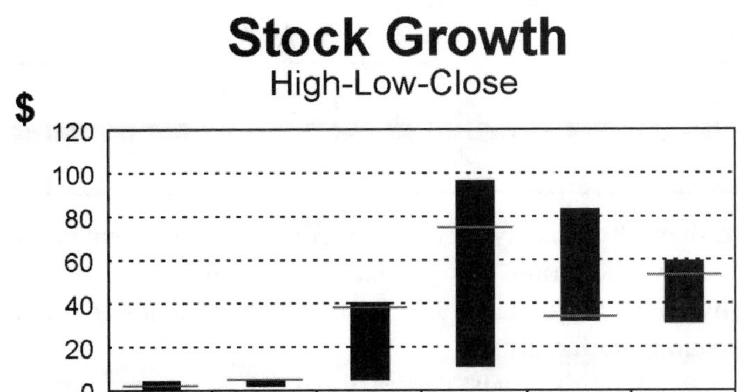

	96	97	98	99	2000	2001*
High	4.44	5.71	40	95.81	83.38	58.88
Low	1.4	1.98	5.16	11.31	32.75	31.5
Close	2.08	5.66	38.78	75.38	34.8	53

*2001 price as of July 1

38

Vishay Intertechnology, Inc.

63 Lincoln Highway
Malvern, PA 19355
610-644-1300
NYSE: VSH
www.vishay.com

Chairman and CEO: Dr. Felix Zandman
President: Gerald Paul

Earnings Progression	★ ★ ★ ★
Revenue Growth	★ ★ ★
Stock Growth	★ ★ ★
Consistency	★ ★ ★
Total	**13 Points**

Chances are there is a Vishay electronics component in your home. The company's passive electronic components are used in the electronic products made by every major U.S. and European electronics manufacturer and many Asian manufacturers.

Vishay is the nation's largest maker of passive electronic components, including resistors, resistive sensors, capacitors, and inductors. The company also makes semiconductor components such as diodes, transistors, optoelectronic products, and power and analog switching circuits. Its components can be found in computers, telephones, TVs, automobiles, household appliances, medical equipment, satellites, and military and aerospace equipment.

Other leading products manufactured by Vishay include fixed resistors, tantalum capacitors, multilayer ceramic chip capacitors, film capacitors, power integrated circuits, signal processing switches, transformers, plasma displays, thermistors, and infrared data transceivers.

The company's passive components are used to adjust and regulate current or store energy and filter frequencies. Its discrete active components, such as diodes and transistors, generate, control, regulate, amplify, or switch electronic signals or energy, and must be interconnected with passive components. Its resistors are used in all forms of electronic circuitry to adjust and regulate levels of voltage and current. Its capacitors perform energy storage, frequency control, timing, and filtering functions in most types of electronic equipment.

The company sells its products through its own sales staff, independent distributors, and manufacturer's representatives in all industrial countries. It has manufacturing facilities in 14 countries and sales and service centers worldwide. In all, the company has 69 manufacturing plants.

Its leading customers include AT&T, Alcatel, Ford, IBM, Intel, Lockheed, Motorola, Samsung, Siemens, Sony, and Sun Microsystems.

Founded in 1962, Vishay began a serious expansion policy in 1985. Since then it has grown rapidly by aggressively acquiring other related manufacturers. The Malvern, Pennsylvania operation has about 22,000 employees and a market capitalization of about $3.5 billion.

EARNINGS PER SHARE PROGRESSION ★★★★

Past 4 years: 797 percent (73 percent per year)

REVENUE GROWTH ★★★

Past 4 years: 124 percent (23 percent per year)

STOCK GROWTH ★★★

Past 4 years: 119 percent (22 percent per year)
Dollar growth: $10,000 over 4 years would have grown to $21,900.

CONSISTENCY ★★★

Increased earnings per share: 3 of the past 4 years
Increased sales: 4 consecutive years

VISHAY INTERTECHNOLOGY AT A GLANCE

Fiscal year ended: Dec. 31
Revenue and net income in $millions

	1996	1997	1998	1999	2000	4-Year Growth: Avg. Annual (%)	4-Year Growth: Total (%)
Revenue ($)	1,098	1,125	1,573	1,760	2,465	23	124
Net income ($)	52.6	55.4	12.0	97.8	542	79	930
Earnings/share ($)	0.41	0.42	0.06	0.65	3.68	73	797
PE ratio range	20–58	22–38	75–192	9–32	3–16		

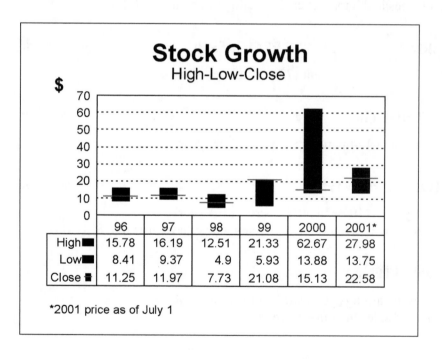

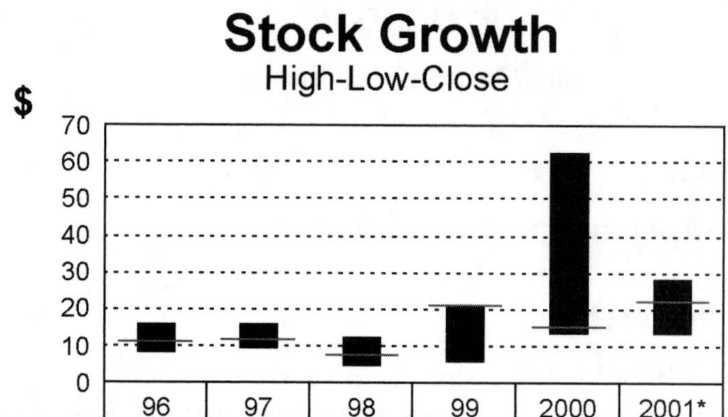

	96	97	98	99	2000	2001*
High	15.78	16.19	12.51	21.33	62.67	27.98
Low	8.41	9.37	4.9	5.93	13.88	13.75
Close	11.25	11.97	7.73	21.08	15.13	22.58

*2001 price as of July 1

Internet

39

Internet Security Systems

6303 Barfield Road
Atlanta, GA 30328
404-236-2943
Nasdaq: ISSX
www.iss.net

Chairman, President, and CEO: Thomas E. Noonan

Earnings Progression	★ ★ ★
Revenue Growth	★ ★ ★ ★
Stock Growth	★ ★ ★
Consistency	★ ★ ★
Total	**13 Points**

Hackers and computer viruses remain a constant threat to corporate and government computer networks around the world. Internet Security Systems (ISS) has turned that threat into a growing business by engineering computer security systems that protect large networks from outside intruders.

ISS designs and manufactures network security monitoring, detection, and response software that protects the security and integrity of computer databases and networks. The ISS system not only repels hackers but also detects and monitors each attempt.

ISS sells its products worldwide to more than 5,500 corporate customers, including 21 of the 25 largest U.S. banks, the top 10 telecommunications companies, and more than 35 government agencies worldwide.

The Atlanta company's core product is the SAFEsuite software package, which incorporates several key components including:

- **Internet Scanner,** which finds and fixes security holes through automated and comprehensive network security vulnerability detection and analysis

- **System Scanner,** which serves as a security assessment system, helping manage security risks through detection and analysis of operating system, application, and user-controlled security weaknesses
- **Database Scanner,** which provides security risk assessment for database management systems
- **Online Scanner,** which provides simple security assessments for home users concerned about their e-commerce transactions
- **RealSecure,** an integrated network- and host-based intrusion detection and response system
- **Intrusion Detection and Response,** which enables organizations to monitor their networks and systems around the clock for attacks and misuse

ISS founder Christopher Klaus developed his first network security software product in 1992 as a 19-year-old college student. In 1994, Klaus teamed up with Thomas Noonan, who still serves as company chairman, president, and CEO, to launch the firm's first commercial security product, Internet Scanner.

ISS went public with its initial stock offering in 1998. It has about 1,200 employees and a market capitalization of about $1 billion.

EARNINGS PER SHARE PROGRESSION ★ ★ ★

The company has gone from losses to a gain in 1999 and 2000.

REVENUE GROWTH ★ ★ ★ ★

Past 4 years: 4,269 percent (157 percent per year)

STOCK GROWTH ★ ★ ★

Past 3 years: 110 percent (29 percent per year)
Dollar growth: $10,000 over 3 years would have grown to $21,000.

CONSISTENCY ★ ★ ★

Positive earnings progression: 3 of the past 4 years
Increased sales: 4 consecutive years

INTERNET SECURITY SYSTEMS AT A GLANCE

Fiscal year ended: Dec. 31
Revenue and net income in $millions

						4-Year Growth	
	1996	1997	1998	1999	2000	Avg. Annual (%)	Total (%)
Revenue ($)	4.46	25.4	57.1	116	195	157	4,269
Net income ($)	–1.13	–3.3	–3.9	7.49	18.3	144	144
Earnings/share ($)	–0.04	–0.18	–0.12	0.17	0.41	141	141
PE range	NA	NA	NA	116–415	113–347		

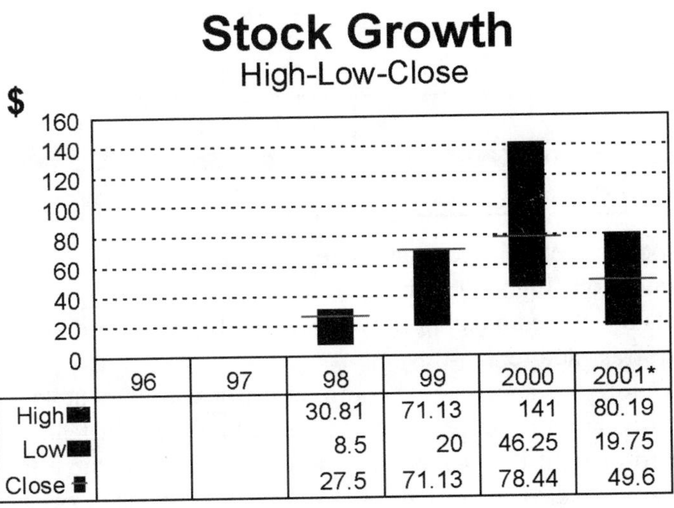

	96	97	98	99	2000	2001*
High			30.81	71.13	141	80.19
Low			8.5	20	46.25	19.75
Close			27.5	71.13	78.44	49.6

*2001 price as of July 1

40

CIENA Corporation

1201 Winterson Road
Linthicum, MD 21090
410-865-8500
Nasdaq: CIEN
www.ciena.com

Chairman and CEO: Patrick Nettles
President: Gary Smith

Earnings Progression	★ ★ ★ ★
Revenue Growth	★ ★ ★ ★
Stock Growth	★ ★ ★ ★
Consistency	★
Total	**13 Points**

New fiber-optics technologies have been raising the speed limit of the telecommunications highway, but CIENA has gone one step further. The company has developed a technology that actually adds more lanes to the phone line infrastructure.

CIENA's long distance optical communications equipment uses dense wavelength division multiplexing (DWDM) technology. Instead of using a single beam of light that sends data through fiber-optic cable in phone line networks, DWDM uses multiple colors of light, each of which is capable of carrying tens of thousands of voice conversations or data transmissions. DWDM is more cost efficient than adding new fibers to the network, and it enables telephone companies to drive significantly more traffic across the long distance networks.

The company sells its optical networking equipment to long-distance carriers, local exchange carriers, Internet service providers, and wireless and wholesale carriers worldwide, including Verizon, BellSouth, Cable & Wireless, Korea Telecom, Sprint, Qwest, MCI WorldCom, and ALLTEL.

The company's optical transport and intelligent optical switching systems, known as CIENA LightWorks, include:

- **Optical transport.** The company's MultiWave line of optical transport products uses DWDM to enable carriers to cost effectively add network bandwidth when and where needed.
- **Intelligent optical core switching.** CIENA's MultiWave CoreDirector equipment enables carriers to manage the bandwidth created with optical transport products.
- **Network management.** CIENA's "On-Center" family of software tools enables phone companies to quickly deploy new and differentiating optical services.

The components of the CIENA LightWorks architecture can be sold separately or together as a complete network. The LightWorks package is designed to simplify a carrier's network by reducing the number of network elements. That simplification should lead to lower capital equipment cost and lower operating cost.

Founded in 1992, CIENA has about 3,000 employees and a market capitalization of about $16 billion.

EARNINGS PER SHARE PROGRESSION ★★★★

Past 4 years: 200 percent (33 percent per year)

REVENUE GROWTH ★★★★

Past 4 years: 870 percent (77 percent per year)

STOCK GROWTH ★★★★

Past 4 years: 284 percent (40 percent per year)
Dollar growth: $10,000 over 4 years would have grown to $38,000.

CONSISTENCY ★

Increased earnings per share: 2 of the past 4 years
Increased sales: 3 of the past 4 years

CIENA AT A GLANCE

Fiscal year ended: Oct. 31
Revenue and net income in $millions

	1996	1997	1998	1999	2000	4-Year Growth Avg. Annual (%)	4-Year Growth Total (%)
Revenue ($)	88.5	413	508	482	859	77	870
Net income ($)	17.3	115.0	45.7	–3.9	81.4	48	370
Earnings/share ($)	0.09	0.55	0.18	–0.01	0.27	33	200
PE range	NA	20–57	22–258	NA	83–555		

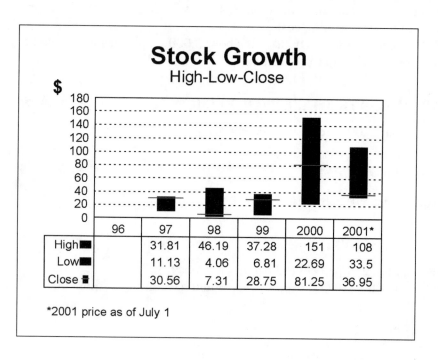

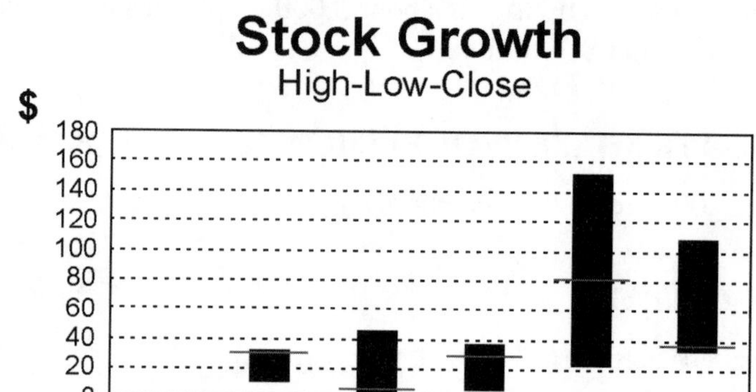

	96	97	98	99	2000	2001*
High		31.81	46.19	37.28	151	108
Low		11.13	4.06	6.81	22.69	33.5
Close		30.56	7.31	28.75	81.25	36.95

*2001 price as of July 1

41

SunGard Data Systems, Inc.

1285 Drummers Lane, Suite 300
Wayne, PA 19087
610-341-8700
NYSE: SDS
www.sungard.com

Chairman and CEO: James L. Mann
President: Christobal Conde

Earnings Progression	★★★★
Revenue Growth	★★★
Stock Growth	★★★
Consistency	★★★
Total	**13 Points**

SunGard Data Systems specializes in software and services that help banks and investment companies simplify the complex task of managing and investing their customers' money.

The company has grown quickly by aggressively acquiring smaller companies that make software for the financial and public sector industries. For instance, in 2000 SunGard acquired ten companies, including Microbank Software, which makes management software for banks; Frontier Analytics, which makes asset allocation software for investors; and Orion Systems Group, which makes administrative software for school districts and agencies.

SunGard focuses on several key areas:

- **Brokerage and execution systems.** The firm offers processing of securities and exchange-traded instruments for banks and brokerages. Services include order routing, execution and clearance, position keeping and tracking, regulatory compliance and reporting, and investment accounting and recordkeeping. The company also sells customer rela-

tionship management software used by brokers to track customer contacts, manage portfolios, and measure performance.
- **Risk and derivatives systems.** SunGard offers software to handle most aspects of risk management and trading operations for capital markets around the world. This software is typically used by traders and market makers of various types of derivative instruments, equities, and fixed-income securities.
- **Asset management systems.** Its software maintains the books of record for large investment portfolios managed by banks, mutual funds, insurance companies, and employee retirement plans.
- **Investor accounting systems.** SunGard's software automates the investment operations and maintains the books associated with defined-contribution retirement plans such as 401(k) plans.
- **Public sector systems.** The company offers fund accounting systems for educational institutions, state and local governments, and other nonprofit organizations.

The company also offers business continuity software and services, Internet hosting services, and a workflow management system for the health care insurance industry.

The Pennsylvania-based operation has about 8,000 employees and a market capitalization of about $7 billion.

EARNINGS PER SHARE PROGRESSION ★★★★

Past 4 years: 283 percent (40 percent per year)

REVENUE GROWTH ★★★

Past 4 years: 133 percent (24 percent per year)

STOCK GROWTH ★★★

Past 4 years: 173 percent (28 percent per year)
Dollar growth: $10,000 over 4 years would have grown to about $27,000.

CONSISTENCY ★★★

Increased earnings per share: 3 of the past 4 years
Increased sales: 4 consecutive years

SUNGARD DATA SYSTEMS AT A GLANCE

Fiscal year ended: Dec. 31
Revenue and net income in $millions

						4-Year Growth	
	1996	1997	1998	1999	2000	Avg. Annual (%)	Total (%)
Revenue ($)	712	1,038	1,312	1,444	1,661	24	133
Net income ($)	40.3	92.9	127	100	213	52	428
Earnings/share ($)	0.41	0.77	1.04	0.85	1.57	40	283
PE range	33–58	24–40	21–39	21–54	14–33		

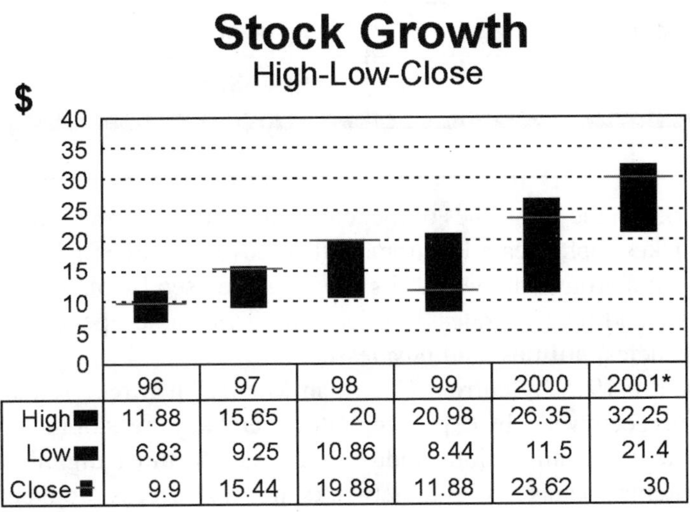

	96	97	98	99	2000	2001*
High	11.88	15.65	20	20.98	26.35	32.25
Low	6.83	9.25	10.86	8.44	11.5	21.4
Close	9.9	15.44	19.88	11.88	23.62	30

*2001 price as of July 1

42

Tellabs, Inc.

4951 Indiana Avenue
Lisle, IL 60532
630-378-8800
Nasdaq: TLAB
www.tellabs.com

Chairman, President, and CEO: Michael J. Birck

Earnings Progression	★ ★ ★ ★
Revenue Growth	★ ★ ★ ★
Stock Growth	★
Consistency	★ ★ ★ ★
Total	**13 Points**

Tellabs works on the front lines of the telecommunications revolution. The company makes sophisticated equipment that moves voices and data across the country and around the world. Its products are used by phone companies, cellular and other wireless service providers, cable operators, government agencies, utilities, and businesses.

Founded in 1975 by current Chairman Michael J. Birck, Tellabs has flourished in recent years by expanding into several key areas of the rapidly expanding telecommunications industry. It manufactures digital cross-connect systems, managed digital networks, network access products, and fiber-optic systems.

The Chicago-area company breaks its operations into three key segments:

- **Optical networking.** The company's Titan family of optical networking systems enables service providers to set up and manage fiber-optic networks. Its focus equipment helps carriers build their own backbone and access networks to provide new services.

- **Next generation switching.** The firm's Salix switches enable service providers to migrate voice and data networks into one telepacket platform that supports converged services.
- **Broadband access.** Its MartisDXX network systems enable service providers to manage wireless voice and wired data networks.

The company's line of advanced digital cross-connection systems are used by telecommunications managers for centralized and remote testing of transmission facilities; grooming of voice, data, and video signals; automated installation of new services; and restoration of failed facilities.

Tellabs's network access products are used in a variety of areas, including echo cancellation (removing feedback from one's own voice on long distance and wireless connections) and voice compression (multiplies the capacity of digital transmission facilities used for voice and data services).

The company has operations worldwide. International sales account for about 30 percent of its total revenue.

Tellabs went public with its initial stock offering in 1980. The company has about 9,000 employees and a market capitalization of about $15 billion.

EARNINGS PER SHARE PROGRESSION ★★★★

Past 4 years: 447 percent (53 percent per year)

REVENUE GROWTH ★★★★

Past 4 years: 290 percent (41 percent per year)

STOCK GROWTH ★

Past 4 years: 71 percent (14 percent per year)
Dollar growth: $10,000 over 4 years would have grown to about $17,000.

CONSISTENCY ★★★★

Increased earnings per share: 4 consecutive years
Increased sales: 4 consecutive years

TELLABS AT A GLANCE

Fiscal year ended: Dec. 31
Revenue and net income in $billions

	1996	1997	1998	1999	2000	4-Year Growth Avg. Annual (%)	4-Year Growth Total (%)
Revenue ($)	0.868	1.28	1.7	2.32	3.39	41	290
Net income ($)	0.118	0.275	0.396	0.559	0.760	59	544
Earnings/share ($)	0.32	0.69	0.98	1.35	1.75	53	447
PE range	23–72	NA	22–67	33–78	20–42		

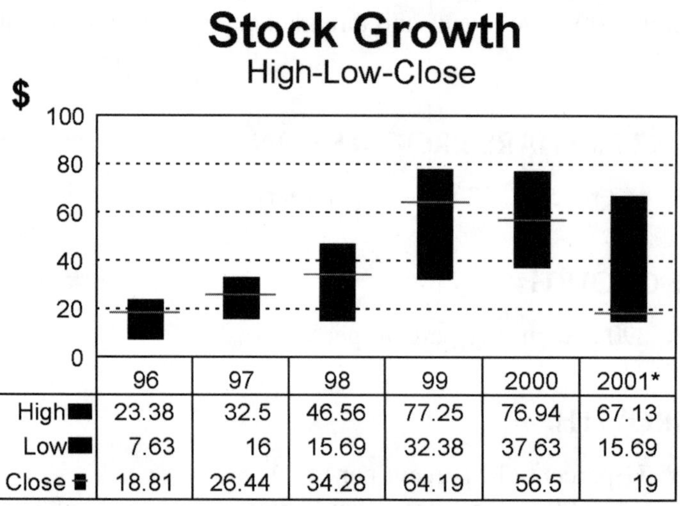

	96	97	98	99	2000	2001*
High	23.38	32.5	46.56	77.25	76.94	67.13
Low	7.63	16	15.69	32.38	37.63	15.69
Close	18.81	26.44	34.28	64.19	56.5	19

*2001 price as of July 1

43

Take-Two Interactive Software

575 Broadway
New York, NY 10012
212-334-6633
Nasdaq: TTWO
www.take2games.com

Chairman: Barry S. Rutcofsky
President: Paul Eibeler
CEO: Ryan A. Brant

Earnings Progression	★ ★ ★ ★
Revenue Growth	★ ★ ★ ★
Stock Growth	★ ★
Consistency	★ ★ ★
Total	**13 Points**

Take to the streets for a day of car racing, bash heads with the best in world soccer, battle it out in the boxing ring, or surf the world's most wicked waves—all from the comfort of your easy chair with Take-Two's growing list of interactive video games.

Take-Two Interactive has developed a line of video games and accessories for PCs, Sony PlayStation and PlayStation2, Nintendo 64, Nintendo Game Boy, and Sega Dreamcast.

The New York operation markets its games through more than 20,000 retail outlets in the U.S., including Wal-Mart, Toys R Us, Best Buy, Ames Department Stores, and other supermarkets, drugstores, and discount stores. Its games are also sold throughout Europe and Asia.

Take-Two produces games under several studios, including Rockstar Games, Mission Studios, GearHead Entertainment, Tarantula Studios, Alternative Reality Technologies, and TalonSoft.

Some of its leading games include Street Racing, Smuggler's Run, Midnight Club (street racing), Billiard's Master, Grand Theft Auto, Black Bass Lure Fishing, Monster Truck Madness, Thrasher, Bass Hunter 64, Monkey Hero, International Soccer, The Operational Art of War, Battle of Britain, Hollywood Pinball, and Las Vegas Cool Hand.

Take-Two has been busy recently turning out new games for Sony's popular new PlayStation2, including new versions of Street Racing, Smuggler's Run, Grand Theft Auto, and Duke Nukem, all of which have been ranked among the top sellers available for PlayStation2.

The company continues to boost its research and development expenses to keep the new hits coming. It spent $5.6 million on R&D in 2000, up from $1.7 million two years earlier.

In addition to its video game development business, Take-Two operates Jack of All Games, which is a distributor of entertainment software with offices worldwide.

Take-Two Interactive has about 700 employees and a market capitalization of about $400 million.

EARNINGS PER SHARE PROGRESSION ★★★★

Past 4 years: 2,100 percent (117 percent per year)

REVENUE GROWTH ★★★★

Past 4 years: 2,996 percent (137 percent per year)

STOCK GROWTH ★★

Past 4 years: 97 percent (18 percent per year)
Dollar growth: $10,000 over 4 years would have grown to $20,000.

CONSISTENCY ★★★

Increased earnings per share: 3 of the past 4 years
Increased sales: 4 consecutive years

TAKE-TWO INTERACTIVE SOFTWARE AT A GLANCE

Fiscal year ended: Oct. 31
Revenue and net income in $millions

						4-Year Growth	
	1996	1997	1998	1999	2000	Avg. Annual (%)	Total (%)
Revenue ($)	12.5	97.3	194	306	387	137	2,996
Net income ($)	0.549	–2.8	7.3	16.4	25.7	176	4,581
Earnings/share ($)	0.04	–0.25	0.42	0.76	0.88	117	2,100
PE range	NA	NA	11–20	9–23	9–21		

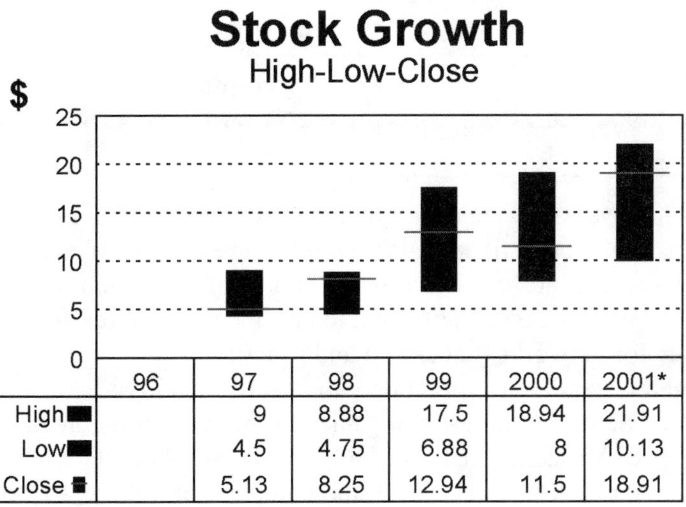

	96	97	98	99	2000	2001*
High		9	8.88	17.5	18.94	21.91
Low		4.5	4.75	6.88	8	10.13
Close		5.13	8.25	12.94	11.5	18.91

*2001 price as of July 1

44

Digital Lightwave, Inc.

15550 Lightwave Drive
Clearwater, FL 33760
727-442-6677
Nasdaq: DIGL
www.digitallightwave.com

Chairman, President, and CEO: Gerry Chastelet

Earnings Progression	★★★
Revenue Growth	★★★★
Stock Growth	★★★★
Consistency	★★
Total	**13 Points**

Digital Lightwave helps telecommunications companies monitor and manage their high-speed fiber-optic networks. The company makes diagnostic products that are used to qualify and verify telecommunications service during network installation and to provide ongoing real-time quality assurance for networks that are up and running.

The small Clearwater, Florida operation sells its software and related products to some of the largest companies in the telecommunications industry, such as Verizon, MCI WorldCom, Qwest, Ameritech, Alcatel, Tellabs, and Nortel Networks. In all, the company has about 150 corporate customers.

Digital Lightwave's leading products include:

- **Portable Network Information Computers.** This line of lightweight computers enables users to verify, qualify, and monitor the performance of telecommunications networks and transmission equipment. It was designed to replace existing network test instruments by incorporating their functions into a software-based information processing system. The specialized computers enable telecommunications service providers and equipment manufacturers to plan for and implement fiber-optic network expansion more cost-effectively. It also allows them to verify and manage information concerning the transmission of voice, data, image, and video traffic. Telecommunications equipment manufacturers also use the Network Information Computer in designing, engineering, and manufacturing their products, installing their products in the networks of their customers, and providing ongoing customer support.

- **Network Access Agents.** This family of network-integrated products provides centralized performance monitoring and analysis of optical networks.
- **Custom optical subsystem technology.** The company's system provides automated optical diagnostic, analysis, and monitoring functions for network operations centers, validation laboratories, and manufacturing facilities.

Digital's sales staff markets its products directly to communications equipment manufacturers, regional Bell companies, local phone carriers, wireless service providers, and private network operators.

Founded in 1991, the company went public with its initial stock offering in 1996. It has about 200 employees and a market capitalization of about $1.5 billion.

EARNINGS PER SHARE PROGRESSION ★ ★ ★

The company has gone from losses to gains the past 4 years.

REVENUE GROWTH ★ ★ ★ ★

Past 4 years: 1,572 percent (103 percent per year)

STOCK GROWTH ★ ★ ★ ★

Past 4 years: 205 percent (75 percent per year)
Dollar growth: $10,000 over 4 years would have grown to about $30,000.

CONSISTENCY ★ ★

Positive earnings progression: 2 of the past 4 years
Increased sales: 4 consecutive years

DIGITAL LIGHTWAVE AT A GLANCE

Fiscal year ended: Dec. 31
Revenue and net income in $millions

	1996	1997	1998	1999	2000	4-Year Growth Avg. Annual (%)	4-Year Growth Total (%)
Revenue ($)	6.04	9.08	24.2	50.5	101	103	1,572
Net income ($)	–2.11	–6.69	–29.8	4.95	31.4	534*	534*
Earnings/share ($)	–0.09	–0.26	–1.13	0.17	0.98	476*	476*
PE range	NA	NA	NA	13–407	25–152		

*Net income and earnings per share figures are based on 1-year earnings growth.

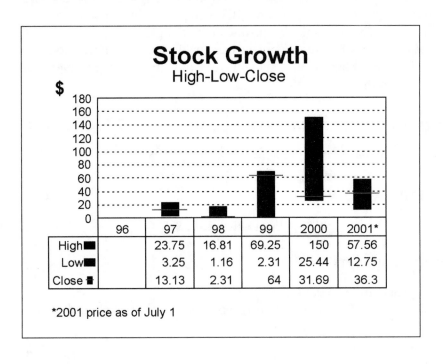

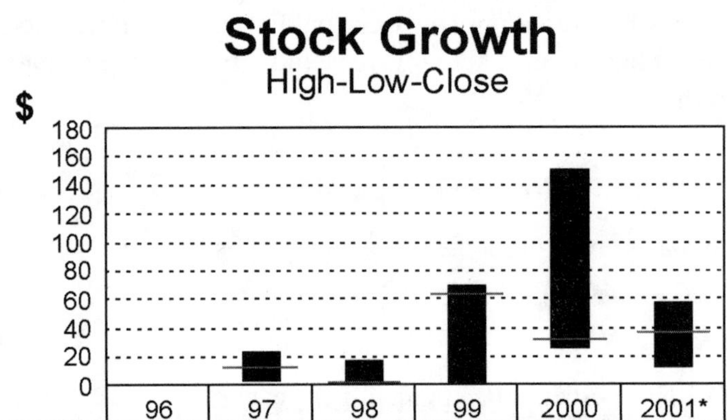

	96	97	98	99	2000	2001*
High		23.75	16.81	69.25	150	57.56
Low		3.25	1.16	2.31	25.44	12.75
Close		13.13	2.31	64	31.69	36.3

*2001 price as of July 1

45

Celestica, Inc.

844 Don Mills Road
Toronto, Ontario
M3C 1V7, Canada
416-448-5800
NYSE: CLS
www.celestica.com

Chairman and CEO: E. Polistuk
President: M. MaGee

Earnings Progression	★ ★ ★
Revenue Growth	★ ★ ★ ★
Stock Growth	★ ★ ★ ★
Consistency	★
Total	**12 Points**

Celestica's earthly mission is to do the heavy lifting for the world's leading electronics manufacturers. It's an unheralded mission, because none of the PCs, workstations, servers, printed circuit assemblies, or networking equipment that is produced at its 36 plants around the world bears the Celestica name.

But Celestica is handsomely rewarded by the manufacturers who are relieved of the burden of directly operating a plant. Celestica is the third-largest electronics manufacturer services (EMS) company in the world.

The EMS business is huge and getting bigger. The industry generates nearly $100 billion in revenue. That figure is expected to double or possibly triple in the next several years. Celestica got into the outsourcing business at just the right moment.

Until 1993, it was the Canadian manufacturing operation of IBM. But Big Blue was in the process of shifting from big-box manufacturing to software and services. But rather than shutter the operation, it was spun off into what's now a $10 billion-plus operation.

IBM is now a customer along with other blue-chip electronics-related companies such as Cisco Systems, Lucent Technologies, Nortel Networks, Hewlett-Packard, EMC Corporation, and Sun Microsystems. In addition to manufacturing, Celestica does testing, design, packaging and distribution, and repair services. It also offers supply chain management, product assurance, and after-sales service.

Driving future growth for the company is the accelerating trend by the telecommunications industry to outsource its manufacturing, the emerging trend by large Japanese manufacturers to outsource their work, and increasing demand for repair services done by EMS plants. Analysts estimate that about 15 percent of the world's $500 billion in electronics manufacturing is currently outsourced, and they project a 25 percent annual growth rate for the industry.

In March 2001, Celestica completed the acquisition of two Motorola manufacturing facilities in Iowa and Ireland where it will make pagers and cellular phones for the telecommunications giant. Celestica has about 14,000 employees and a market capitalization of about $10 billion.

EARNINGS PER SHARE PROGRESSION ★ ★ ★

Past 4 years: 133 percent (24 percent per year)

REVENUE GROWTH ★ ★ ★ ★

Past 4 years: 383 percent (48 percent per year)

STOCK GROWTH ★ ★ ★ ★

Past 3 years: 248 percent (51 percent per year)
Dollar growth: $10,000 over 3 years would have grown to $35,000.

CONSISTENCY ★

Increased earnings per share: 2 of the past 4 years
Increased sales: 3 consecutive years

CELESTICA AT A GLANCE

Fiscal year ended: Dec. 31
Revenue and net income in $millions

	1996	1997	1998	1999	2000	4-Year Growth Avg. Annual (%)	4-Year Growth Total (%)
Revenue ($)	2,017	2,007	3,249	5,297	9,752	48	383
Net income ($)	29	–6.9	–48.5	68.4	207	63	614
Earnings/share ($)	0.42	–0.10	–0.53	0.38	0.98	24	133
PE range	NA	NA	NA	31–150	36–89		

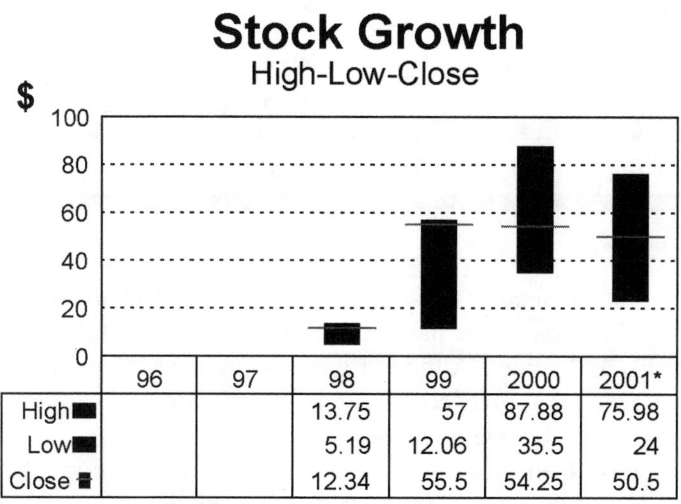

	96	97	98	99	2000	2001*
High			13.75	57	87.88	75.98
Low			5.19	12.06	35.5	24
Close			12.34	55.5	54.25	50.5

*2001 price as of July 1

46

Linear Technology Corporation

1630 McCarthy Boulevard
Milpitas, CA 95035
408-432-1900
Nasdaq: LLTC
www.linear-tech.com

Chairman and CEO: Robert Swanson, Jr.
President: Clive Davies

Earnings Progression	★ ★ ★
Revenue Growth	★ ★
Stock Growth	★ ★ ★ ★
Consistency	★ ★ ★
Total	**12 Points**

The computer semiconductor market continues to be characterized by volatile swings in demand that have sent most chip manufacturers through a serious of ups and downs. Although it is not immune to cyclical downturns, Linear Technology has continued to rack up impressive growth of revenue and earnings for many years.

The Milpitas, California operation makes a broad line of high-performance linear integrated circuits (in which a number of transistors and other elements are combined to form more complicated electronic circuits).

Semiconductor components are the electronic building blocks used in electronic systems and equipment. Linear circuits, which are a form of semiconductor, are used primarily to monitor, condition, amplify, and transform continuous analog signals associated with physical properties, such as temperature, pressure, weight, light, sound, or speed.

Linear Tech's integrated circuits are used in a wide variety of applications, such as wireless communications, notebook and handheld computing, computer peripherals, medical systems, factory automation, network products, satellites, military and space systems, and automotive electronics.

In all, the company sells about 5,600 products, including:

- **Amplifiers,** which amplify the voltage or output current of a device
- **High-speed amplifiers,** which are used to amplify signals above 5MHz for applications such as video, fast data acquisition, and data communication
- **Voltage regulators,** which control the voltage of a device or circuit at a specified level
- **Voltage reference circuits,** which serve as electronic benchmarks providing a constant voltage for system usage
- **Data converters,** which change linear (analog) signals into digital signals or vice versa

The company's other linear circuits include buffers, battery monitors, motor controllers, hot swap circuits, comparators, sample-and-hold devices, and filters.

Linear markets its products worldwide to about 15,000 original manufacturers.

Founded in 1981, the company has about 2,800 employees and a market capitalization of about $14 billion.

EARNINGS PER SHARE PROGRESSION ★ ★ ★

Past 4 years: 105 percent (20 percent per year)

REVENUE GROWTH ★ ★

Past 4 years: 87 percent (17 percent per year)

STOCK GROWTH ★ ★ ★ ★

Past 4 years: 347 percent (46 percent per year)
Dollar growth: $10,000 over 4 years would have grown to $44,700.

CONSISTENCY ★ ★ ★

Increased earnings per share: 3 consecutive years
Increased sales: 4 consecutive years

LINEAR TECHNOLOGY AT A GLANCE

Fiscal year ended: June 30
Revenue and net income in $millions

	1996	1997	1998	1999	2000	4-Year Growth Avg. Annual (%)	4-Year Growth Total (%)
Revenue ($)	378	379	485	507	706	17	87
Net income ($)	134	134	181	194	288	21	115
Earnings/share ($)	0.43	0.43	0.57	0.61	0.88	20	105
PE range	12–29	23–43	17–39	34–68	39–85		

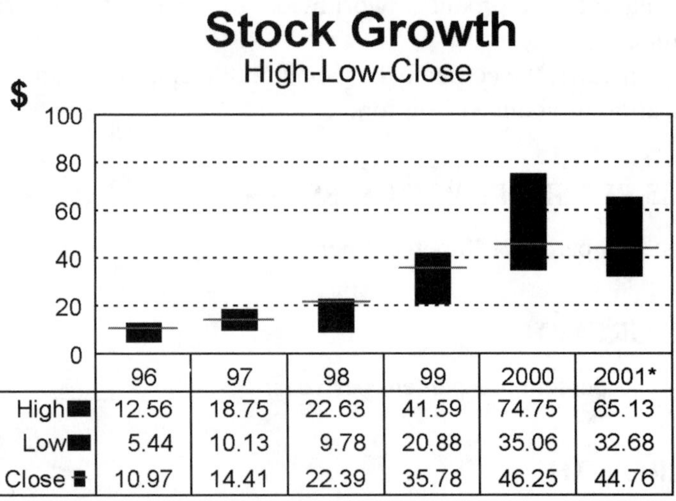

	96	97	98	99	2000	2001*
High	12.56	18.75	22.63	41.59	74.75	65.13
Low	5.44	10.13	9.78	20.88	35.06	32.68
Close	10.97	14.41	22.39	35.78	46.25	44.76

*2001 price as of July 1

47

Applied Materials

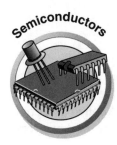

3050 Bowers Avenue
Santa Clara, CA 95054
408-727-5555
Nasdaq: AMAT
www.appliedmaterials.com

Chairman and CEO: James Morgan
President: Dan Maydan

Earnings Progression	★★★★
Revenue Growth	★★★
Stock Growth	★★★★
Consistency	★
Total	**12 Points**

The world has developed an insatiable appetite for microchips. And Applied Materials, the world's largest manufacturer of semiconductor manufacturing equipment, is only too happy to meet the demand.

Fueling the growth of the chip market is the ever-increasing demand for cell phones, personal computers, computer games, automotive electronics, and the Internet. It requires more than 500 semiconductor chips to get an Internet user online.

The surge in demand for new generations of chips is driving the expansion of chip-making equipment that helps to create a chip that consists of microscopically thin layers of materials, including thousands or even millions of transistors.

Applied Material's chip manufacturing equipment addresses nearly all of the primary process steps used to make microchips. It also makes spare parts for the chip manufacturing systems. In 1990, the number of chips made worldwide was 134 billion. By 2004, that figure is expected to reach more than 700 billion chips.

A chip (or integrated circuit) is a fingernail-sized sliver of silicon with layers of precise circuitry. They are made in specialized factories called "fabs" or fabrication plants. Applied Materials supplies the manufacturing equipment to more than 900 fabs around the world. Applied Materials management likes to say that it helps make every chip, every day, everywhere in the world.

The company's substantial investments in research and development have allowed it to bring new technologies to the market, enabling its fab customers to shrink chip sizes, build millions more transistors onto each chip, and dramatically cut costs. To help maintain Applied Materials's more than over 10,000 chip-making systems in customer fabs throughout the world, more than 2,500 highly trained process support and customer engineers work in or near fab sites from the United States to Japan.

Founded in 1967, the company has about 19,000 employees and a market capitalization of about $38 billion.

EARNINGS PER SHARE PROGRESSION ★★★★

Past 4 years: 193 percent (31 percent per year)

REVENUE GROWTH ★★★

Past 4 years: 131 percent (23 percent per year)

STOCK GROWTH ★★★★

Past 4 years: 551 percent (59 percent per year)
Dollar growth: $10,000 over 4 years would have grown to $65,100.

CONSISTENCY ★

Increased earnings per share: 2 of the past 4 years
Increased sales: 3 of the past 4 years

APPLIED MATERIALS AT A GLANCE

Fiscal year ended: Oct. 31
Revenue and net income in $billions

	1996	1997	1998	1999	2000	4-Year Growth Avg. Annual (%)	4-Year Growth Total (%)
Revenue ($)	4.14	4.07	4.33	5.10	9.56	23	131
Net income ($)	0.599	0.498	0.356	0.693	2.06	36	244
Earnings/share ($)	0.82	0.66	0.38	0.88	2.40	31	193
PE ratio range	6–13	13–41	28–61	24–72	14–47		

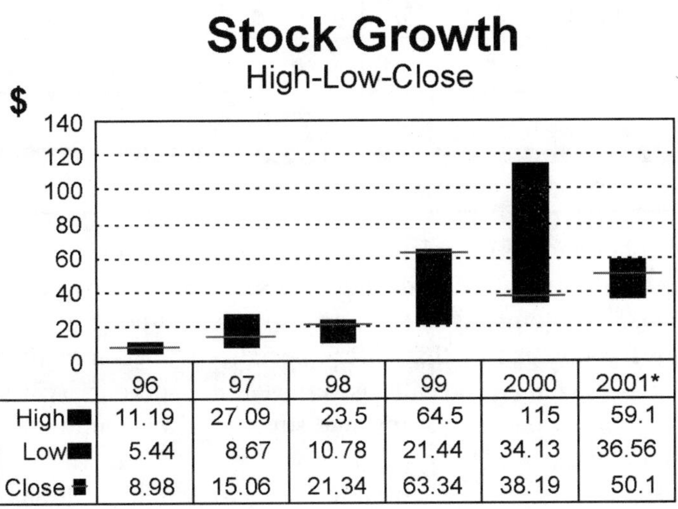

	96	97	98	99	2000	2001*
High	11.19	27.09	23.5	64.5	115	59.1
Low	5.44	8.67	10.78	21.44	34.13	36.56
Close	8.98	15.06	21.34	63.34	38.19	50.1

*2001 price as of July 1

48

Comverse Technology, Inc.

170 Crossways Park Drive
Woodbury, NY 11797
516-677-7200
Nasdaq: CMVT
www.comverse.com

Chairman and CEO: Kobi Alexander
President: Itsik Danziger

Earnings Progression	★ ★ ★ ★
Revenue Growth	★ ★ ★
Stock Growth	★ ★ ★ ★
Consistency	★
Total	**12 Points**

Comverse Technology helps telecommunications companies cash in on the ever-growing universe of voice and data services used by businesses and consumers. The company is the world's leading supplier of software and systems for companies that offer specialized telecommunications services such as voice mail and call answering. These add-on services have become an important part of the revenue stream for telecommunications companies around the world.

Comverse sells its products to more than 350 communications companies operating in more than 100 countries. It counts among its customers 14 of the world's 20 largest telephone companies, including AT&T, Bell Atlantic, Cable & Wireless, Deutsche Telekom, and Sprint PCS. Telecommunications companies generally offer Comverse's specialized services to their customers on a subscription or pay-per-usage basis.

Among Comverse's leading service options are call answering, voice mail, fax mail, unified messaging (voice, fax, and e-mail in a single mailbox), prepaid calling services, short text messaging, and interactive voice response. The company also offers a number of wireless data and Internet-based services, such as Internet messaging and Internet call management, and it provides a number of voice-activated options, such as voice dialing, voice-activated Web browsing, and voice-activated messaging.

The Woodbury, New York operation also offers some related services through its subsidiaries. Its Comverse Infosys subsidiary provides digital monitoring and recording systems for call centers, customer relationship management applications, public networks, and government agencies.

Its Ulticom subsidiary sells network signaling software for wireless, wireline, and Internet communication services known as Signalware. Signalware enables communications service providers to offer such options as voice-activated dialing, prepaid calling, caller ID, and text messaging. Comverse holds about an 80 percent stake of Ulticom, which trades separately on the Nasdaq exchange.

Comverse Technology has about 5,000 employees and a market capitalization of about $10 billion.

EARNINGS PER SHARE PROGRESSION ★★★★

Past 4 years: 215 percent (32 percent per year)

REVENUE GROWTH ★★★

Past 4 years: 124 percent (22 percent per year)

STOCK GROWTH ★★★★

Past 4 years: 455 percent (53 percent per year)
Dollar growth: $10,000 over 4 years would have grown to about $55,000.

CONSISTENCY ★

Increased earnings per share: 2 of the past 4 years
Increased sales: 3 of the past 4 years

COMVERSE TECHNOLOGY AT A GLANCE

Fiscal year ended: Jan. 31
Revenue and net income in $millions

	1996	1997	1998	1999	2000	4-Year Growth Avg. Annual (%)	4-Year Growth Total (%)
Revenue ($)	390	489	15.8	696	872	22	124
Net income ($)	42.1	34.5	–115	111	170	41	304
Earnings/share ($)	0.34	0.25	–0.89	0.78	1.07	32	215
PE range	16–41	41–73	NA	27–93	57–115		

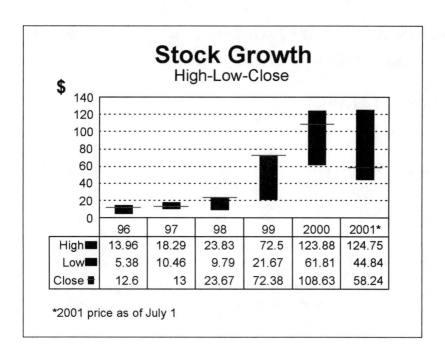

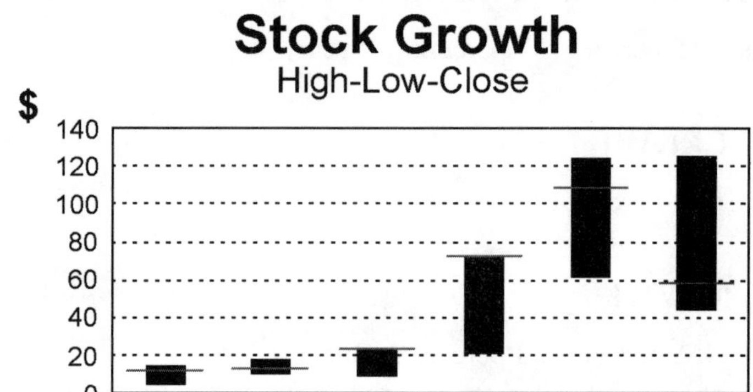

	96	97	98	99	2000	2001*
High	13.96	18.29	23.83	72.5	123.88	124.75
Low	5.38	10.46	9.79	21.67	61.81	44.84
Close	12.6	13	23.67	72.38	108.63	58.24

*2001 price as of July 1

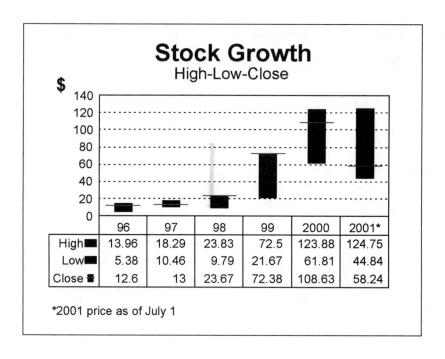

49

Analog Devices, Inc.

One Technology Way
Norwood, MA 02062
781-329-4700
NYSE: ADI
www.analogdevices.com

Chairman: Ray Stata
President and CEO: Jerald G. Fishman

Earnings Progression	★ ★ ★ ★
Revenue Growth	★ ★ ★
Stock Growth	★ ★ ★ ★
Consistency	★
Total	**12 Points**

Founded in 1965, Analog Devices continues to find new and better ways to monitor and measure real-world phenomena, such as temperature, pressure, sound, speed, and acceleration.

Through analog sensors, this information can be detected and measured by continuously varying voltages and currents. Analog Devices makes devices that measure and monitor this information and convert it to digital form to be stored, displayed, or manipulated.

The Boston operation makes about 2,000 products, most of which use high-performance integrated circuits that incorporate analog mixed signal and digital signal processing technologies.

The company offers products for a wide range of applications, including:

- **Communications.** The company makes signal processing devices for audio, data, image, and video communications, as well as products for broadband and wireless communications applications involving digital subscriber line modems, cellular phones, base station equipment, and remote access servers.

- **Computers and computer peripherals.** The firm makes integrated circuits for graphics displays, power and battery management controls, and interface devices that link PCs and peripherals.
- **Consumer electronics.** The company makes integrated circuits for DVD players, digital camcorders and cameras, compact disc players, and other electronics devices.
- **Industrial.** The company's chips are used in data acquisition systems, automatic process control systems, robotics, environmental control systems, and automatic test equipment.
- **Instrumentation.** The firm's microchips are used in engineering, medical, and scientific instruments.
- **Automotive.** Analog Devices supplies microchips for crash sensors in automobile airbag systems.
- **Aerospace and defense.** The company's integrated circuits are used in broadcast satellites and other commercial space applications, as well as related military devices.

Analog Devices sells its products worldwide, with sales offices in 18 countries. Nearly 50 percent of its revenue is generated outside the U.S.

The company has about 9,000 employees and a market capitalization of about $13 billion.

EARNINGS PER SHARE PROGRESSION ★★★★

Past 4 years: 192 percent (31 percent per year)

REVENUE GROWTH ★★★

Past 4 years: 116 percent (21 percent per year)

STOCK GROWTH ★★★★

Past 4 years: 285 percent (41 percent per year)
Dollar growth: $10,000 over 4 years would have grown to about $39,000.

CONSISTENCY ★

Increased earnings per share: 2 of the past 4 years
Increased sales: 3 of the past 4 years

ANALOG DEVICES AT A GLANCE

Fiscal year ended: Oct. 31
Revenue and net income in $millions

						4-Year Growth	
	1996	1997	1998	1999	2000	Avg. Annual (%)	Total (%)
Revenue ($)	1,194	1,243	1,231	1,450	2,577	21	116
Net income ($)	172	178	119	197	607	37	253
Earnings/share ($)	0.52	0.52	0.25	0.55	1.52	31	192
PE range	12–25	19–35	17–56	22–86	6–64		

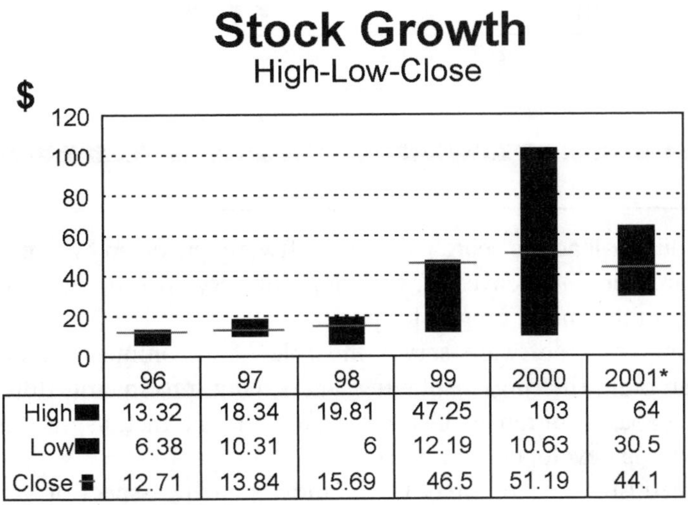

*2001 price as of July 1

Internet

50

Verity, Inc.

894 Ross Drive
Sunnyvale, CA 94089
408-541-1500
Nasdaq: VRTY
www.verity.com

Chairman and CEO: Gary Sbona
President: Anthony J. Bettencourt III

Earnings Progression	★ ★ ★
Revenue Growth	★ ★ ★ ★
Stock Growth	★ ★ ★ ★
Consistency	★
Total	**12 Points**

Verity's industry-leading search engine software picks up where other Internet search engines leave off, ferreting out very specific information instantly on an unlimited range of topics.

The company's software serves the role of an online librarian by quickly searching, filtering, displaying, and saving information stored on corporate databases, intranets, CD-ROMs, and the Internet, using classification standards developed by librarians.

The speed of the search may be the most amazing aspect of Verity's K2 search engine. It can search hundreds of millions of documents in less than a second.

The Sunnyvale, California operation is the leading provider of knowledge retrieval software. Its software products are used by more than 1,000 corporations, e-commerce sites, government agencies, online service providers, Internet publishers, and software developers, including most of the Fortune 100 companies.

Verity offers a family of software products, including:

- **Verity Portal One,** an integrated business portal package that provides all of the essential technology capabilities and service support needed for a corporate desktop. Capabilities include personalization, search, navigate and view, unified access, intelligent classification, and enterprise strength.
- **Knowledge Organizer,** a program similar to the Yahoo search engine
- **Document Navigator,** a program designed to help users search long articles in academic journals
- **Information Server,** a program that enables administrators to organize, build, and centrally maintain indices of documents stored on Web and file servers
- **Internet Spider,** a search tool used to index multiple domains
- **Agent Server,** a program that enables proactive notification and dissemination of specific information to users and workgroups

The company also offers a variety of application development tools that allow customers to integrate Verity's search tools into their own applications, products, or services.

Founded in 1988, Verity went public with its initial stock offering in 1995. The company has about 370 employees and a market capitalization of about $1 billion.

EARNINGS PER SHARE PROGRESSION ★★★

The company has gone from losses to gains the past 4 years.

REVENUE GROWTH ★★★★

Past 4 years: 213 percent (33 percent per year)

STOCK GROWTH ★★★★

Past 4 years: 202 percent (33 percent per year)
Dollar growth: $10,000 over 4 years would have grown to about $30,000.

CONSISTENCY ★

Positive earnings progression: 2 of the past 4 years
Increased sales: 3 of the past 4 years

VERITY AT A GLANCE

Fiscal year ended: May 31
Revenue and net income in $millions

	1996	1997	1998	1999	2000	4-Year Growth Avg. Annual (%)	4-Year Growth Total (%)
Revenue ($)	30.7	42.7	38.8	64.4	96.1	33	213
Net income ($)	–0.313	–17.7	–16.5	12.1	33.0	NA	NA
Earnings/share ($)	–0.06	–0.08	–0.73	0.50	1.10	NA	NA
PE range	NA	NA	NA	29–140	13–67		

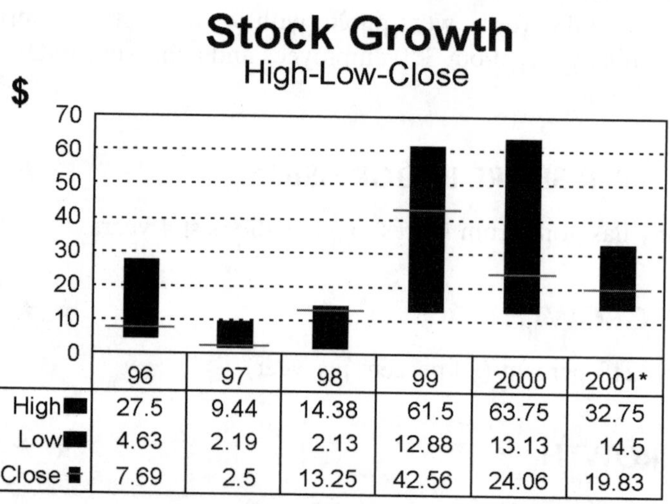

	96	97	98	99	2000	2001*
High	27.5	9.44	14.38	61.5	63.75	32.75
Low	4.63	2.19	2.13	12.88	13.13	14.5
Close	7.69	2.5	13.25	42.56	24.06	19.83

*2001 price as of July 1

51

Electronic Arts, Inc.

209 Redwood Shores Parkway
Redwood City, CA 94065
650-628-1500
Nasdaq: ERTS
www.ea.com

Chairman and CEO: L. F. Probst III
President: John Riccitiello

Earnings Progression	★ ★ ★
Revenue Growth	★ ★ ★
Stock Growth	★ ★ ★
Consistency	★ ★ ★
Total	**12 Points**

Every time Sony comes up with a new generation of its famous PlayStation, or Nintendo upgrades its own video game software, they are creating a new profit opportunity for Electronic Arts.

The Redwood City, California operation is the world's leading independent video game manufacturer, pumping out a new crop of top-selling games year after year.

Among its leading sellers are FIFA Soccer, Madden NFL (football), NASCAR, NBA Live (basketball), Need for Speed (auto racing), NHL Hockey, Tiger Woods and the PGA Tour Golf, Road Rash, Triple Play Baseball, and Wing Commander.

Electronic Arts markets its products worldwide under six brand names, including EA SPORTS, ORIGIN Systems, Jane's Combat Simulations, Bullfrog Production, Maxis, and Westwood Studios.

The company has produced well over 100 video game titles and has distributed more than 50 other titles developed by other software publishers. Worldwide, it has distributed more than a thousand "affiliated label" titles.

Reflecting the turnover in the computer game hardware market, the company has developed games for about 40 different computer hardware platforms, from the old Commodore 64 and Apple II computers to the new Nintendo 64 systems and the Sony PlayStation II. But while the popularity of some of those platforms has come and gone, Electronic Arts continues to turn out award-winning software year in and year out. The firm has garnered more than 700 awards for software design in the U.S. and Europe.

About 41 percent of the company's revenue comes from games designed for the Sony PlayStation, and 8 percent comes from the Nintendo 64 games. Other revenue comes from games designed for personal computers and other platforms.

First incorporated in 1982, Electronic Arts has about 3,100 employees and a market capitalization of about $7 billion.

EARNINGS PER SHARE PROGRESSION ★★★

Past 4 years: 120 percent (22 percent per year)

REVENUE GROWTH ★★★

Past 4 years: 142 percent (25 percent per year)

STOCK GROWTH ★★★

Past 4 years: 274 percent (28.5 percent per year)
Dollar growth: $10,000 over 4 years would have grown to $37,000.

CONSISTENCY ★★★

Increased earnings per share: 3 of the past 4 years
Increased sales: 4 consecutive years

ELECTRONIC ARTS AT A GLANCE

Fiscal year ended: March 31
Revenue and net income in $millions

	1996	1997	1998	1999	2000	4-Year Growth Avg. Annual (%)	4-Year Growth Total (%)
Revenue ($)	587	673	909	1,221	1,420	25	142
Net income ($)	47	50	72.5	73	117	25.5	149
Earnings/share ($)	0.40	0.43	0.59	0.58	0.88	22	120
PE range	26–49	22–46	27–48	32–108	27–65		

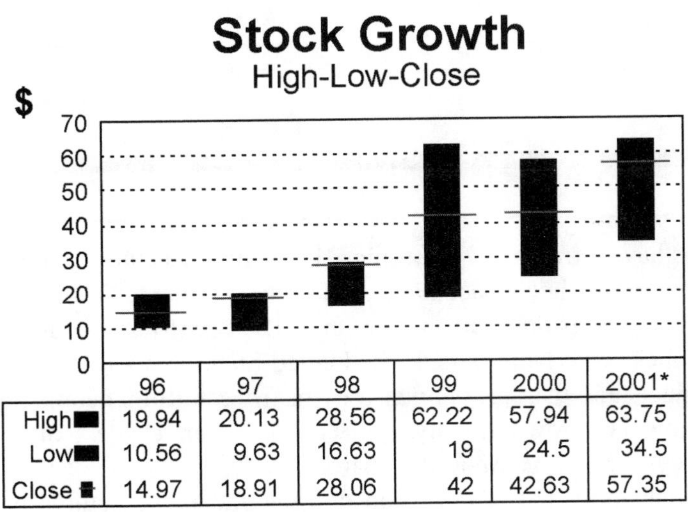

	96	97	98	99	2000	2001*
High	19.94	20.13	28.56	62.22	57.94	63.75
Low	10.56	9.63	16.63	19	24.5	34.5
Close	14.97	18.91	28.06	42	42.63	57.35

*2001 price as of July 1

52

Medtronic, Inc.

7000 Central Avenue N.E.
Minneapolis, MN 55432
763-514-4000
NYSE: MDT
www.medtronic.com

Chairman and CEO: William W. George
President: Arthur D. Collins Jr.

Earnings Progression	★ ★ ★
Revenue Growth	★ ★
Stock Growth	★ ★ ★
Consistency	★ ★ ★
Total	**11 Points**

Weak hearts have a friend in Medtronic. The company is the world's leading manufacturer of heart pacemakers and other implantable biomedical devices. It markets its products in more than 120 countries. About 40 percent of its sales come from outside the United States.

Its products and therapies are used by nearly 3 million people a year. The company has grown rapidly, with 15 consecutive years of record sales, earnings, and book-value-per-share.

The Minneapolis-based operation designs and manufactures pacing devices for patients whose heartbeats are irregular or too slow, as well as for patients whose hearts beat too rapidly. Medtronic's pacing devices can adjust electrical pulse intensity, duration, rate, and other characteristics.

Medtronic's pacemakers are small, coin-sized, implantable pulse generators with extended battery life. The implantable pacemaker is among a growing line of biomedical devices that Medtronic manufactures as part of its mission to "alleviate pain, restore health, and extend life."

The company's pacing business—its cardiac rhythm management division—accounts for about 50 percent of its $5 billion in annual sales.

Cardiovascular products such as blood pumps, heart valves, oxygenators, catheters, and other blood management systems contribute about 16 percent of the company's sales. In addition to its line of cardiovascular products, Medtronic provides such value-added services as physician education programs.

Cardiac surgery products, such as heart valves, perfusion systems, cannulae, and surgical accessories, account for about 9 percent of sales.

The company also makes neurological devices used for treating pain and controlling movement disorders. The company makes implantable neurostimulation devices used for spinal cord and brain stimulation to treat pain and tremors. It also makes drug delivery systems, neurosurgery products, and diagnostic systems. Neurological devices account for about 25 percent of total sales and represent the fastest growing sector of the company's business.

Medtronic pioneered the pacemaker 42 years ago when Dr. C. Walton Lillehei of the University of Minnesota Medical School identified a medical need for young heart block patients. Working with Earl Bakken, an electrical engineer, Dr. Lillehei developed the first wearable, external, battery-generated pulse generator.

Founded in 1949 and incorporated in 1957, Medtronic has about 25,000 employees. The company has a market capitalization of about $59 billion.

EARNINGS PER SHARE PROGRESSION ★ ★ ★

Past 4 years: 114 percent (21 percent per year)

REVENUE GROWTH ★ ★

Past 4 years: 89 percent (17 percent per year)

STOCK GROWTH ★ ★ ★

Past 4 years: 168 percent (28 percent per year)
Dollar growth: $10,000 over 4 years would have grown to $26,800.

CONSISTENCY ★ ★ ★

Increased earnings per share: 3 of the past 4 years
Increased sales: 4 consecutive years

MEDTRONIC AT A GLANCE

Fiscal year ended: April 30
Revenue and net income in $billions

	1997	1998	1999	2000	2001	4-Year Growth Avg. Annual (%)	4-Year Growth Total (%)
Revenue ($)	2.94	3.42	4.23	5.01	5.55	17	89
Net income ($)	0.583	0.594	0.476	1.09	1.28	22	119
Earnings/share ($)	0.49	0.50	0.39	0.90	1.05	21	114
PE range	28–52	44–75	75–113	36–68	NA		

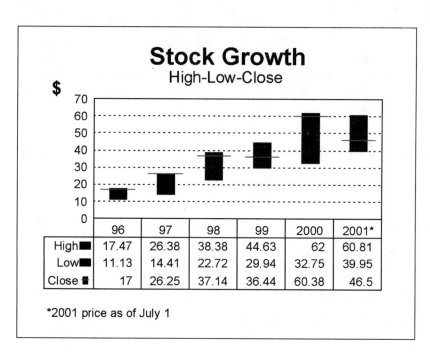

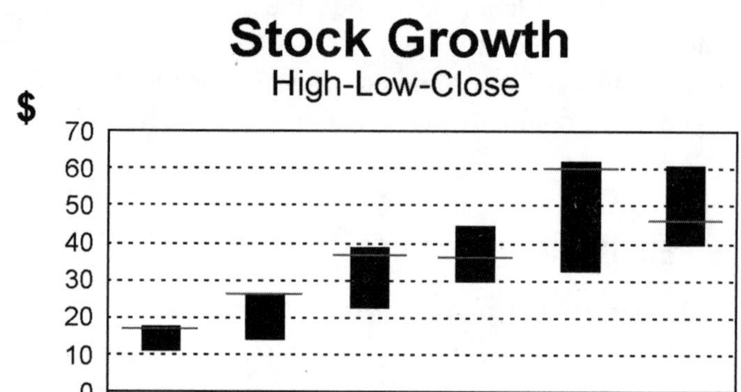

	96	97	98	99	2000	2001*
High	17.47	26.38	38.38	44.63	62	60.81
Low	11.13	14.41	22.72	29.94	32.75	39.95
Close	17	26.25	37.14	36.44	60.38	46.5

*2001 price as of July 1

53

PMC-Sierra, Inc.

900 East Hamilton Avenue, Suite 250
Campbell, CA 95008
408-626-2000
Nasdaq: PMCS
www.pmcsierra.com

Chairman, President, and CEO: Robert L. Bailey

Earnings Progression	★ ★
Revenue Growth	★ ★ ★ ★
Stock Growth	★ ★ ★ ★
Consistency	★
Total	**11 Points**

PMC-Sierra has enjoyed exceptional growth in recent years by developing specialized semiconductors used for high-speed transmission and networking systems within the telecommunications and data communications infrastructure.

The Internet is made up of a complex web of linked networks, many of which are owned and operated by separate organizations. These networks typically use a variety of equipment from a diverse range of manufacturers.

PMC-Sierra helps its manufacturing customers conform to network standards by designing semiconductor-based products that perform the most common networking functions and can be used in the majority of applications used in the Internet infrastructure.

The Santa Clara, California operation designs products for a wide variety of networking equipment, including:

- **Wide area network (WAN) equipment.** The company makes products for WAN Access Equipment and WAN Transmission and Switching Equipment, including remote access equipment, WAN edge switches, frame relay access devices, routers, wireless basestations, WAN core switches, digital loop carriers, digital cross connects, frame relay switches, add-drop multiplexers, Internet access concentrators, terminal multiplexers, and digital subscriber line access multiplexers.

- **Local area network (LAN) equipment.** The firm makes semiconductors for routers, switches, network interface cards, and network appliances.

The company has grown quickly through an aggressive acquisition strategy, including seven new acquisitions in 2000 alone. Among its recent acquisitions are Toucan Technology, which is involved in digital signal processing, Extreme Packet Devices, which provides Internet traffic management products, and AANetcome, which manufactures high-speed serial devices and deserialisers.

PMC-Sierra markets its products worldwide through its own sales staff and through distributors, independent representatives, and manufacturing subcontractors. About 38 percent of its revenue is generated outside the U.S. market.

First incorporated in 1983, PMC-Sierra has 1,700 employees and a market capitalization of about $7 billion.

EARNINGS PER SHARE PROGRESSION ★★

Past 3 years: 58 percent (16 percent per year)

REVENUE GROWTH ★★★★

Past 4 years: 270 percent (54 percent per year)

STOCK GROWTH ★★★★

Past 4 years: 920 percent (79 percent per year)
Dollar growth: $10,000 over 4 years would have grown to $102,000.

CONSISTENCY ★

Positive earnings progression: 2 of the past 4 years
Increased sales: 3 of the past 4 years

PMC-SIERRA AT A GLANCE

Fiscal year ended: Dec. 31
Revenue and net income in $millions

	1996	1997	1998	1999	2000	4-Year Growth Avg. Annual (%)	4-Year Growth Total (%)
Revenue ($)	188	127	174	296	695	54	270
Net income ($)	–48.2	34.2	–21.7	71.8	75.3	30*	120*
Earnings/share ($)	–0.40	0.26	–0.16	0.45	0.41	16*	58*
PE range	NA	13–33	NA	26–135	144–617		

*Net income and earnings per share growth figures are based on 3-year growth.

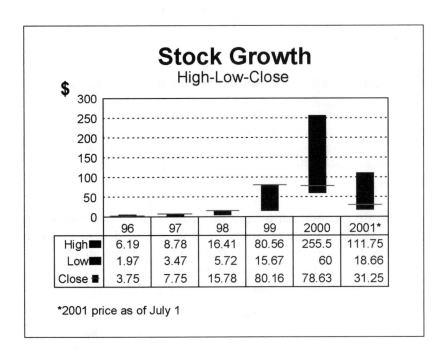

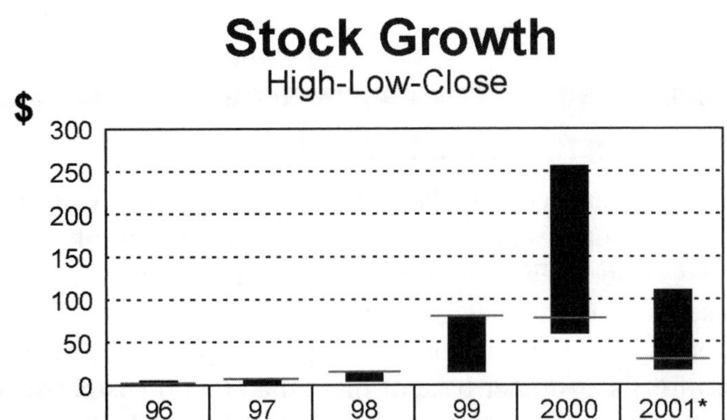

	96	97	98	99	2000	2001*
High	6.19	8.78	16.41	80.56	255.5	111.75
Low	1.97	3.47	5.72	15.67	60	18.66
Close	3.75	7.75	15.78	80.16	78.63	31.25

*2001 price as of July 1

Instruments and Equipment

54

BEI Technologies, Inc.

One Post Street, Suite 2500
San Francisco, CA 94104
415-956-4477
Nasdaq: BEIQ
www.bei-tech.com

Chairman and CEO: Charles Crocker

Earnings Progression	★ ★
Revenue Growth	★ ★ ★
Stock Growth	★ ★ ★ ★
Consistency	★ ★
Total	**11 Points**

BEI's specialized sensors help keep Cadillacs, BMWs, Volkswagens, Volvos, Audis, and other cars on the road and under control. The company's steering sensors help prevent spinouts and rollovers for many of the world's top-selling automobiles.

Steering sensors are just one of many types of sensors and motors BEI manufactures for its customer base of more than 6,000 businesses in the automotive, heavy equipment, medical, industrial, office automation, aerospace, and telecommunications markets. About 50 percent of its revenue comes from sales to the automotive market.

The company breaks its product line into three segments:

- **Traditional sensors and related products.** Its leading sensor is the shaft encoder, which translates the motion of rotating shafts directly into digitally coded electronic signals that are used to control the operation of machinery and equipment. Other sensors include precision potentiometers, which help control the throttle, steering, suspension, and seat and mirror position controls in autos and some heavy equipment; and magnetic actuators, which are used for precise control of short stroke linear or limited rotary motion in motors.

- **Micromachined sensors.** The company makes rate sensors and accelerometers, used to provide precise and reliable measurement of minute linear and angular motion for control, guidance, and instrumentation of vehicles, and GyroChip sensors, used in vehicles for stability control and spinout prevention and for navigation of robotic-guided vehicles.
- **Engineered subsystems.** The company's inertial measurement units are a fundamental element of virtually all inertial navigation and position or attitude reporting systems. Its scanner assemblies are used in the optics of military night vision systems, and its Servo System is a closed-loop electronic system that controls the position or velocity of rotating shafts.

The company was formed in 1997 through a spin-off from BEI Electronics. It has about 1,100 employees and a market capitalization of about $350 million.

EARNINGS PER SHARE PROGRESSION ★★

Past 4 years: 97 percent (18.5 percent)

REVENUE GROWTH ★★★

Past 4 years: 126 percent (23 percent per year)

STOCK GROWTH ★★★★

Past 3 years: 255 percent (52 percent per year)
Dollar growth: $10,000 over 3 years would have grown to $35,500.

CONSISTENCY ★★

Positive earnings progression: 2 of the past 4 years
Increased sales: 4 consecutive years

BEI TECHNOLOGIES AT A GLANCE

Fiscal year ended: Sept. 30
Revenue and net income in $millions

	1996	1997	1998	1999	2000	4-Year Growth Avg. Annual (%)	4-Year Growth Total (%)
Revenue ($)	96.7	101	124	159	219	23	126
Net income ($)	2.87	3.0	2.51	5.34	9.61	35	235
Earnings/share ($)	0.33	0.32	0.18	0.35	0.65	18.5	97
PE range	NA	24–32	15–59	9–25	8–45		

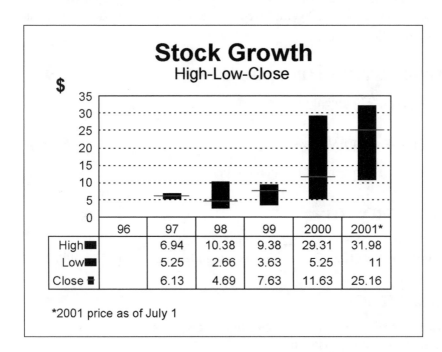

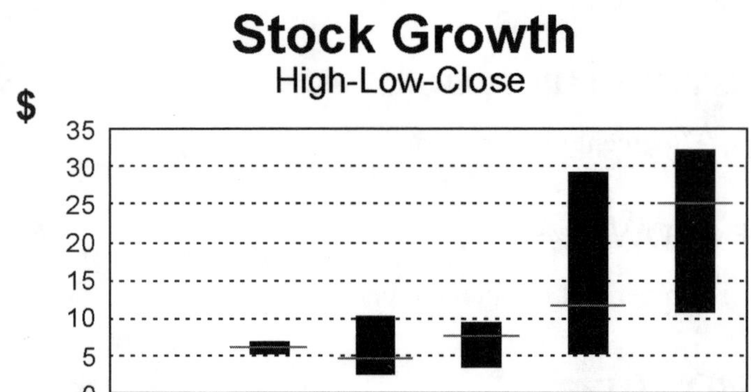

	96	97	98	99	2000	2001*
High		6.94	10.38	9.38	29.31	31.98
Low		5.25	2.66	3.63	5.25	11
Close		6.13	4.69	7.63	11.63	25.16

*2001 price as of July 1

55

BEA Systems, Inc.

2315 North First Street
San Jose, CA 95131
408-570-8000
Nasdaq: BEAS
www.bea.com

Chairman and CEO: William T. Coleman, III
President: Alfred S. Chuang

Earnings Progression	★
Revenue Growth	★ ★ ★ ★
Stock Growth	★ ★ ★ ★
Consistency	★ ★
Total	**11 Points**

BEA Systems is one of the leading developers of e-commerce infrastructure software that helps businesses build e-commerce systems. The firm has more than 8,000 customers around the world, including the majority of Fortune Global 100 companies. In fact, BEA claims as customers 100 percent of the Fortune Global 500 telecommunications companies, computer and office equipment makers, and financial companies.

The company's signature software product is the Weblogic E-Business Platform, a software package that provides the infrastructure for high-volume transaction systems, such as telecommunications billing applications, commercial bank ATM networks and account management systems, credit card billing systems, and securities trading account management systems.

BEA software solves a lot of problems for Web-based operations. In order to perform a single e-business transaction, an e-commerce system must process several distinct computer transactions. A typical e-commerce transaction generates a series of interconnected computer transactions, such as determining whether the ordered item is in stock, determining where the item is located, scheduling the item for shipping, processing payment, and recording the transaction in the company's financial records.

In addition, many Web sites now gather information about users as they navigate the site. This information is stored, identified with the particular user, and compared with past behavior of the same and other users in order to personalize online interaction by recommending specific merchandise, offering personalized pricing, and displaying targeted advertising.

BEA's software enables its customers to handle all of those tasks smoothly, efficiently, and automatically. In fact, its software is the de facto standard for more than 1,000 systems integrators, independent software vendors, and application services providers. The company also offers professional services to help customers design and build their e-commerce sites in a matter of weeks.

Founded in 1995, BEA has about 2,000 employees and a market capitalization of about $12 billion.

EARNINGS PER SHARE PROGRESSION ★

Past 4 years: The company is not yet profitable, although losses have declined in recent years.

REVENUE GROWTH ★ ★ ★ ★

Past 4 years: 8,950 percent (140 percent per year)

STOCK GROWTH ★ ★ ★ ★

Past 4 years: 2,592 percent (228 percent per year)
Dollar growth: $10,000 over 3 years would have grown to $270,000.

CONSISTENCY ★ ★

Positive earnings progression 2 of the past 4 years
Increased sales: 4 consecutive years

BEA SYSTEMS AT A GLANCE

Fiscal year ended: Jan. 31
Revenue and net income in $millions

	1996	1997	1998	1999	2000	4-Year Growth Avg. Annual (%)	4-Year Growth Total (%)
Revenue ($)	5.13	64.6	166	289	464	140	8,950
Net income ($)	–17.7	–87.8	–22.9	–51.6	–19.6	NA	NA
Earnings/share ($)	–0.09	–2.21	–0.11	–0.18	–0.06	NA	NA
PE range	NA	NA	NA	NA	NA		

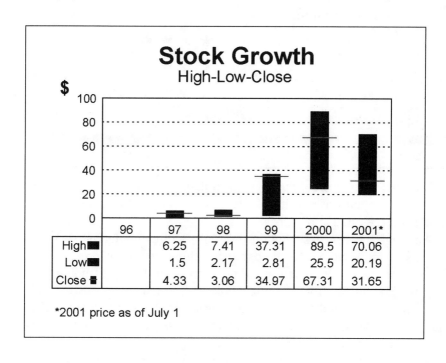

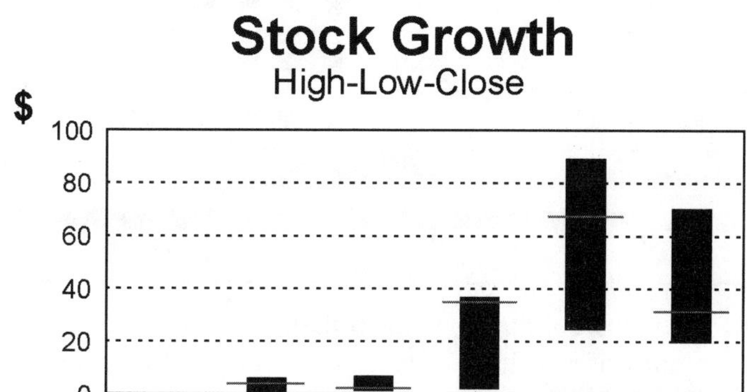

	96	97	98	99	2000	2001*
High		6.25	7.41	37.31	89.5	70.06
Low		1.5	2.17	2.81	25.5	20.19
Close		4.33	3.06	34.97	67.31	31.65

*2001 price as of July 1

56

Veritas Software Corporation

1600 Plymouth Street
Mountain View, CA 94043
650-335-8000
Nasdaq: VRTS
www.veritas.com

Chairman: Mark Leslie
President and CEO: Gary Bloom

Earnings Progression	
Revenue Growth	★ ★ ★ ★
Stock Growth	★ ★ ★ ★
Consistency	★ ★ ★
Total	**11 Points**

Veritas Software helps corporations keep their computer systems up and running. Companies use Veritas software to ensure that their data is protected and accessible at all times.

Although there is no such thing as a fail-proof computer network protection system, Veritas software can make things easier. It protects data loss and file corruption, allows rapid recovery after disk or computer system failure, enables information technology (IT) managers to work efficiently with large numbers of files, and makes it possible to manage data distributed on large networks of computer systems without harming productivity or interrupting users.

Veritas offers software for several key applications, including:

- **File and volume management.** The company's software helps companies improve the manageability and performance of business-critical data. Its volume manager software protects against data loss due to hardware failure and accelerates system performance by allowing files to be spread across multiple disks. It also lets IT managers reconfigure data locations without interrupting users. Its file system software enables fast system recovery, generally within seconds, from operating system failure or disruption.

- **Data protection.** This software is used to back up and restore data.
- **Clustering and replication.** The company provides software that improves availability of key applications in complex computing environments.
- **Desktop and mobile.** This software is used to protect data on a wide range of devices in the home, small office, and mobile business environments.

The company markets its software to original equipment manufacturers and indirect sales channels, such as resellers, value-added resellers, hardware distributors, application software vendors, and systems integrators. Among its leading customers are Compaq, Dell, EMC, Amazon.com, American Airlines, AT&T, IBM, Yahoo, Ford, GTE, Oracle, Sun Microsystems, Microsoft, and eBay.

Veritas has about 5,000 employees and a market capitalization of about $27 billion.

EARNINGS PER SHARE PROGRESSION

The company has gone from gains to losses the past 4 years.

REVENUE GROWTH ★★★★

Past 4 years: 1,560 percent (107 percent per year)

STOCK GROWTH ★★★★

Past 4 years: 1,152 percent (88 percent per year)
Dollar growth: $10,000 over 4 years would have grown to about $125,000.

CONSISTENCY ★★★

Positive earnings progression: 3 of the past 4 years
Increased sales: 4 consecutive years

VERITAS SOFTWARE AT A GLANCE

Fiscal year ended: Dec. 31
Revenue and net income in $millions

	1996	1997	1998	1999	2000	4-Year Growth Avg. Annual (%)	4-Year Growth Total (%)
Revenue ($)	72.7	121	211	596	1,207	107	1,560
Net income ($)	12.1	22.7	51.6	–503	–620	NA	NA
Earnings/share ($)	0.06	0.10	0.22	–1.59	–1.55	NA	NA
PE range	28–95	22–78	23–65	NA	NA		

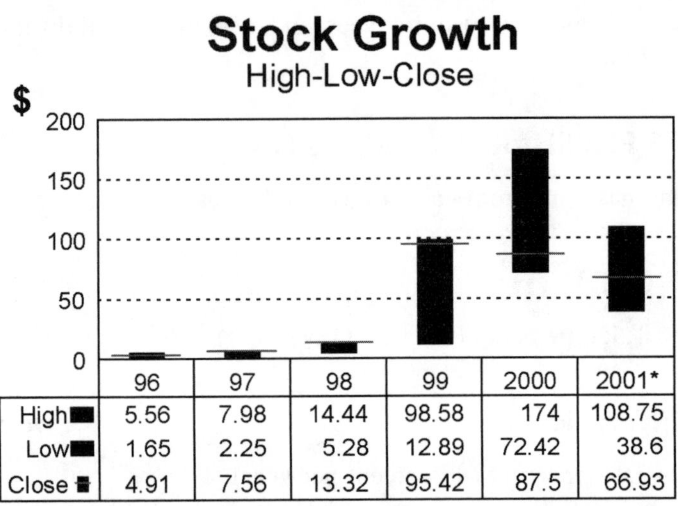

	96	97	98	99	2000	2001*
High	5.56	7.98	14.44	98.58	174	108.75
Low	1.65	2.25	5.28	12.89	72.42	38.6
Close	4.91	7.56	13.32	95.42	87.5	66.93

*2001 price as of July 1

57

China Mobile Limited

16/F Dah Sing
Financial Center
108 Gloucester Road
Wanchai, Hong Kong China
212-815-2221
NYSE: CHL
www.chinamobile.com

Chairman and President: Xiaochu Wang

Earnings Progression	
Revenue Growth	★ ★ ★ ★
Stock Growth	★ ★ ★ ★
Consistency	★ ★ ★
Total	**11 Points**

Think of the growth possibilities in a country of more than 1 billion people where only 8 percent own a mobile phone. China Mobile (Hong Kong) Limited, China's dominant provider of cellular communications, is rapidly putting mobile phones into the hands of the residents of the world's most populous nation.

The number of China Mobile's subscribers is skyrocketing—from about 15 million at the end of 1999 to about 50 million by the end of 2001's first quarter. The cost of handsets and monthly connection fees are falling rapidly, making cellular service a genuine option in a country that has had a low penetration of fixed-wire phone service and personal computer ownership.

The company commands about 78 percent of the total cellular market in China, where it serves 18 of the nation's provinces. There's competition on the way in the increasingly privatized Chinese marketplace, but China Mobile has staked out the territory well ahead of them. China Mobile

Communications, the former state-owned mobile phone monopoly, owns 75 percent of China Mobile (Hong Kong). Vodafone, the British-based telecom giant, holds a 2 percent stake in the company.

To further its growth, the company is committed to expanding its network capacity, improving the network's efficiency, controlling operating costs, and adding new wireless data services that use the latest telecommunications technologies. China Mobile is keenly focused on further developing its wireless data services, which have been launched with short messaging services (SMS), mobile banking, and information-on-demand services.

To capture the capitalistic spirit in its workforce, the company adopted an employee incentive program that's based on the employee's performance and the company's financial performance. The company has a customer-oriented management philosophy that focuses on providing high-quality communications for its growing legion of mobile phone users.

The company was incorporated in Hong Kong in 1997. It has about 13,000 employees and a market capitalization of about $60 billion.

EARNINGS PER SHARE PROGRESSION

Past 4 years: 21 percent (5 percent per year)

REVENUE GROWTH ★★★★

Past 4 years: 408 percent (50 percent per year)

STOCK GROWTH ★★★★

Past 3 years: 184 percent (42 percent per year)
Dollar growth: $10,000 over 3 years would have grown to about $28,000.

CONSISTENCY ★★★

Increased earnings per share: 3 of the past 4 years
Increased sales: 4 consecutive years

CHINA MOBILE AT A GLANCE

Fiscal year ended: Dec. 31
Revenue and net income in $millions

	1996	1997	1998	1999	2000	4-Year Growth: Avg. Annual (%)	4-Year Growth: Total (%)
Revenue ($)	7.6	10.4	15.5	26.3	38.6	50	408
Net income ($)	4.6	4.5	5.0	6.9	4.8	1	4
Earnings/share ($)	0.51	0.58	0.75	0.79	0.62	4	21
PE range	NA	14–21	11–22	21–85	NA		

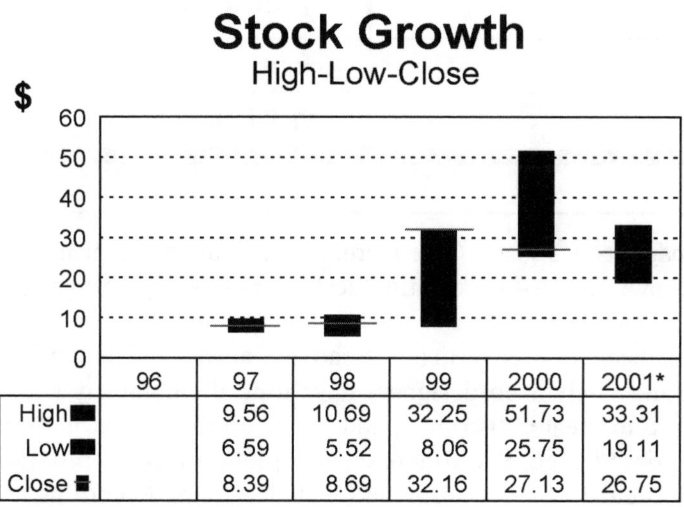

	96	97	98	99	2000	2001*
High		9.56	10.69	32.25	51.73	33.31
Low		6.59	5.52	8.06	25.75	19.11
Close		8.39	8.69	32.16	27.13	26.75

*2001 price as of July 1

58

Adobe Systems, Inc.

345 Park Avenue
San Jose, CA 95110
408-536-6000
Nasdaq: ADBE
www.adobe.com

Co-Chairman: John E. Warnock
Co-Chairman: Charles M. Geschke

Earnings Progression	★ ★ ★
Revenue Growth	★ ★
Stock Growth	★ ★ ★ ★
Consistency	★ ★
Total	**11 Points**

Stealing a page from Johann Gutenberg, Adobe launched a printing revolution of its own in 1984 by creating desktop publishing software. It has never looked back.

Graphic designers, advertising creatives, newspaper and magazine publishers, and lately Web designers have used the company's leading-edge software to create, distribute, and manage information both online and on the printed page. Photoshop, one of Adobe's leading programs, is the industry standard for both print and Web designers. According to a recent survey in *Publish* magazine, 89 percent of Web designers used Adobe Photoshop to design Web pages.

Adobe seized on the rapid growth of the Internet by developing a multifaceted online strategy, including an updated version of Photoshop that features advanced capabilities for Web graphics production—video, digital photographic images, animation, navigational buttons, and banners. The company is committed to rolling out new Web-focused software and Web-savvy updates of its leading software products.

Adobe's next-generation page layout program, Adobe InDesign, was well received by the advertising and publishing industries. Such organizations as McCann-Erickson, DDB Needham, Young & Rubicam, and CAPPS Digital quickly adopted the new program to streamline page layout.

Adobe's reputation for creating multimedia tools was enhanced with the introduction of Adobe LiveMotion, a high-end software solution that creates dynamic Web animation in a matter of seconds. Film and video professionals use Adobe's After Effects program to precisely shape footage.

Businesses that need to manage electronic and paper documents simultaneously use Adobe ePaper Solutions. Based on the industry-standard Adobe Acrobat technology, ePaper Solutions can convert just about any kind of information, including Microsoft Office documents, to compressed Adobe .pdf files that can be easily shared across a variety of computing platforms. Employees at companies with multiple sites can collaborate electronically via e-mail, the Web, and corporate intranets with the Acrobat Business tools.

Founded in 1982, the company has about 3,000 employees and a market capitalization of about $7 billion.

EARNINGS PER SHARE PROGRESSION ★★★

Past 4 years: 120 percent (21 percent per year)

REVENUE GROWTH ★★

Past 4 years: 61 percent (13 percent per year)

STOCK GROWTH ★★★★

Past 4 years: 403 percent (50 percent per year)
Dollar growth: $10,000 over 4 years would have grown to about $50,000.

CONSISTENCY ★★

Increased earnings per share: 3 of the past 4 years
Increased sales: 3 of the past 4 years

ADOBE SYSTEMS AT A GLANCE

Fiscal year ended: Nov. 30
Revenue and net income in $millions

	1996	1997	1998	1999	2000	4-Year Growth Avg. Annual (%)	4-Year Growth Total (%)
Revenue ($)	787	912	895	1,015	1,266	13	61
Net income ($)	153	187	105	238	288	17	88
Earnings/share ($)	0.51	0.63	0.39	0.92	1.12	21	120
PE range	13–31	12–21	15–33	10–42	23–77		

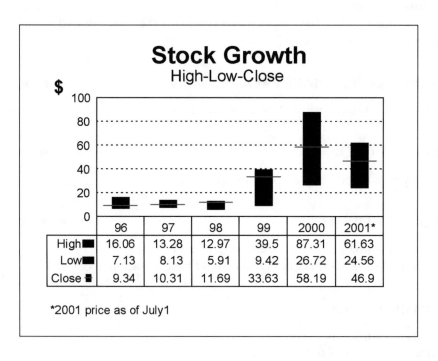

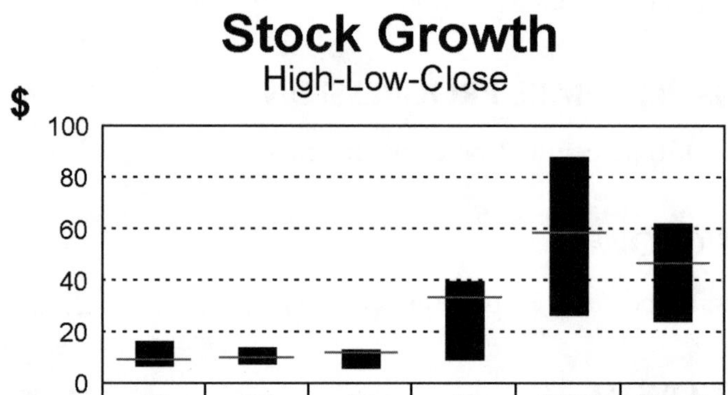

	96	97	98	99	2000	2001*
High	16.06	13.28	12.97	39.5	87.31	61.63
Low	7.13	8.13	5.91	9.42	26.72	24.56
Close	9.34	10.31	11.69	33.63	58.19	46.9

*2001 price as of July1

59

Rational Software Corporation

18880 Homestead Road
Cupertino, CA 95014
408-863-9900
Nasdaq: RATL
www.rational.com

Chairman: Paul D. Levy
President: Thomas F. Bogan
CEO: Michael T. Devlin

Earnings Progression	★★
Revenue Growth	★★★★
Stock Growth	★★
Consistency	★★★
Total	**11 Points**

Rational Software helps companies develop new software for Internet applications quickly and, as its name suggests, logically.

Rational provides a set of tools, training services, and software engineering best-practices that allows companies to automate the software development process instead of tediously writing a program line by line. Customer companies then gain a competitive advantage because they can rapidly develop and deploy high-quality, mission-critical software.

Rational is focusing on Internet-connected global companies that fall into three categories:

- **E-business customers.** Organizations using the power of the Internet to boost fortunes through B2B or B2C software. Customers include Charles Schwab, E*Trade, Merrill Lynch, and Siebel Systems.

- **E-infrastructure companies.** Companies building the physical and software infrastructure for the Internet. Customers include America Online, Cisco, Ericsson, IBM, Lucent, Microsoft, and Sun Microsystems.
- **E-devices customers.** Customers making devices with software that provide connectivity to the Internet and intranets. Hewlett-Packard, Motorola, Nokia, Palm, and Sony are among Rational's customers in this category.

The company is well positioned to take advantage of the need for software and software development, because software plays a critical role in the development of e-commerce Web sites. Rational's software products include design tools such as Rational Rose and Rational Robot, which let the user create, modify, and run automated tests on the Web and other systems.

In addition to reducing a customer's time to market, Rational aims to improve the quality of its customers' software, help companies identify performance bottlenecks, and manage change more effectively.

Rational targets professionals on software development teams employed by businesses across a variety of industries and sells its product through the Web, its field sales force, and distributors.

Founded in 1981, the company has about 2,700 employees and a market capitalization of about $7 billion.

EARNINGS PER SHARE PROGRESSION ★★

The company has gone from losses to gains the past 4 years.

REVENUE GROWTH ★★★★

Past 4 years: 193 percent (31 percent per year)

STOCK GROWTH ★★

Past 4 years: 18 percent (4 percent per year)
Dollar growth: $10,000 over 4 years would have grown to $11,800.

CONSISTENCY ★★★

Positive earnings progression: 3 of the past 4 years
Increased sales: 4 consecutive years

RATIONAL SOFTWARE AT A GLANCE

Fiscal year ended: March 31
Revenue and net income in $millions

	1997	1998	1999	2000	2001	4-Year Growth Avg. Annual (%)	4-Year Growth Total (%)
Revenue ($)	278	311	412	572	815	31	193
Net income ($)	–49.6	–38.3	59.2	84.2	56.8	NA	NA
Earnings/share ($)	–0.31	–0.22	0.32	0.45	0.35	NA	NA
PE range	NA	NA	33–83	47–158	NA		

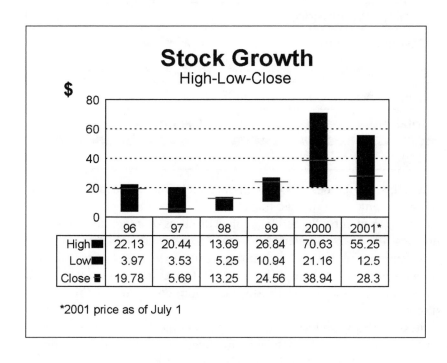

Stock Growth
High-Low-Close

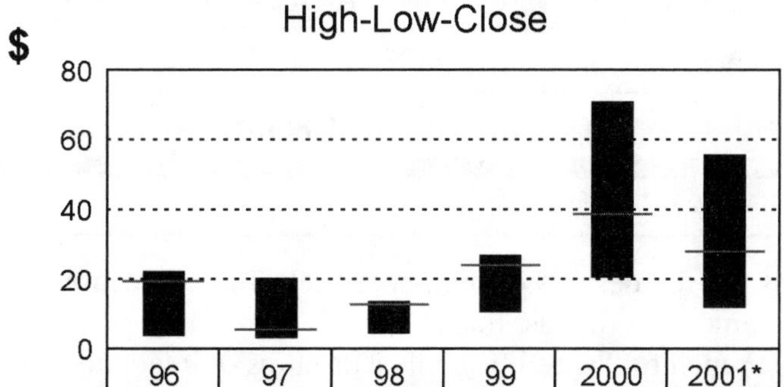

	96	97	98	99	2000	2001*
High	22.13	20.44	13.69	26.84	70.63	55.25
Low	3.97	3.53	5.25	10.94	21.16	12.5
Close	19.78	5.69	13.25	24.56	38.94	28.3

*2001 price as of July 1

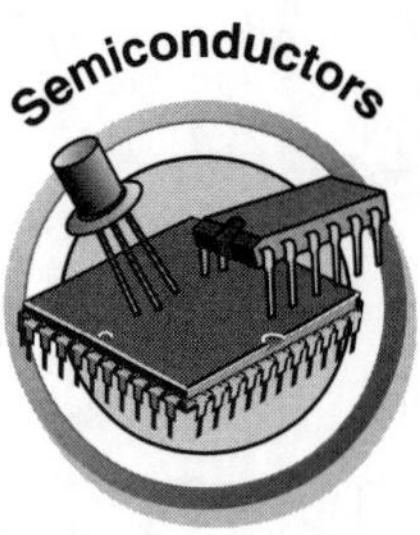

60
Vitesse Semiconductor Corporation

741 Calle Plano
Camarillo, CA 93012
805-388-3700
Nasdaq: VTSS
www.vitesse.com

Chairman: Pierre R. Lamond
President and CEO: Louis R. Tomasetta

Earnings Progression	
Revenue Growth	★ ★ ★ ★
Stock Growth	★ ★ ★ ★
Consistency	★ ★ ★
Total	**11 Points**

Vitesse helps put the designs of high-speed telecommunications and networking equipment on the fast track.

Vitesse (French for "speed") supplies its chips or integrated circuits to companies like Cisco, Lucent, Ericsson, Alcatel, and IBM that must get their products to market on Internet time. Customers are fond of Vitesse's gallium arsenide (GaAs) chips, because electronic signals are transmitted through them five to six times faster than more conventional chips made of silicon.

Vitesse's chips are harder to make, but engineers designing the optical infrastructure of today's telecommunications and data communications swear by them. They have reduced the time to market of their designs by about half.

Makers of automated test equipment also use the chips in their designs. About half the company's sales are to telecom companies, and the remaining sales are evenly divided between data communications equipment and automated test equipment. International sales account for about a quarter of the company's total revenue.

Vitesse was a spin-off of Rockwell International, where Lou Tomasetta, Vitesse's president and CEO, and others developed a way to make digital circuits on gallium arsenide. Vitesse also developed the international standard for high-speed fiber-optic transmission that is used by long distance telephone carriers and local operating companies worldwide.

As the need for more and faster data such as streaming video and MP3 files grows, so too will the demand for Vitesse's high-speed chips. The company believes it's well positioned to handle the world's growing appetite for increased bandwidth and additional capacity needs of data storage equipment. The company manufactures chips at its fabrication plant in Camarillo, California, and in Colorado Springs, Colorado.

Founded in 1987, the company has about 1,100 employees and a market capitalization of about $10 billion.

EARNINGS PER SHARE PROGRESSION

Past 4 years: 36 percent (8 percent per year)

REVENUE GROWTH ★★★★

Past 4 years: 570 percent (62 percent per year)

STOCK GROWTH ★★★★

Past 4 years: 352 percent (46 percent per year)
Dollar growth: $10,000 over 4 years would have grown to about $45,000.

CONSISTENCY ★★★

Increased earnings per share: 3 of the past 4 years
Increased sales: 4 consecutive years

VITESSE SEMICONDUCTOR AT A GLANCE

Fiscal year ended: Sept. 30
Revenue and net income in $millions

	1996	1997	1998	1999	2000	4-Year Growth Avg. Annual (%)	4-Year Growth Total (%)
Revenue ($)	66	105	181	282	442	62	570
Net income ($)	12.6	29.5	48.6	61.1	27.9	22	121
Earnings/share ($)	0.11	0.19	0.29	0.34	0.15	8	36
PE range	15–80	27–73	29–84	59–161	242–786		

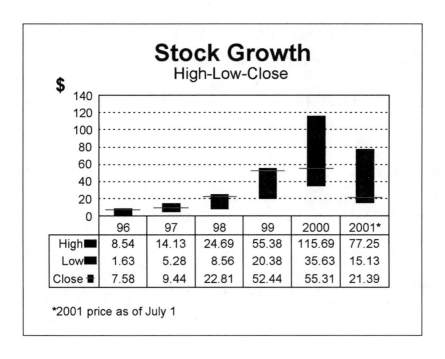

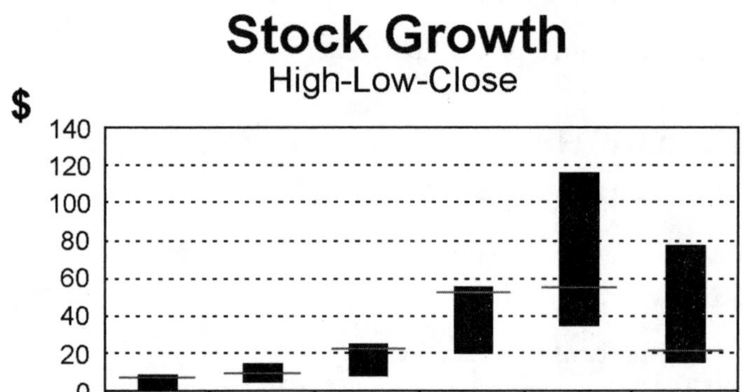

	96	97	98	99	2000	2001*
High	8.54	14.13	24.69	55.38	115.69	77.25
Low	1.63	5.28	8.56	20.38	35.63	15.13
Close	7.58	9.44	22.81	52.44	55.31	21.39

*2001 price as of July 1

61

The InterCept Group, Inc.

3150 Holcomb Bridge Road, Suite 200
Norcross, GA 30071
770-248-9600
Nasdaq: ICPT
www.tellerplus.com

Chairman and CEO: John W. Collins
President: Donny R. Jackson

Earnings Progression	
Revenue Growth	★ ★ ★ ★
Stock Growth	★ ★ ★ ★
Consistency	★ ★ ★
Total	**11 Points**

Small community banks can use the same type of electronic transaction processes as the big institutions, thanks to a comprehensive line of banking software offered by the InterCept Group.

InterCept provides software and services for electronic funds transfer services, data communication management, check imaging, Internet banking, client-server enterprise software, and other processing solutions for more than 1,400 community banks and savings institutions.

The firm focuses on financial institutions with assets of under $500 million. Most of its corporate customers are located in the southern United States.

The Georgia-based operation is also the largest third-party processor of automatic teller machine transactions in the southeastern U.S.

InterCept's key services for savings institutions include:

- **Electronic funds transfer.** The firm offers automatic funds transfer services for banks, including transactions for money machines, point of sale, debit card and scrip debit transactions, funds transfers, and remote banking transactions.

- **Core data processing.** InterCept supplies software and services to help its customers with general ledger, loan and deposit operations, financial accounting and reporting, and customer information file maintenance.
- **Data communications management.** Through its InterCept Frame Relay Network, the company manages data communications and voice-over-frame communications, which eliminate certain long distance charges for its customers. It also designs and manages local and wide area data communications networks for its customers and offers them certain Internet services, including managed firewall and e-mail service.
- **Check imaging.** InterCept's check imaging software creates computerized images of checks, deposit slips, and related paper documents for electronic storage and retrieval.
- **Internet banking.** Through its Netzee, Inc. affiliate, the company offers Internet and telephone banking products and services.

First incorporated in 1996, InterCept went public with its initial stock offering in 1998. The company has about 320 employees and a market capitalization of about $300 million.

EARNINGS PER SHARE PROGRESSION

The company had a loss in 2000 after 2 years of profits.

REVENUE GROWTH ★★★★

Past 4 years: 380 percent (48 percent per year)

STOCK GROWTH ★★★★

Past 3 years: 254 percent (51 percent per year)
Dollar growth: $10,000 over 3 years would have grown to about $35,000.

CONSISTENCY ★★★

Positive earnings progression: 3 of the past 4 years
Increased sales: 4 consecutive years

INTERCEPT AT A GLANCE

Fiscal year ended: Dec. 31
Revenue and net income in $millions

	1996	1997	1998	1999	2000	4-Year Growth	
						Avg. Annual (%)	Total (%)
Revenue ($)	14.5	23.2	33.2	52.3	69.6	48	380
Net income ($)	–1.4	–0.434	2.67	25.4	13.9	110*	420*
Earnings/share ($)	–0.24	–0.06	0.30	0.94	–1.31	NA	NA
PE range	NA	NA	15–29	7–32	NA		

*Net income growth figures are based on 2-year growth.

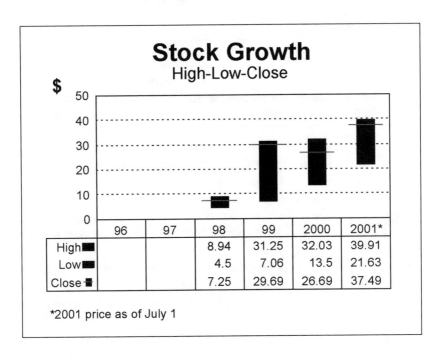

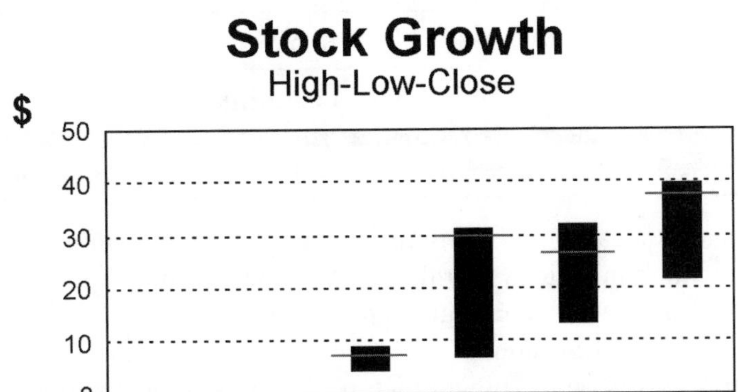

	96	97	98	99	2000	2001*
High			8.94	31.25	32.03	39.91
Low			4.5	7.06	13.5	21.63
Close			7.25	29.69	26.69	37.49

*2001 price as of July 1

62

ADC Telecommunications

12501 Whitewater Drive
Minnetonka, MN 55343
952-938-8080
Nasdaq: ADCT
www.adc.com

Chairman and CEO: Richard R. Roscitt
President: Lynn Davis

Earnings Progression	★ ★ ★ ★
Revenue Growth	★ ★ ★ ★
Stock Growth	
Consistency	★ ★ ★
Total	**11 Points**

ADC Telecommunications has built its business on the little things that tie the vast telecommunications world together, such as plugs and routers, patch cords, jacks, cables, and digital enhancers.

But while the Minneapolis operation continues to push the small parts, its emphasis is on the bigger picture. It has become a major player in the broadband industry, manufacturing fiber optics and network equipment and software.

The company markets its products primarily to long distance phone companies, cable television operators, Internet service providers, wireless service providers, private network operators, and broadcast television operators.

In recent years, ADC has focused much of its research and development efforts on helping telephone companies keep up with the rapidly rising demand for service. Increased demand for Internet access, cable television, fax machines, and interactive services has put a strain on line capacity. ADC's transmission products help ease the communications bottleneck and increase the speed and efficiency of the communications network. Its broadband telecommunications equipment is designed to increase line capacity both on traditional copper-based networks and fiber-optic and wireless transmission networks.

ADC divides its business into three main groups, including broadband connectivity, broadband access, and transport and integrated solutions.

The company has expanded rapidly in recent years through a series of acquisitions. ADC currently has operations in more than 30 countries and sells its products in about 100 countries around the world.

ADC Telecommunications was founded in 1935 by Ralph Allison, a young engineer who opened shop in the basement of his Minneapolis home. The company's first product was the "audiometer," an electronic device designed to test hearing. Along with fellow engineer Walt Lehnert, Allison continued to add to the mix of products, including jacks, plugs, and patch cords that served as the firm's entrée into the communications industry.

ADC has about 22,000 employees and a market capitalization of about $8 billion.

EARNINGS PER SHARE PROGRESSION ★★★★

Past 4 years: 194 percent (31 percent per year)

REVENUE GROWTH ★★★★

Past 4 years: 297 percent (41 percent per year)

STOCK GROWTH

Past 4 years: 15 percent (3 percent per year)
Dollar growth: $10,000 over 4 years would have grown to $11,500.

CONSISTENCY ★★★

Increased earnings per share: 3 of the past 4 years
Increased sales: 4 consecutive years

ADC TELECOMMUNICATIONS AT A GLANCE

Fiscal year ended: Oct. 31
Revenue and net income in $millions

	1996	1997	1998	1999	2000	4-Year Growth Avg. Annual (%)	4-Year Growth Total (%)
Revenue ($)	828	1,271	1,830	2,152	3,288	41	297
Net income ($)	87.5	133	210	197	384.4	45	338
Earnings/share ($)	0.17	0.23	0.29	0.29	0.50	31	194
PE range	21–60	23–50	12–33	75–166	13–43		

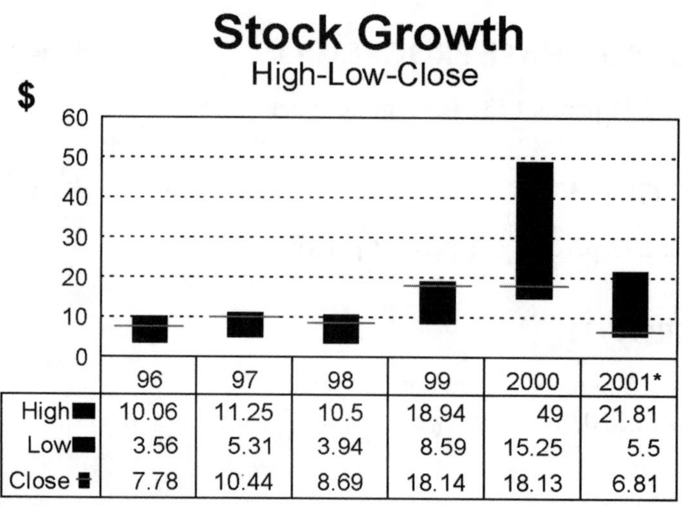

	96	97	98	99	2000	2001*
High	10.06	11.25	10.5	18.94	49	21.81
Low	3.56	5.31	3.94	8.59	15.25	5.5
Close	7.78	10.44	8.69	18.14	18.13	6.81

*2001 price as of July1

63

Microchip Technology, Inc.

2355 West Chandler Boulevard
Chandler, AZ 85224
480-792-7200
Nasdaq: MCHP
www.microchip.com

Chairman, President, and CEO: Steve Sanghi

Earnings Progression	★★★
Revenue Growth	★★★
Stock Growth	★★
Consistency	★★★
Total	**11 Points**

Tiny microcontrollers serve as the brains of thousands of modern devices, from TV remote controls and garage door openers to handheld tools, cell phones, and major appliances. Microchip Technology is one of the leading makers of microcontrollers and related products.

Microprocessors have become popular for several important reasons. They're very small and very powerful, they work well under low voltage, and they're very cheap. The price of Microchip's microcontrollers ranges from about 80 cents to $10 each. The company has shipped more than a billion microcontrollers to its corporate customers since the company began manufacturing operations in 1990.

In addition to microcontrollers, Microchip Technology also makes products in three other broad categories, including:

- **Development systems.** This software product enables system designers to quickly program a microcontroller for specific applications. Its software operates in the standard Windows environment on standard PC hardware. Entry-level systems are priced at less than $200. A fully configured system, which also provides in-circuit emulation hardware, performance simulators, and software debuggers, is priced at approximately $2,000.

- **Application specific standard products (ASSPs).** These specialized integrated circuits are designed to perform specific end-user applications, such as automotive remote keyless entry systems, automatic garage and gate openers, and smart cards.
- **Mixed signal products.** These products consist of a growing portfolio of stand-alone analog devices that are used primarily in embedded control systems to convert or buffer input and output signals to or from a microcontroller.

In addition to its high volume chips, which are referred to as OTP (one-time programmable), Microchip Technology also makes a line of specialty memory chips, such as erasable programmable read-only memory chips (EPROMs) and ROM (read-only memory) devices. The company also makes a variety of specialized integrated circuits, including KEELOQ security products and Quick ASIC gate array devices.

First incorporated in 1989, Microchip Technology has about 2,700 employees and a market capitalization of about $4 billion.

EARNINGS PER SHARE PROGRESSION ★ ★ ★

Past 4 years: 148 percent (25 percent per year)

REVENUE GROWTH ★ ★ ★

Past 4 years: 114 percent (21 percent per year)

STOCK GROWTH ★ ★

Past 4 years: 86 percent (17 percent per year)
Dollar growth: $10,000 over 4 years would have grown to $18,600.

CONSISTENCY ★ ★ ★

Increased earnings per share: 3 of the past 4 years
Increased sales: 4 consecutive years

MICROCHIP TECHNOLOGY AT A GLANCE

Fiscal year ended: March 31
Revenue and net income in $millions

	1997	1998	1999	2000	2001	4-Year Growth Avg. Annual (%)	4-Year Growth Total (%)
Revenue ($)	334	397	406	553	716	21	114
Net income ($)	51.1	64.4	50.0	115	143	29	180
Earnings/share ($)	0.42	0.51	0.42	0.88	1.04	25	148
PE range	24–52	14–35	27–82	23–61	NA		

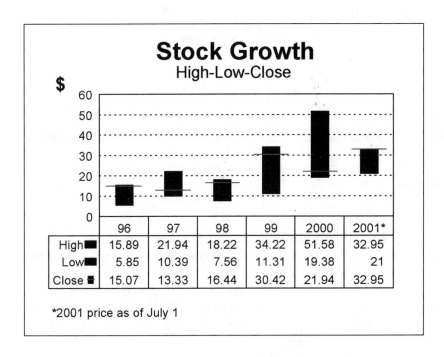

Stock Growth
High-Low-Close

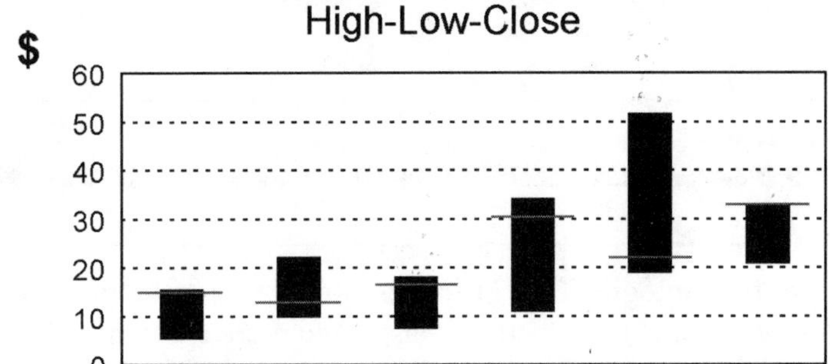

	96	97	98	99	2000	2001*
High	15.89	21.94	18.22	34.22	51.58	32.95
Low	5.85	10.39	7.56	11.31	19.38	21
Close	15.07	13.33	16.44	30.42	21.94	32.95

*2001 price as of July 1

64

Cable Design Technologies

Foster Plaza 7
661 Anderson Drive
Pittsburgh, PA 15220
412-937-2300
NYSE: CDT
www.cdtc.com

Chairman: Bryan Cressey
President and CEO: Paul M. Olson

Earnings Progression	★ ★ ★ ★
Revenue Growth	★ ★ ★
Stock Growth	
Consistency	★ ★ ★ ★
Total	**11 Points**

Cable Design Technologies (CDT) makes products that help move data across the telecommunications network faster and more efficiently. The firm manufactures a broad line of specialty electronic data transmission products, such as fiber-optic network cables and connectors, network wiring components, assemblies, electronic and fiber-optic components, and cables for computer and communication switching applications.

CDT markets its products to leading manufacturers of communications products, regional Bell phone companies, and independent distributors. In all, the company has more than 10,000 corporate customers worldwide.

The firm has grown quickly through a series of acquisitions, buying about 20 other companies since 1984.

The Pittsburgh-based operation breaks its product offerings into two key groups:

- **Network communication products** (68 percent of revenue). The company makes a wide range of products for the electronic transmission of voice, data, and multimedia over local and wide area networks and the local loop communication infrastructures. Products include fiber-optic and twisted pair and coaxial copper cables and connectors, wiring racks and panels, outlets and interconnecting hardware for end-to-end network structured wiring systems, fiber-optic assemblies and patch cords, and communication cable products for outside communication and central office switchboard and equipment applications.

- **Specialty electronics** (32 percent of revenue). The company makes highly engineered wire and cable products that address a wide range of specialized markets, including commercial aviation, automotive and medical electronics, electronic testing equipment, robotics, and factory equipment. It also makes cables for automation applications, such as climate control, premise video distribution and sophisticated security, and signal systems.

The firm has sales operations worldwide. International sales account for about 38 percent of total revenue.

CDT was founded in 1984 and incorporated in 1988. It went public with its initial stock offering in 1993. The company has about 4,000 employees and a market capitalization of about $600 million.

EARNINGS PER SHARE PROGRESSION ★ ★ ★ ★

Past 4 years: 247 percent (37 percent per year)

REVENUE GROWTH ★ ★ ★

Past 4 years: 123 percent (22 percent per year)

STOCK GROWTH

Past 4 years: 20 percent (4 percent per year)
Dollar growth: $10,000 over 4 years would have grown to about $12,000.

CONSISTENCY ★ ★ ★ ★

Increased earnings per share: 4 consecutive years
Increased sales: 4 consecutive years

CABLE DESIGN TECHNOLOGIES AT A GLANCE

Fiscal year ended: July 31
Revenue and net income in $millions

	1996	1997	1998	1999	2000	4-Year Growth Avg. Annual (%)	4-Year Growth Total (%)
Revenue ($)	357	517	652	684	798	22	123
Net income ($)	15.9	36.0	40.5	39.6	54.9	36	245
Earnings/share ($)	0.36	0.78	0.86	0.91	1.25	37	247
PE range	26–59	9–24	7–24	7–18	11–23		

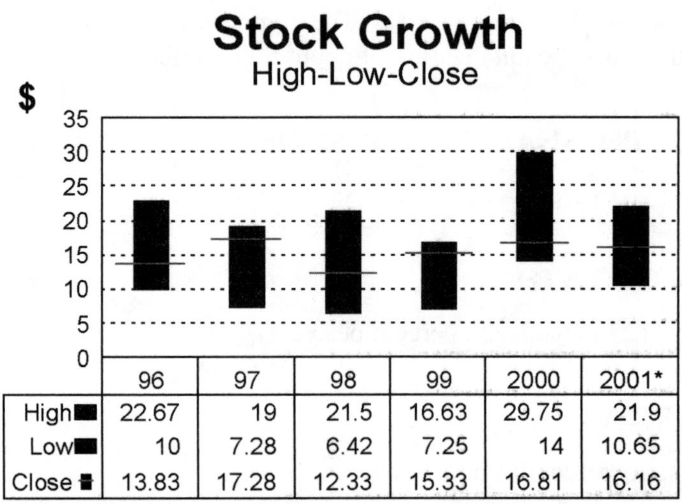

*2001 price as of July 1

65

Vodafone Group PLC

The Courtyard, 2-4
London Road
Newbury, Berkshire
RG14 1JX, United Kingdom
800-233-5601
NYSE: VOD
www.vodafone.com

Chairman: Lord MacLaurin
CEO: Christopher C. Gent

Earnings Progression	
Revenue Growth	★ ★ ★ ★
Stock Growth	★ ★ ★ ★
Consistency	★ ★ ★
Total	**11 Points**

Vodafone wants to create a seamless worldwide mobile phone network. The world's largest wireless company is well on its way to that goal with ownership stakes in wireless carriers in some 30 countries throughout Asia/Pacific, Europe, the U.S., Africa, and the Middle East.

Vodafone's largest presence is in its home turf of the UK, Germany, and the U.S. Vodafone owns 45 percent of Verizon Wireless, America's largest wireless provider.

In an effort to create a powerful global brand for the various wireless companies under its control, Vodafone will begin renaming the companies under its own name to foster instant customer recognition of its wireless network. By 2004, the company hopes to own one of the world's most familiar and valuable brand names.

Vodafone, with about 25 percent of the world's mobile phone users, has a global customer base of more than 80 million. It makes savvy use of its customer relationship system to get to know users' preferences and what additional services and products they might need.

Users of mobile phones or palmtop devices are developing a strong appetite for wireless data services, such as Internet access and short messaging. Nearly half of Vodafone's European customers are using its short messaging services, or SMS.

Vodafone is establishing a global Internet services platform that will allow access to the Net from mobile phones, PCs, and palmtops from across the Vodafone operating companies.

To expand its wireless data services, Vodafone entered into a joint venture with Vivendi Universal, one of Europe's leading media companies, to create Vizzavi, an Internet portal designed for consumers. Customers will be able to visit any content site via their mobile phone, PDA, or digital TV. Vizzavi expects to have more than two million registered users by the end of 2001.

Vodafone has about 29,000 employees and a market capitalization of about $160 billion.

EARNINGS PER SHARE PROGRESSION

Past 4 years: 5 percent (1 percent per year)

REVENUE GROWTH ★★★★

Past 4 years: 461 percent (54 percent per year)

STOCK GROWTH ★★★★

Past 4 years: 268 percent (39 percent per year)
Dollar growth: $10,000 over 4 years would have grown to about $37,000.

CONSISTENCY ★★★

Increased earnings per share: 3 of the past 4 years
Increased sales: 4 consecutive years

VODAFONE AT A GLANCE

Fiscal year ended: March 31
Revenue and net income in $millions
(.7 British pound = 1 U.S. dollar)

	1996	1997	1998	1999	2000	4-Year Growth: Avg. Annual (%)	4-Year Growth: Total (%)
Revenue ($)	1,402	1,749	2,471	3,360	7,873	54	461
Net income ($)	310	367	447	683	664	21	114
Earnings/share ($)	0.19	0.22	0.24	0.33	0.20	1	5
PE range	23–31	24–46	38–94	69–112	114–219		

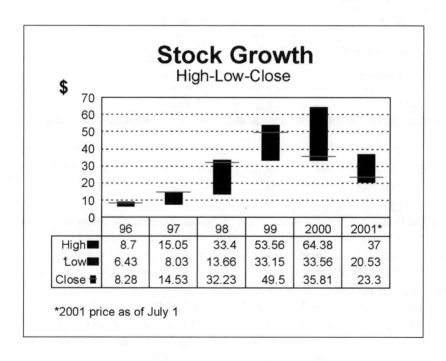

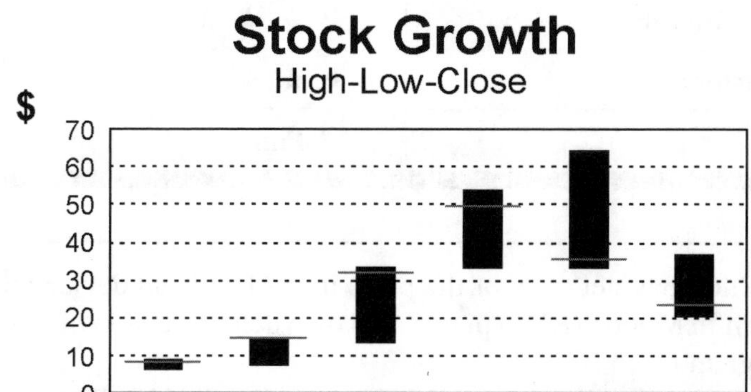

	96	97	98	99	2000	2001*
High	8.7	15.05	33.4	53.56	64.38	37
Low	6.43	8.03	13.66	33.15	33.56	20.53
Close	8.28	14.53	32.23	49.5	35.81	23.3

*2001 price as of July 1

66

Research In Motion, Ltd.

295 Phillip Street
Waterloo, Ontario
N2L 3W8 Canada
519-888-7465
Nasdaq: RIMM
www.rim.net

Chairman and Co-CEO: Jim Balsillie
Co-CEO: Mike Lazaridis

Earnings Progression	
Revenue Growth	★ ★ ★ ★
Stock Growth	★ ★ ★ ★
Consistency	★ ★ ★
Total	**11 Points**

The Palm Pilot may get most of the press in the handheld device market, but Research In Motion (RIM) puts out its own deluxe version of the wireless super-gizmo.

The company's palm-sized RIM Wireless Handhelds allow users to send and receive wireless e-mail from anywhere. The unit has a keyboard, thumb-operated trackwheel, backlit screen, and intuitive menu-driven interface. The RIM Handheld is always on, with no dialing in, no initiating connections, and no antennas to raise. Your e-mails automatically find you.

The company's flagship model is the BlackBerry handheld device, available in both pager-sized and palm-sized units. In addition to providing ongoing e-mail access, the units also include a personal organizer with a calendar, address book, memo pad, and task list feature. The unit works easily with office computers. By simply placing the BlackBerry unit in its cradle and clicking the special icon on the monitor, information is automatically synchronized and updated between the handheld unit and the PC.

The Ontario, Canada operation has developed some strategic alliances with some of the leading technology companies, such as America Online, Compaq, Nortel Networks, and Sun Microsystems to develop its next generation of wireless devices.

In addition to its handheld units, the company also makes a line of embedded radio modems that can be integrated into laptop computers and other portable devices. RIM typically sells the radio-frequency modems to manufacturers of laptop computers and other portable devices to be inserted during the original manufacturing process.

The devices are also used in point-of-sale terminals, bank machines, billboards and other displays, monitoring and metering equipment, vending machines, and automobiles.

RIM also offers software development tools that enable BlackBerry users to customize the features on their devices.

Founded in 1984, Research In Motion has about 800 employees and a market capitalization of about $2 billion.

EARNINGS PER SHARE PROGRESSION

The company had a loss in fiscal 2001 after several years of positive earnings.

REVENUE GROWTH ★ ★ ★ ★

Past 4 years: 3,459 percent (142 percent per year)

STOCK GROWTH ★ ★ ★ ★

Past 2 years (since its IPO): 200 percent (73 percent per year)
Dollar growth: $10,000 over 2 years would have grown to about $30,000.

CONSISTENCY ★ ★ ★

Positive earnings progression: 3 of the past 4 years
Increased sales: 4 consecutive years

RESEARCH IN MOTION AT A GLANCE

Fiscal year ended: Feb. 28
Revenue and net income in $millions

	1997	1998	1999	2000	2001	4-Year Growth Avg. Annual (%)	4-Year Growth Total (%)
Revenue ($)	6.35	20.1	45.5	74.9	226	142	3,459
Net income ($)	0.28	0.349	6.16	10.5	–6.21	NA	NA
Earnings/share ($)	0.00	0.01	0.09	0.14	–0.08	NA	NA
PE range	NA	NA	72–671	167–1264	NA		

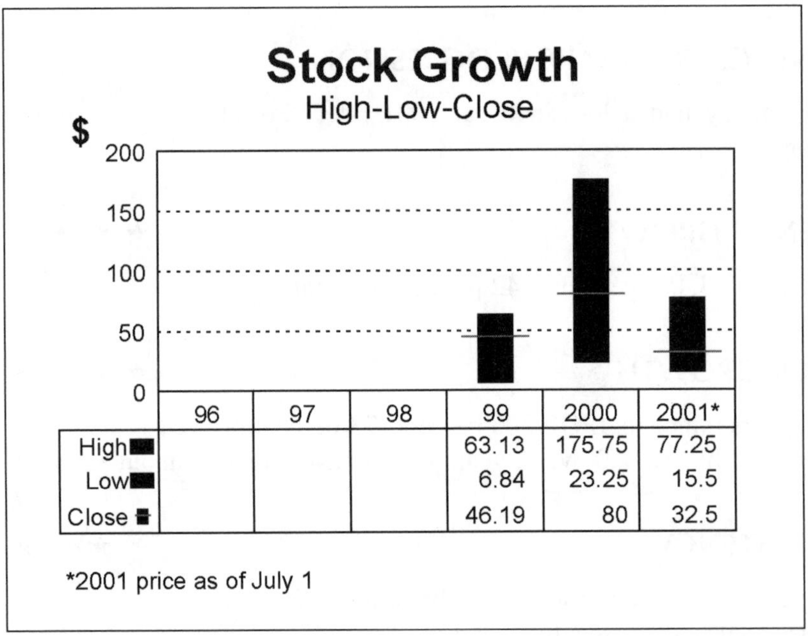

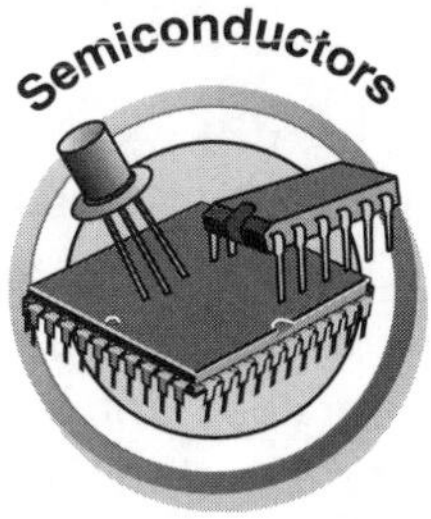

67

Advanced Micro Devices

One AMD Place
Sunnyvale, CA 94088
408-732-2400
NYSE: AMD
www.amd.com

Chairman and CEO: W.J. Sanders III
President: H. de J. Ruiz

Earnings Progression	★ ★
Revenue Growth	★ ★ ★
Stock Growth	★ ★ ★
Consistency	★ ★ ★
Total	**11 Points**

Advanced Micro Devices (AMD) created the world's fastest, most-powerful microprocessor for the PC in the form of its Athlon chip in the ever-escalating battle with Intel for supremacy in the semiconductor market.

Intel, which AMD describes as the industry's 800-pound gorilla, retains its leading market position with its line of Pentium chips, but AMD holds a solid second place position in the lucrative microprocessor industry. A technology powerhouse, AMD is continuously upgrading the speed and functionality of its chips, which can now process more than 1 billion instructions per second.

To maintain its leadership, AMD is committed to doubling the performance of its microprocessors every 18 months. In 2001, the U.S. Patent and Trademark Office ranked AMD No. 5 among U.S.-based companies and 12th in the world for the number of patents it was awarded. It was the third year in a row that AMD was ranked among the top 25 companies in the number of U.S. patents received. AMD was awarded 1,055 patents in 2000, placing it ahead of Hewlett-Packard (904), arch rival Intel (797), and GE (790). Hector Ruiz, AMD's president, said: "We think there is a strong connection between AMD innovations, our continued success, and the number of awards won by our microprocessors and flash memory devices in recent years."

Flash memory chips are the primary memory devices for cellular telephones, set-top PC boxes, and the Internet—all vibrant industries with unlimited growth potential. It's expected that demand for the flash memory chips will exceed supply in the near term and possibly beyond.

AMD Athlon's chips power PCs made by Compaq (its largest customer), Gateway, Hewlett-Packard, and other leading manufacturers. AMD has established a number of strategic alliances—such as a technology development program with Motorola—with infrastructure providers around the world to present a viable alternative to the chips made by Intel.

Founded in 1969, AMD has about 14,000 employees and a market capitalization of about $7 billion.

EARNINGS PER SHARE PROGRESSION ★★

Past 4 years: The company has gone from losses to a large gain in 2000.

REVENUE GROWTH ★★★

Past 4 years: 138 percent (24 percent per year)

STOCK GROWTH ★★★

Past 4 years: 125 percent (22 percent per year)
Dollar growth: $10,000 over 4 years would have grown to $22,500.

CONSISTENCY ★★★

Positive earnings progression: 3 of the past 4 years
Increased sales: 4 consecutive years

ADVANCED MICRO DEVICES AT A GLANCE

Fiscal year ended: Dec. 31
Revenue and net income in $millions

	1996	1997	1998	1999	2000	4-Year Growth Avg. Annual (%)	4-Year Growth Total (%)
Revenue ($)	1,953	2,356	2,542	2,858	4,644	24	138
Net income ($)	–124	–45.7	–115	–93.7	793.8	NA	NA
Earnings/share ($)	–0.25	–0.07	–0.36	–0.30	2.36	NA	NA
PE range	NA	NA	NA	NA	4–16		

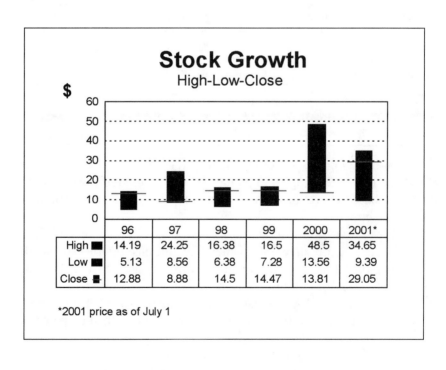

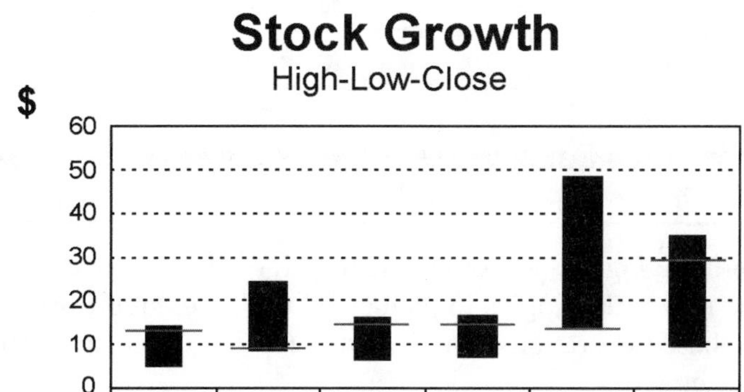

	96	97	98	99	2000	2001*
High	14.19	24.25	16.38	16.5	48.5	34.65
Low	5.13	8.56	6.38	7.28	13.56	9.39
Close	12.88	8.88	14.5	14.47	13.81	29.05

*2001 price as of July 1

68

CheckFree Corporation

4411 East Jones Bridge Road
Norcross, GA 30092
678-375-3000
Nasdaq: CKFR
www.checkfree.com

Chairman and CEO: Peter Kight
President: Peter Sinisgalli

Earnings Progression	★
Revenue Growth	★ ★ ★ ★
Stock Growth	★ ★ ★
Consistency	★ ★ ★
Total	**11 Points**

Electronic bill-paying has become a reality for millions of consumers, thanks to the new technologies implemented by CheckFree Corporation. The Georgia-based operation is the leading provider of electronic billing and payment services.

CheckFree provides electronic transaction services for about 4 million consumers through more than 350 financial institutions, Internet financial sites, and personal financial management software such as Quicken. It handles about 200 million transactions annually.

CheckFree has developed relationships with well over 1,000 merchants nationwide that enable the company to remit more than 60 percent of all its bill payments electronically. The company also delivers more than 100,000 bills per month electronically.

Consumers have become increasingly interested in the electronic bill-paying concept for a variety of reasons. The technology allows consumers to receive electronic bills through the Internet and pay their bills—electronic or paper—to a growing legion of participating businesses. Check-Free's customers can also perform a number of banking transactions (such as balance inquiries and transfers between accounts) 24 hours a day, seven days a week.

CheckFree introduced its "E-bill" technology in 1997, enabling merchants to deliver billing and marketing materials interactively to their customers over the Internet.

The company is also a leading provider of institutional portfolio management and information services. It provides electronic commerce and financial applications software and services for businesses and financial institutions. Related services include data conversion, personnel training, trading systems, graphical client reporting, technical network support and interface setup, and Depository Trust Corp. interfacing.

CheckFree also offers institutional clients financial planning software that includes retirement and estate planning modules, cash flow, tax and education planning modules, asset allocation modules, and an investment manager performance database system.

CheckFree has about 2,500 employees and a market capitalization of about $5 billion.

EARNINGS PER SHARE PROGRESSION ★

The company has seen its losses decline in recent years.

REVENUE GROWTH ★ ★ ★ ★

Past 4 years: 508 percent (57 percent per year)

STOCK GROWTH ★ ★ ★

Past 4 years: 119 percent (22 percent per year)
Dollar growth: $10,000 over 4 years would have grown to $21,900.

CONSISTENCY ★ ★ ★

Positive earnings progression: 3 of the past 4 years
Increased sales: 4 consecutive years

CHECKFREE AT A GLANCE

Fiscal year ended: June 30
Revenue and net income in $millions

	1996	1997	1998	1999	2000	4-Year Growth Avg. Annual (%)	4-Year Growth Total (%)
Revenue ($)	51	176	234	250	310	57	508
Net income ($)	–138	–162	–3.7	10.4	–32.3	NA	NA
Earnings/share ($)	–3.70	–3.44	–0.07	0.18	–0.61	NA	NA
PE range	NA	NA	NA	111–581	NA		

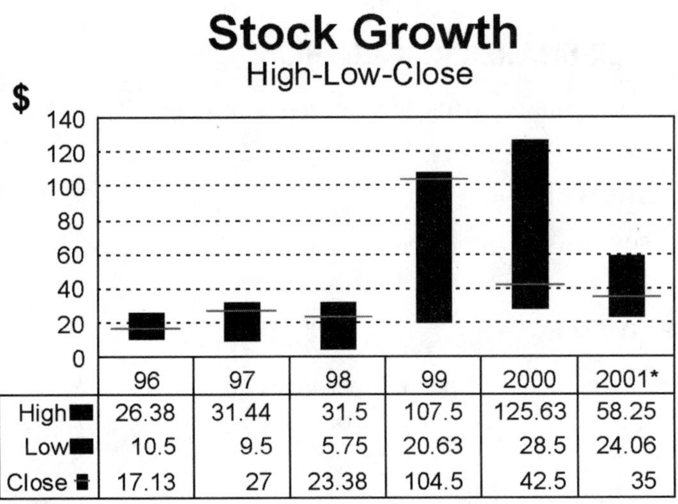

	96	97	98	99	2000	2001*
High	26.38	31.44	31.5	107.5	125.63	58.25
Low	10.5	9.5	5.75	20.63	28.5	24.06
Close	17.13	27	23.38	104.5	42.5	35

*2001 price as of July 1

69

Micromuse, Inc.

139 Townsend Street
San Francisco, CA 94107
415-538-9090
Nasdaq: MUSE
www.micromuse.com

Chairman and CEO: Gregory Brown

Earnings Progression	
Revenue Growth	★ ★ ★ ★
Stock Growth	★ ★ ★ ★
Consistency	★ ★
Total	**10 Points**

Micromuse helps telecommunications companies and Internet service providers keep their networks up and running. The company's Netcool software monitors large-scale networks 24 hours a day, alerting network operators at the first sign of trouble.

The company's software keeps watch over a wide range of elements in a network infrastructure, including network devices, computing systems, and other software. The Netcool software suite actively collects and consolidates high volumes of computer network information, enters it in a high-speed database, processes the information in real time, and rapidly distributes graphical views of the information to operators and administrators monitoring service levels.

The company also offers Netcool ObjectServer software, which includes a library of off-the-shelf software modules that collect computer event information from more than 300 network environments, including management applications, voice and data networking equipment, Internet and wide area services, and computer systems.

Other Netcool software options include:

- **Netcool OMNIbus.** The company's flagship product, first developed in 1994, allows network service providers to manage service levels and maintain availability of their voice, data, and Internet services.
- **Netcool Reporter.** This multi-threaded Java-based application allows network operations center personnel to analyze key historical information over the Web using standard Web browsers. It can also create a wide variety of charts, graphs, or text-based reports.
- **Netcool Impact.** This software allows service providers and corporate enterprises to determine how Netcool-collected faults will impact information technology business processes, network-based services, or any revenue-generating system on the network.
- **Netcool Internet Service Monitor.** Internet service providers use this software to receive real-time Internet availability and response time information for 18 different Internet protocols and applications through regular testing.

The company has marketed its software to about 1,000 corporate customers, including AirTouch, America Online, AT&T, Cable & Wireless, Cellular One, Charles Schwab, Deutsche Telekom, GTE, and MCI Worldcom.

Micromuse went public with its initial stock offering in 1998. The company has about 500 employees and a market capitalization of about $3 billion.

EARNINGS PER SHARE PROGRESSION

The company has had losses 3 of the past 4 years.

REVENUE GROWTH ★ ★ ★ ★

Past 4 years: 2,627 percent (129 percent per year)

STOCK GROWTH ★ ★ ★ ★

Past 2 years: 799 percent (181 percent per year)
Dollar growth: $10,000 over 2 years would have grown to about $90,000.

CONSISTENCY ★ ★

Positive earnings progression: 2 of the past 4 years
Increased sales: 4 consecutive years

MICROMUSE AT A GLANCE

Fiscal year ended: Sept. 30
Revenue and net income in $millions

						4-Year Growth	
	1996	1997	1998	1999	2000	Avg. Annual (%)	Total (%)
Revenue ($)	4.51	9.29	28.3	58.1	123	129	2,627
Net income ($)	–0.805	–8.93	–0.838	7.89	–2.09	NA	NA
Earnings/share ($)	–0.01	–0.34	–0.05	0.11	–0.03	NA	NA
PE range	NA	NA	NA	44–403	NA		

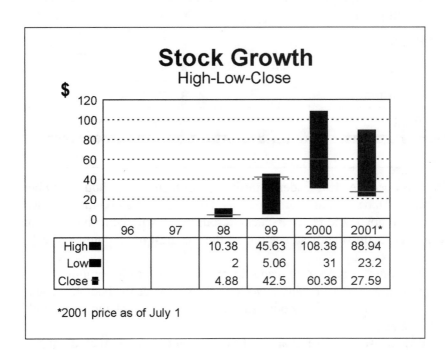

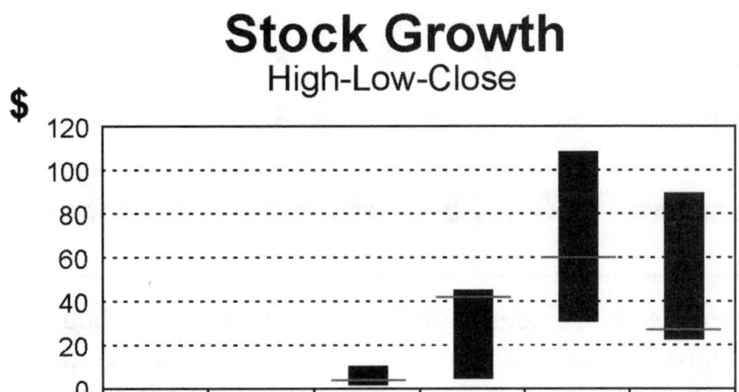

	96	97	98	99	2000	2001*
High			10.38	45.63	108.38	88.94
Low			2	5.06	31	23.2
Close			4.88	42.5	60.36	27.59

*2001 price as of July 1

70

International Business Machines

One New Orchard Road
Armonk, NY 10504
914-499-1900
NYSE: IBM
www.ibm.com

Chairman and CEO: Louis V. Gerstner
President: Samuel J. Palmisano

Earnings Progression	★ ★
Revenue Growth	
Stock Growth	★ ★ ★ ★
Consistency	★ ★ ★ ★
Total	**10 Points**

IBM was once the clear leader in the computer technology industry. Other competitors have certainly emerged to challenge IBM's dominance, such as Dell, Compaq, and Hewlett-Packard, but in the volatile tech market of recent years, Big Blue has been one of the steadiest of all computer technology stocks.

The company is a world leader in several areas of the computer technology market. It does business worldwide, with sales in about 150 countries. International sales account for about 58 percent of the company's total revenue.

IBM focuses on several areas of the computer market, including:

- **Technology.** The firm makes peripheral equipment such as storage devices, networking components, advanced function printers, and display devices.

- **Personal systems.** The company makes a broad line of computer systems, including Aptiva home personal computers, IntelliStation workstations, IBM xSeries servers, and NetVista and ThinkPad mobile systems.
- **Enterprise systems.** IBM makes a variety of disk storage products, including the Enterprise Storage Server, tape subsystems, and storage area networking programs.
- **Global Services Consulting.** IBM is the world's largest information technology services provider. It offers a variety of services for its corporate customers, including setting up and operating a company's entire computer network.
- **Software.** The company provides operating system software for its servers and e-business enabling software for both IBM and non-IBM platforms.
- **Global Financing.** IBM is the world's largest provider of financing services for information technology equipment.

Hardware accounts for about 43 percent of total sales, global services makes up about 37 percent, software accounts for 14 percent, global financing makes up 4 percent, and other areas account for the remaining 2 percent.

IBM was first incorporated in 1911 as the Computing-Tabulating-Recording Company. It took the name International Business Machines Corp. in 1924. The company has about 320,000 employees and a market capitalization of about $200 billion.

EARNINGS PER SHARE PROGRESSION ★ ★

Past 4 years: 78 percent (15 percent per year)

REVENUE GROWTH

Past 4 years: 16 percent (3 percent per year)

STOCK GROWTH ★ ★ ★ ★

Past 4 years: 230 percent (35 percent per year)
Dollar growth: $10,000 over 4 years would have grown to $33,000.

CONSISTENCY ★ ★ ★ ★

Increased earnings per share: 4 consecutive years
Increased sales: 4 consecutive years

IBM AT A GLANCE

Fiscal year ended: Dec. 31
Revenue and net income in $billions

	1996	1997	1998	1999	2000	4-Year Growth Avg. Annual (%)	4-Year Growth Total (%)
Revenue ($)	75.9	78.5	81.7	87.5	88.4	3	16
Net income ($)	5.43	6.09	6.33	7.71	8.09	11	49
Earnings/share ($)	2.50	3.00	3.28	4.11	4.44	15	78
PE range	8–16	10–18	14–28	19–33	18–30		

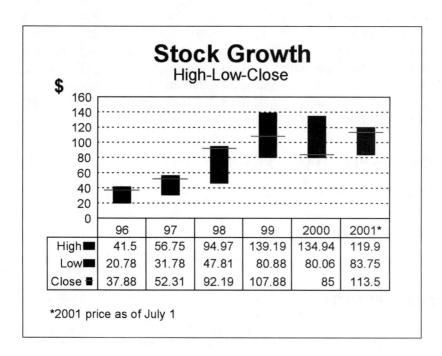

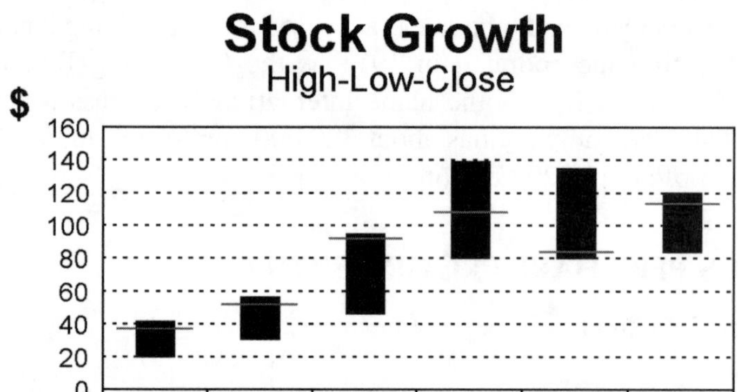

	96	97	98	99	2000	2001*
High	41.5	56.75	94.97	139.19	134.94	119.9
Low	20.78	31.78	47.81	80.88	80.06	83.75
Close	37.88	52.31	92.19	107.88	85	113.5

*2001 price as of July 1

Biotech and Medical

71

Amgen, Inc.

One Amgen Center Drive
Thousand Oaks, CA 91320
805-447-1000
Nasdaq: AMGN
www.amgen.com

Chairman, President, and CEO: Kevin W. Sharer

Earnings Progression	★ ★
Revenue Growth	★
Stock Growth	★ ★ ★ ★
Consistency	★ ★ ★
Total	**10 Points**

Amgen is one of the true pioneers of the biotechnology revolution. Founded in 1980, Amgen has been profitable for many years. The Silicon Valley operation is the world's largest independent biotechnology company.

Amgen has been a leader in discovering, developing, and manufacturing cost-effective human therapeutics that are based on advances in cellular and molecular biology.

Its profits are driven by three highly successful drugs:

- **Epogen.** This is the company's oldest and most profitable drug, with annual sales of about $2 billion, making it one of the top-selling pharmaceuticals in the world. First patented in 1987, Epogen stimulates and regulates the production of red blood cells.
- **Infergen.** The newest of Amgen's three main products, Infergen was approved by the FDA for the treatment of chronic hepatitis C viral (HCV) infections.
- **Neupogen.** With annual sales of about $1.2 billion, Neupogen is used for a variety of cancer-related applications. It helps reduce the incidence

of infection associated with some forms of chemotherapy, and it is used to shorten the recovery time for some chemotherapy patients.

Amgen has a number of new products in the pipeline that focus on such areas as oncology, hephrology, and rheumatology. The company often works in collaboration with other companies in developing new treatments, including Praecis Pharmaceuticals, Regeneron, Yamanouchi Pharmaceutical, and the Massachusetts Institute of Technology. In 1997, Amgen formed a collaboration with Guilford Pharmaceuticals, which granted Amgen worldwide rights to Guilford's FKBP-neuroimmunophilin ligands, a class of small molecule neurotrophic agents that are being investigated for the treatment of neurodegenerative disorders.

The company is worldwide in scope, with offices throughout Europe, China, Australia, and North America. Amgen has about 7,000 employees and a market capitalization of about $65 billion.

EARNINGS PER SHARE PROGRESSION ★★

Past 4 years: 73 percent (15 percent per year)

REVENUE GROWTH ★

Past 4 years: 62 percent (13 percent per year)

STOCK GROWTH ★★★★

Past 4 years: 367 percent (47 percent per year)
Dollar growth: $10,000 over 4 years would have grown to $47,000.

CONSISTENCY ★★★

Increased earnings per share: 3 of the past 4 years
Increased sales: 4 consecutive years

AMGEN AT A GLANCE

Fiscal year ended: Dec. 31
Revenue and net income in $billions

	1996	1997	1998	1999	2000	4-Year Growth Avg. Annual (%)	4-Year Growth Total (%)
Revenue ($)	2.24	2.40	2.72	3.34	3.63	13	62
Net income ($)	0.680	0.644	0.863	1.1	1.14	14	68
Earnings/share ($)	0.64	0.61	0.85	1.07	1.11	15	73
PE range	21–27	19–29	14–33	25–65	47–76		

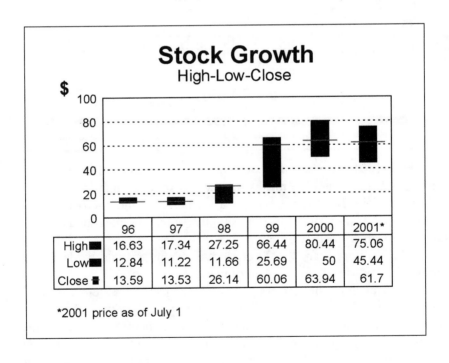

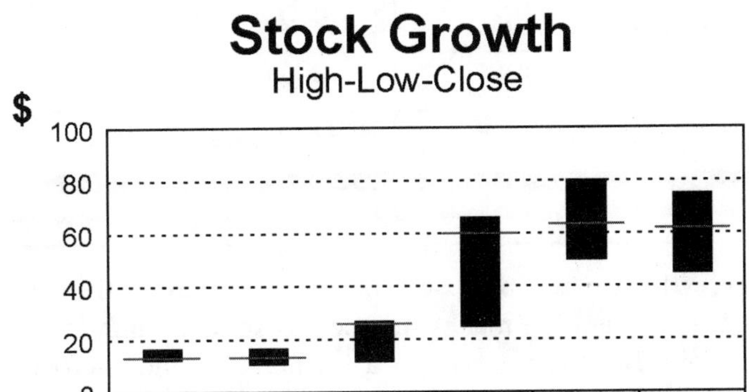

	96	97	98	99	2000	2001*
High	16.63	17.34	27.25	66.44	80.44	75.06
Low	12.84	11.22	11.66	25.69	50	45.44
Close	13.59	13.53	26.14	60.06	63.94	61.7

*2001 price as of July 1

Semiconductors

72

Texas Instruments

12500 TI Boulevard
P.O. Box 660199
Dallas, TX 75266
800-336-5236
NYSE: TXN
www.texasinstruments.com

Chairman, President, and CEO: T. J. Engibous

Earnings Progression	★ ★ ★ ★
Revenue Growth	
Stock Growth	★ ★ ★ ★
Consistency	★ ★
Total	**10 Points**

They say everything's big in Texas—but not at Texas Instruments (TI). The Dallas-based operation makes microchips so small they could fit on the head of a pin. But the company is a *big* player in the microchip market. In fact, TI is the world's leading supplier of analog integrated circuits and digital signal processors.

TI claims more than 30,000 corporate customers worldwide in the commercial, industrial, and consumer markets.

TI's digital signal processors and analog chips work together in digital electronic devices such as cell phones, computers, printers, hard disk drives, modems, networking equipment, digital cameras, motor controls, automobiles, and home appliances. Analog technology converts analog signals such as sound, light, temperature, and pressure into the digital language of numbers, which can be processed in real time by a digital signal processor. Analog integrated circuits also translate digital signals back to analog.

In addition to its strong position in the analog microchip market, TI is also a world leader in the production of other types of semiconductor products, such as standard logic chips, application-specific integrated circuits, reduced instruction-set computing chips, microcontrollers, and digital imaging devices.

Semiconductor sales account for about 84 percent of the company's total revenue. The firm is also in two other businesses. Its Materials and Controls division, which accounts for 11 percent of revenue, sells electrical and electronic controls, electronic connectors, sensors, and radio-frequency identification systems to the commercial and industrial markets.

Its Educational and Productivity Solutions division, which accounts for 5 percent of revenue, sells educational and graphing calculators through retailers and schools.

TI sells its products primarily to original equipment manufacturers and through independent distributors worldwide. TI has sales or manufacturing operations in 27 countries.

Founded in 1930, TI has about 40,000 employees and a market capitalization of about $70 billion.

EARNINGS PER SHARE PROGRESSION ★★★★

Past 4 years: 4,175 percent (156 percent per year)

REVENUE GROWTH

Past 4 years: 20 percent (3.5 percent per year)

STOCK GROWTH ★★★★

Past 4 years: 370 percent (46 percent per year)
Dollar growth: $10,000 over 4 years would have grown to $47,000.

CONSISTENCY ★★

Increased earnings per share: 3 of the past 4 years
Increased sales: 3 of the past 4 years

TEXAS INSTRUMENTS AT A GLANCE

Fiscal year ended: Dec. 31
Revenue and net income in $billions

	1996	1997	1998	1999	2000	4-Year Growth Avg. Annual (%)	4-Year Growth Total (%)
Revenue ($)	9.94	9.97	8.87	9.76	11.9	3.5	20
Net income ($)	–.046	.339	.452	1.45	3.09	102*	811*
Earnings/share ($)	0.04	1.13	0.26	0.83	1.71	156	4,175
PE range	NA	37–85	39–89	25–66	20–57		

*Net income growth is based on 3-year growth.

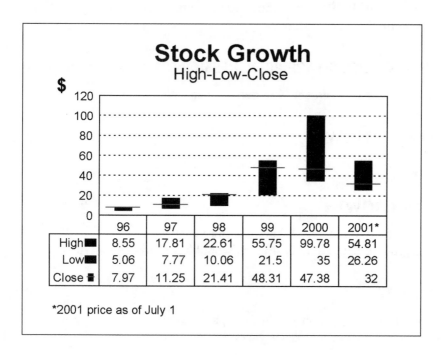

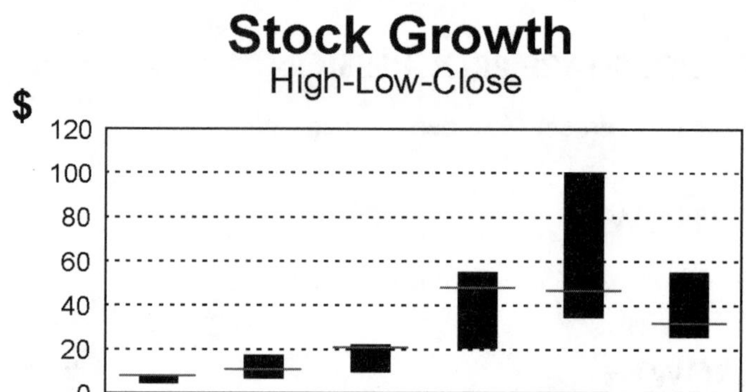

	96	97	98	99	2000	2001*
High	8.55	17.81	22.61	55.75	99.78	54.81
Low	5.06	7.77	10.06	21.5	35	26.26
Close	7.97	11.25	21.41	48.31	47.38	32

*2001 price as of July 1

73

Avant! Corporation

46871 Bayside Parkway
Fremont, CA 94538
510-413-8000
Nasdaq: AVNT
www.avanticorp.com

Chairman, President, and CEO: Gerald C. Hsu

Earnings Progression	★ ★ ★ ★
Revenue Growth	★ ★ ★ ★
Stock Growth	
Consistency	★ ★
Total	**10 Points**

As microchips get smaller and smaller, semiconductor design engineers require increasingly sophisticated tools to create the next generation of chips. Avant! Corporation makes specialized software that helps electronics engineers design advanced microscopic chips for such devices as cell phones, digital watches, and automotive components.

But making microchips even smaller is no small task. Today's chips contain millions of "gates" connected by circuitry wires that are only 0.18 microns wide (a micron is one-millionth of a meter). In order to design and test their handiwork, designers must turn to electronic design automation, or EDA, the driving force of the electronics industry. Avant!'s EDA software enables designers to quickly design new chip circuitry even on the more complex "systems on a chip."

Without EDA, it would be impossible to make integrated circuits such as memory chips or microcontrollers that serve as the brains of the futuristic, increasingly miniature devices that are becoming part of everyday life. Avant!'s software has been used on more than 7,500 designs.

Avant! (pronounced A-van-tee) generates about two-thirds of its revenues through the licensing of its software to customers. The remaining third is generated by various support services it provides customers. About 70 percent of its sales are to U.S. and Canadian customers. The company has more than 50 offices in 16 countries.

Much of its services are provided through its Web site, which includes a direct link to edamall.com, Avant!'s e-commerce site where U.S. and Canadian customers can license the company's design tools over the Web.

In addition to its software for integrated circuit design, Avant! makes software for process simulation, device modeling, mask synthesis, and related functions. The company is also the leading maker of physical foundation IP libraries for integrated circuit design.

Avant! went public with its initial stock offer in 1995. It has about 1,000 employees and a market capitalization of about $327 million.

EARNINGS PER SHARE PROGRESSION ★ ★ ★ ★

Past 4 years: 193 percent (31 percent per year)

REVENUE GROWTH ★ ★ ★ ★

Past 4 years: 189 percent (30 percent per year)

STOCK GROWTH

Past 4 years: –37 percent
Dollar growth: $10,000 over 4 years would have declined to $6,300.

CONSISTENCY ★ ★

Increased earnings per share: 2 of the past 4 years
Increased sales: 4 consecutive years

AVANT! AT A GLANCE

Fiscal year ended: Dec. 31
Revenue and net income in $millions

	1996	1997	1998	1999	2000	4-Year Growth Avg. Annual (%)	4-Year Growth Total (%)
Revenue ($)	124	181	248	304	358	30	189
Net income ($)	13.7	2.4	22.6	56.6	52.8	40	285
Earnings/share ($)	0.45	0.06	0.59	1.42	1.32	31	193
PE range	31–82	150–623	17–50	7–17	6–14		

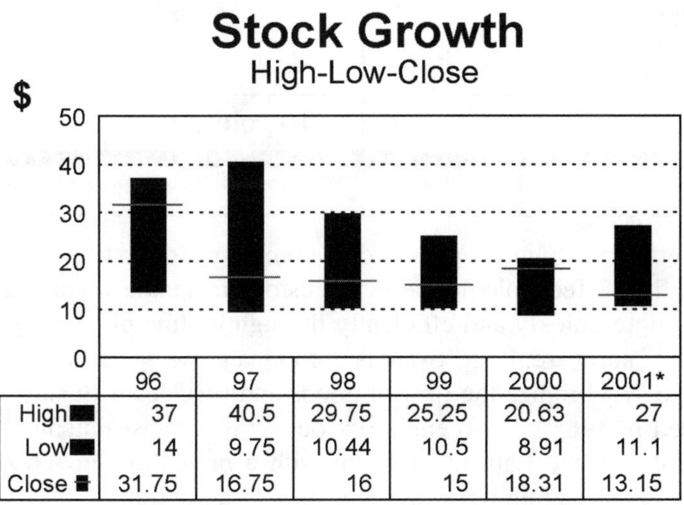

	96	97	98	99	2000	2001*
High	37	40.5	29.75	25.25	20.63	27
Low	14	9.75	10.44	10.5	8.91	11.1
Close	31.75	16.75	16	15	18.31	13.15

*2001 price as of July 1

74

i2 Technologies, Inc.

One i2 Place
11701 Luna Road
Dallas, TX 75234
469-357-1000
Nasdaq: ITWO
www.i2.com

Chairman and CEO: Sanjiv S. Sidhu

Earnings Progression	
Revenue Growth	★ ★ ★ ★
Stock Growth	★ ★ ★ ★
Consistency	★ ★
Total	**10 Points**

Increased efficiencies in all phases of a company's operations mean increased profits. i2 Technologies helps its customers handle a wide range of operations more quickly and efficiently through its line of "supply chain management" software. Its software is used by a growing number of manufacturers to synchronize the flow of goods and services with suppliers.

Founded in 1988 by two engineers out of Texas Instruments' famed Artificial Intelligence Lab, i2 came up with a breakthrough scheduling technology for managing business-to-business transactions.

i2's Rhythm software enables companies to manage inventories and factory floors with greater precision and efficiency. Rhythm ultimately evolved into an Internet product, because digital marketplaces also need software to handle logistics in order to form online exchanges for complex products. Rhythm offers several key modules, including:

- **Supply chain management.** The company's flagship product fine-tunes business e-commerce from bid through delivery.

- **Inter-process planning.** This application tracks relationships between tasks and the resources needed to execute them and helps companies schedule tasks more efficiently.
- **Product lifecycle management.** This speeds up product development by finding reusable components and identifying potential production bottlenecks.
- **Rhythm eCustomer Marketing Suite.** This software is used to profile and target customers, configure and price complex products, and even schedule field technician service calls.

The Dallas-based operation also offers another line of software called TradeMatrix that is geared to buyers, sellers, designers, service providers, and end-customers in the digital marketplace. TradeMatrix helps customers with planning, procurement, commerce, fulfillment, customer care, retail, strategic sourcing, and product development.

i2 sells its software to companies across a broad range of industries. Among its leading customers are Ford, General Motors, 3M, IBM, Merck, Nike, General Electric, Philips, and Motorola.

i2 Technologies went public with its initial stock offering in 1996. The company has about 6,000 employees and a market capitalization of about $6 billion.

EARNINGS PER SHARE PROGRESSION

The company had its biggest loss in 2000.

REVENUE GROWTH ★★★★

Past 4 years: 1,026 percent (83 percent per year)

STOCK GROWTH ★★★★

Past 4 years: 256 percent (37 percent per year)
Dollar growth: $10,000 over 4 years would have grown to about $36,000.

CONSISTENCY ★★

Increased earnings per share: 2 of the past 4 years
Increased sales: 4 consecutive years

i2 TECHNOLOGIES AT A GLANCE

Fiscal year ended: Dec. 31
Revenue and net income in $millions

	1996	1997	1998	1999	2000	4-Year Growth Avg. Annual (%)	4-Year Growth Total (%)
Revenue ($)	100	222	369	571	1,126	83	1,026
Net income ($)	6.79	–1.75	5.22	23.5	–1,752	NA	NA
Earnings/share ($)	0.03	–0.01	0.02	0.07	–4.83	NA	NA
PE range	114–281	NA	136–621	63–778	NA		

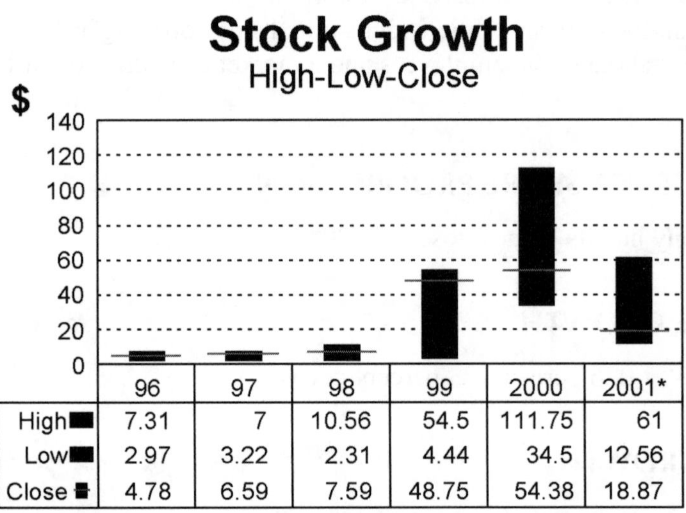

	96	97	98	99	2000	2001*
High	7.31	7	10.56	54.5	111.75	61
Low	2.97	3.22	2.31	4.44	34.5	12.56
Close	4.78	6.59	7.59	48.75	54.38	18.87

*2001 price as of July 1

75

Tech Data Corporation

5350 Tech Data Drive
Clearwater, FL 33760
727-539-7429
Nasdaq: TECD
www.techdata.com

Chairman and CEO: S. Raymond

Earnings Progression	★ ★ ★
Revenue Growth	★ ★ ★ ★
Stock Growth	
Consistency	★ ★ ★
Total	**10 Points**

Tech Data serves as a middleman in the computer technology business, buying in volume from major manufacturers and reselling to a vast universe of corporate customers.

The Clearwater, Florida distributor sells products from most of the major computer and software manufacturers, including Adobe, Apple, Cisco, Compaq, NEC, Palm, Epson, Hewlett-Packard, IBM, Intel, Lexmark, Microsoft, Sony, Toshiba, and Nortel.

In all, the company sells about 75,000 different hardware and software products. It claims a customer base of more than 100,000 companies and resellers around the world. Among its leading products are peripherals, which account for 44 percent of revenue; computer systems, 28 percent; networking devices, 17 percent; and software, 11 percent.

Typically, Tech Data ships out products from its 34 distribution centers the same day as orders are received. The company provides its customers with a high level of technical support to get the products up and running. Its customers tend to be retailers, direct marketers, value-added resellers, Internet service providers, Web integrators, corporate resellers, systems integrators, system builders, government resellers, exporters, e-tailers, direct marketers, catalogers, and Internet resellers. Value-added resellers make up about 55 percent of Tech Data's customer base.

The firm markets its products through some 2,300 field representatives and inside telemarketing sales reps. The company has also focused increasingly on sales through the Internet. Customers can go online to get information on pricing and availability of products, as well as to order products.

The company was incorporated in 1974 to market data processing supplies such as tape, disk packs, and related computer equipment. It has continued to broaden its product line and customer base ever since. It now sells its products in more than 70 countries around the world. International sales account for about 45 percent of total revenue.

Tech Data has about 10,000 employees and a market capitalization of about $2 billion.

EARNINGS PER SHARE PROGRESSION ★★★

Past 4 years: 132 percent (23.5 percent per year)

REVENUE GROWTH ★★★★

Past 4 years: 344 percent (45 percent per year)

STOCK GROWTH

Past 4 years: 30 percent (6 percent per year)
Dollar growth: $10,000 over 4 years would have grown to about $13,000.

CONSISTENCY ★★★

Increased earnings per share: 3 of the past 4 years
Increased sales: 4 consecutive years

TECH DATA AT A GLANCE

Fiscal year ended: Jan. 31
Revenue and net income in $millions

	1997	1998	1999	2000	2001	4-Year Growth: Avg. Annual (%)	4-Year Growth: Total (%)
Revenue ($)	4,599	7,057	11,529	16,992	20,428	45	344
Net income ($)	57	90	130	128	178	33	212
Earnings/share ($)	1.35	1.92	2.47	2.34	3.14	23.5	132
PE range	14–38	17–27	5–18	8–23	NA		

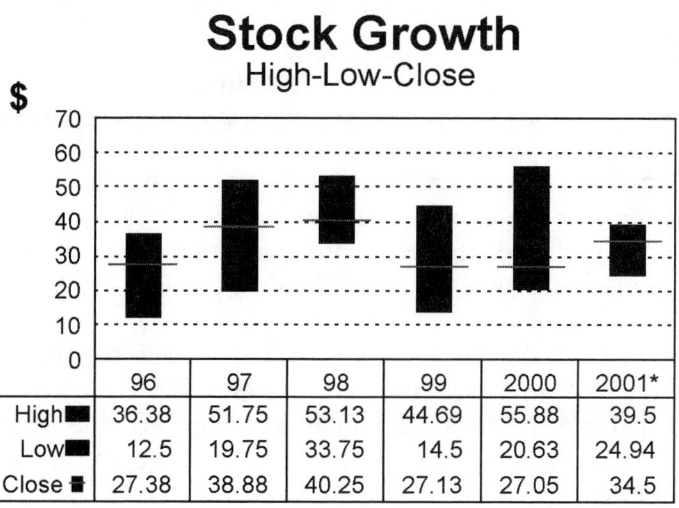

	96	97	98	99	2000	2001*
High	36.38	51.75	53.13	44.69	55.88	39.5
Low	12.5	19.75	33.75	14.5	20.63	24.94
Close	27.38	38.88	40.25	27.13	27.05	34.5

*2001 price as of July 1

76

Macromedia, Inc.

600 Townsend Street
San Francisco, CA 94103
415-252-2000
Nasdaq: MACR
www.macromedia.com

Chairman, President, and CEO: Robert K. Burgess

Earnings Progression	★ ★ ★
Revenue Growth	★ ★ ★ ★
Stock Growth	
Consistency	★ ★ ★
Total	**10 Points**

More sound, more motion, more interactivity—that's what Macromedia brings to the World Wide Web. The company makes software that enables Web designers to create state-of-the-art Web sites with all the latest bells and whistles.

Founded in 1992, the San Francisco operation originally made tools to develop multimedia software for local networks. It translated that into an early start in Internet software. Its suite of development tools covers the gamut of Web programming needs. The company breaks its product line into three groups:

- **Design and development.** The company offers a number of software products that help designers create Web sites, including its flagship product Dreamweaver, which is the world's top-selling product for visual Web site design. Other leading products include Fireworks, used to design Web graphics; HomeSite, an HTML code text editor; Flash 5, used to create animated vector-based content; and JRun Studio, used to accelerate development of JavaServer pages.

- **Players.** Macromedia offers a Flash player to view high-impact, animated Web content, and a Shockwave player to view entertaining rich media content.
- **Servers.** The company offers the ColdFusion Server, used to quickly build and deploy data-driven Web applications; Generator 2 Developer Edition, used to automate Macromedia Flash content updates, Generator 2 Enterprise Edition, used to provide personalized on-the-fly Web site graphics; and JRun Server, used to develop scalable Java applications.

Some Macromedia products have almost gained the status of industry standards. For example, Flash ships with Microsoft's Windows operating system and Internet Explorer browser, and with AOL's Netscape browser.

The company also operates a consumer-oriented Web site, Shockwave .com, that offers online games, music, puzzles, cartoons, and other types of entertainment for Web surfers.

Macromedia went public with its initial stock offering in 1994. It has about 1,600 employees and a market capitalization of about $1.2 billion.

EARNINGS PER SHARE PROGRESSION ★ ★ ★

The company has gone from losses to gains the past 4 years.

REVENUE GROWTH ★ ★ ★ ★

Past 4 years: 264 percent (38 percent per year)

STOCK GROWTH

Past 4 years: 19 percent (3 percent per year)
Dollar growth: $10,000 over 4 years would have grown to about $12,000.

CONSISTENCY ★ ★ ★

Positive earnings progression: 3 consecutive years
Increased sales: 4 consecutive years

MACROMEDIA AT A GLANCE

Fiscal year ended: March 31
Revenue and net income in $millions

	1997	1998	1999	2000	2001	4-Year Growth Avg. Annual (%)	4-Year Growth Total (%)
Revenue ($)	107	114	153	264	390	38	264
Net income ($)	–5.92	–15.6	2.61	8.77	13.4	NA	NA
Earnings/share ($)	–0.16	–0.40	0.05	0.12	0.24	NA	NA
PE range	NA	NA	497–1673	210–601	NA		

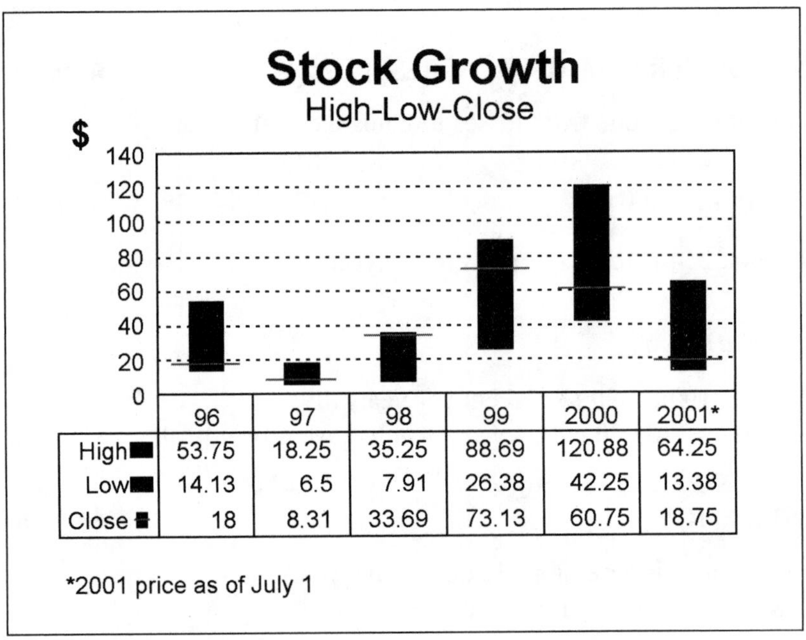

77

Foundry Networks, Inc.

2100 Gold Street
P.O. Box 649100
San Jose, CA 95164
408-586-1700
Nasdaq: FDRY
www.foundrynetworks.com

Chairman, President, and CEO: Bobby R. Johnson, Jr.

Earnings Progression	★ ★ ★
Revenue Growth	★ ★ ★ ★
Stock Growth	
Consistency	★ ★ ★
Total	**10 Points**

Corporations, organizations, and Internet service providers use Foundry's computer hardware to build and maintain their high-speed computer networks.

The Sunnyvale, California operation makes specialized routers, switches, and Internet traffic management systems. Its line of equipment is centered around the Gigabit Ethernet local area networking (LAN) protocol. Focusing on a single standard allows Foundry to offer high-performance products at a competitive price.

In fact, Foundry's business model bears a strong resemblance to that used by Sun Microsystems in its early years. Sun made its mark pushing hot computers running the then-new Unix operating system at low price points and rode the Unix craze to the top. Foundry hopes to do the same with its high-speed Gigabit Ethernet network equipment.

Foundry's product lineup includes:

- **Internet core switches.** These are the most critical network component, serving as the convergence point for the most network traffic.

- **Gigabit Ethernet edge switches.** These connect individuals and groups of workstations to the network.
- **Internet traffic management systems.** Used in Web-hosting facilities and server farmers, these systems provide centralized collection points for server-based applications used by enterprises, Web-based businesses, and Internet service providers.
- **BigIron switching routers.** These are used in big data centers to manage local traffic.

Foundry products are installed in the world's largest Internet service providers, including Yahoo!, America Online, AT&T WorldNet, MSN, and Cable & Wireless. Foundry products are also used by midsized and large companies across a broad range of industries, as well as portals, e-commerce sites, universities, and government organizations. International sales account for about 30 percent of the company's total revenue.

Foundry went public with its initial stock offering in 1999. The company has about 600 employees and a market capitalization of about $2 billion.

EARNINGS PER SHARE PROGRESSION ★★★

The company has gone from losses to gains the past 4 years.

REVENUE GROWTH ★★★★

Past 3 years: 11,054 percent (380 percent per year)

STOCK GROWTH

Past 2 years (since its IPO): –69 percent
Dollar growth: $10,000 over 2 years would have declined to about $3,000.

CONSISTENCY ★★★

Positive earnings progression: 3 of the past 4 years
Increased sales: 4 consecutive years

FOUNDRY NETWORKS AT A GLANCE

Fiscal year ended: Dec. 31
Revenue and net income in $millions

	1996	1997	1998	1999	2000	3-Year Growth Avg. Annual (%)	3-Year Growth Total (%)
Revenue ($)	0	3.38	17	133	377	380	11,054
Net income ($)	–2.01	–9.01	–9.35	22.9	88.1	NA	NA
Earnings/share ($)	–0.50	–0.66	–0.35	0.20	0.69	NA	NA
PE range	NA	NA	NA	273–836	17–305		

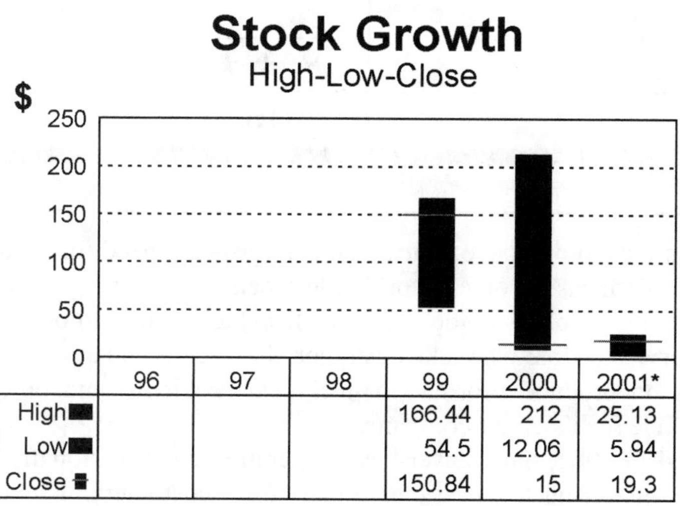

	96	97	98	99	2000	2001*
High				166.44	212	25.13
Low				54.5	12.06	5.94
Close				150.84	15	19.3

*2001 price as of July 1

78

TeleTech Holdings, Inc.

1700 Lincoln Street, Suite 1400
Denver, CO 80203
303-894-4000
Nasdaq: TTEC
www.teletech.com

Chairman: Kenneth Tuchman
Interim CEO: Joseph Livingston

Earnings Progression	★ ★ ★
Revenue Growth	★ ★ ★ ★
Stock Growth	
Consistency	★ ★ ★
Total	**10 Points**

Advances in technology have spurred an ever-growing need for customer support. TeleTech has become a worldwide specialist in serving customers of hundreds of technology companies. The firm has a staff of thousands of customer service people who take customer phone calls and answer Internet e-mails on product information, technical problems, and other inquiries for TeleTech's client companies.

Founded in 1982, the Denver-based operation has traditionally been involved in answering toll-free phone calls from customers of its client companies. But in the past three years, TeleTech has also ramped up its Internet customer service operation. For many of its newer customers, the company handles inquiries both from phone calls and e-mail.

TeleTech jobs out its customer service reps to some of the nation's biggest corporations, including Ford Motor, the U. S. Postal Service, American Express, Verizon, UPS, and Allstate Insurance.

TeleTech offers a variety of specialties, including presales product or service education, processing and fulfilling information requests for products or services, verifying sales and activating services, directing callers to product or service sources, receiving orders for and processing purchases of products or services, and providing initial postsales support, including operating instructions for new products.

The firm also provides comprehensive analytical reports on the customer base to help client companies better understand and retain their customers.

The company has used an aggressive acquisition strategy to expand around the world. It has offices in 11 countries, including New Zealand, Australia, Argentina, Mexico, Brazil, Singapore, China, Spain, the United Kingdom, and Canada.

The company has nearly 20,000 customer services representatives. Its target market includes organizations involved in telecommunications, financial services, technology, government, and transportation industries.

TeleTech went public with its initial stock offering in 1996. It has about 21,000 employees and a market capitalization of about $500 million.

EARNINGS PER SHARE PROGRESSION ★ ★ ★

Past 4 years: 287 percent (40 percent per year; earnings have been sagging in 2001)

REVENUE GROWTH ★ ★ ★ ★

Past 4 years: 417 percent (52 percent per year)

STOCK GROWTH

Past 4 years: –73 percent
Dollar growth: $10,000 over 4 years would have declined to about $3,000.

CONSISTENCY ★ ★ ★

Increased earnings per share: 3 of the past 4 years
Increased sales: 4 consecutive years

TELETECH HOLDINGS AT A GLANCE

Fiscal year ended: Dec. 31
Revenue and net income in $millions

	1996	1997	1998	1999	2000	4-Year Growth Avg. Annual (%)	4-Year Growth Total (%)
Revenue ($)	171	279	425	604	885	52	417
Net income ($)	13.9	21.3	17.1	36.8	75.4	53	442
Earnings/share ($)	0.24	0.35	0.22	0.49	0.93	40	287
PE range	65–169	28–98	28–82	11–70	17–46		

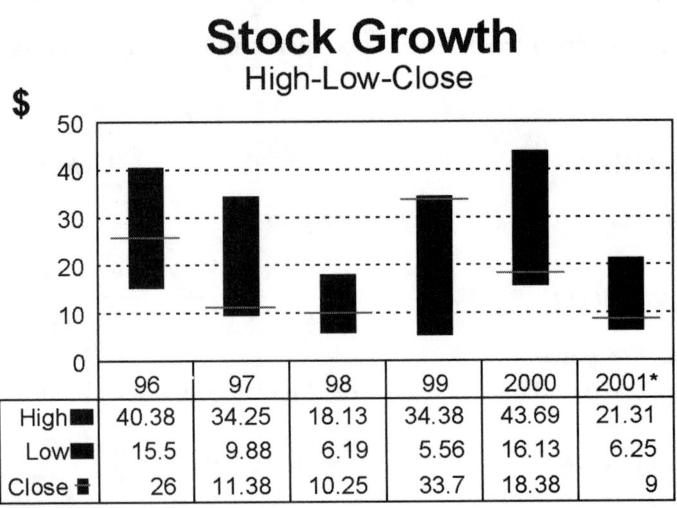

	96	97	98	99	2000	2001*
High	40.38	34.25	18.13	34.38	43.69	21.31
Low	15.5	9.88	6.19	5.56	16.13	6.25
Close	26	11.38	10.25	33.7	18.38	9

*2001 price as of July 1

79

JDS Uniphase Corporation

210 Baypointe Parkway
San Jose, CA 95134
408-434-1800
Nasdaq: JDSU
www.jdsuniphase.com

Chairman: Martin Kaplan
President: Charles J. Abbe
CEO: Jozef Straus

Earnings Progression	
Revenue Growth	★ ★ ★ ★
Stock Growth	★ ★ ★ ★
Consistency	★
Total	**9 Points**

The future of telecommunications is riding the high-speed highway of fiber optics, and JDS Uniphase (JDSU) is leading the charge. With its recent acquisition of SDL, Inc., JDSU has become the dominant player in the worldwide fiber-optics market.

JDSU makes the basic building blocks of fiber-optic networks, including semiconductor lasers, high-speed external modulators, transmitters, amplifiers, couplers, multiplexers, circulators, tunable filters, optical switches, and isolators for fiber-optic applications. JDSU also supplies manufacturers with test instruments for both system production applications and network installation.

The firm also makes laser subsystems for a broad range of manufacturing applications, optical display and projection products used in computer displays and other similar applications, and light interference pigments used in security products and decorative surface treatments. Through its SDL acquisition, the company is also a leader in manufacturing semiconductor lasers, laser-based systems, and fiber-optic-related software.

The company sells its products to telecommunications and cable television system and subsystem providers around the world, including Alcatel, CIENA, Cisco, Corning, Lucent, Motorola, and Nortel.

JDSU divides its product line into three categories, including:

- **Components.** These include source lasers that power the initial signal transmitted over the optical network, modulators, pump lasers, optical photo-detectors and receivers, couplers, filters, isolators, and switches.
- **Modules.** The firm makes amplifiers to boost optical signals, multiplexers, transmitters, cable television transmitters and amplifiers, test instruments, and telecommunications specialty modules and instruments.
- **Other products.** JDSU manufactures laser subsystems and optical display and projection products for computer displays and similar applications.

The San Jose operation was started in a Silicon Valley garage in 1979, and went public with its initial stock offering in 1993. Uniphase merged with Canadian optical components maker JDS Fitel in 1999. JDSU has about 19,000 employees and market capitalization of about $35 billion.

EARNINGS PER SHARE PROGRESSION

The company has posted rising losses the past few years.

REVENUE GROWTH ★★★★

Past 4 years: 1,969 percent (153 percent per year)

STOCK GROWTH ★★★★

Past 4 years: 586 percent (62 percent per year)
Dollar growth: $10,000 over 4 years would have grown to about $70,000.

CONSISTENCY ★

Positive earnings progression: None
Increased sales: 4 consecutive years

JDS UNIPHASE AT A GLANCE

Fiscal year ended: June 30
Revenue and net income in $millions

	1996	1997	1998	1999	2000	4-Year Growth Avg. Annual (%)	4-Year Growth Total (%)
Revenue ($)	69.1	113	185	283	1,430	153	1,969
Net income ($)	2.79	–17.8	–19.6	–171.0	–904.7	NA	NA
Earnings/share ($)	0.01	–0.07	–0.07	–0.53	–1.27	NA	NA
PE range	71–290	NA	NA	NA	NA		

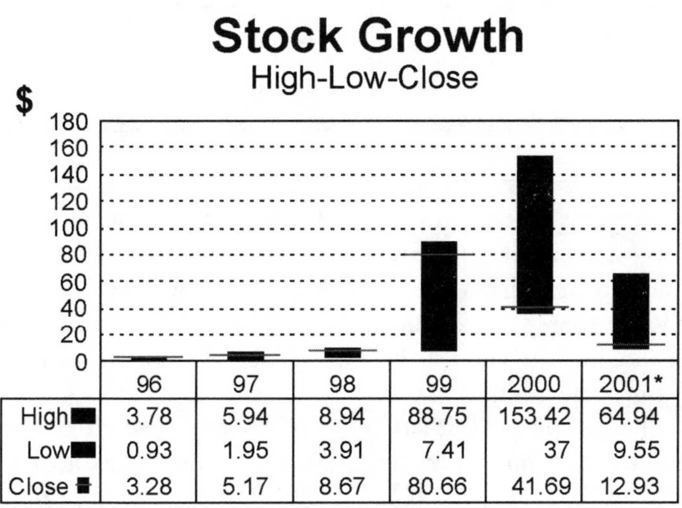

	96	97	98	99	2000	2001*
High	3.78	5.94	8.94	88.75	153.42	64.94
Low	0.93	1.95	3.91	7.41	37	9.55
Close	3.28	5.17	8.67	80.66	41.69	12.93

*2001 price as of July 1

Semiconductors

80

Novellus Systems, Inc.

4000 North First Street
San Jose, CA 95134
408-943-9700
Nasdaq: NVLS
www.novellus.com

Chairman, President, and CEO: Richard Hill

Earnings Progression	
Revenue Growth	★ ★ ★
Stock Growth	★ ★ ★ ★
Consistency	★ ★
Total	**9 Points**

In the semiconductor manufacturing market there is a concept known as Moore's Law—named for Intel cofounder Gordon Moore—which states that the number of transistors on an integrated circuit doubles every 18 months. Now that some semiconductor components are as small as 1/500th the diameter of a human hair, it is becoming increasingly difficult to keep the shrinking process going.

But Novellus is doing all it can to keep Moore's Law alive. The San Jose, California operation is a leading maker of semiconductor manufacturing equipment. Founded in 1984, Novellus has continued to find new ways to manufacture smaller, more powerful chips.

The company's most recent innovation to slim down and speed up the chips is a process that uses copper in place of aluminum to reduce resistance and improve the conductivity of the interconnect material. Chip speed can be increased by decreasing resistance or decreasing capacitance, and Novellus is attempting to do both with its new manufacturing techniques.

Novellus manufactures a wide range of tools and equipment that addresses the entire semiconductor manufacturing process. Since introducing its original Concept One Dielectric system in 1987, the company has developed a family of processing systems for the dielectric and metal deposition markets.

The Concept One Dielectric deposits a variety of insulating or "dielectric" films on wafers including Oxide, Nitride, and TEOS. Its Concept One-W system, introduced in 1990, deposits tungsten metal films on wafers primarily as the metal interconnect between conductor layers in the integrated circuit layers.

Its Concept Two system, introduced in 1991, is a modular, integrated production system capable of depositing both dielectric and conductive metal layers by combining one or more processing chambers around a common, automated robotic wafer handler. The company has continued to add new generations of semiconductor production equipment throughout the past decade.

Novellus has about 3,000 employees and a market capitalization of about $7 billion.

EARNINGS PER SHARE PROGRESSION

Past 4 years: 18 percent (3 percent per year)

REVENUE GROWTH ★ ★ ★

Past 4 years: 154 percent (26 percent per year)

STOCK GROWTH ★ ★ ★ ★

Past 4 years: 485 percent (55 percent per year)
Dollar growth: $10,000 over 4 years would have grown to $809,000.

CONSISTENCY ★ ★

Positive earnings progression: 3 of the past 4 years
Increased sales: 3 of the past 4 years

NOVELLUS SYSTEMS AT A GLANCE

Fiscal year ended: Dec. 31
Revenue and net income in $millions

	1996	1997	1998	1999	2000	4-Year Growth Avg. Annual (%)	4-Year Growth Total (%)
Revenue ($)	462	534	519	593	1,174	26	154
Net income ($)	94	–95.6	52.8	76.5	236	26	151
Earnings/share ($)	0.95	–0.96	0.50	0.64	1.12	3	18
PE range	5–11	NA	13–39	23–67	14–40		

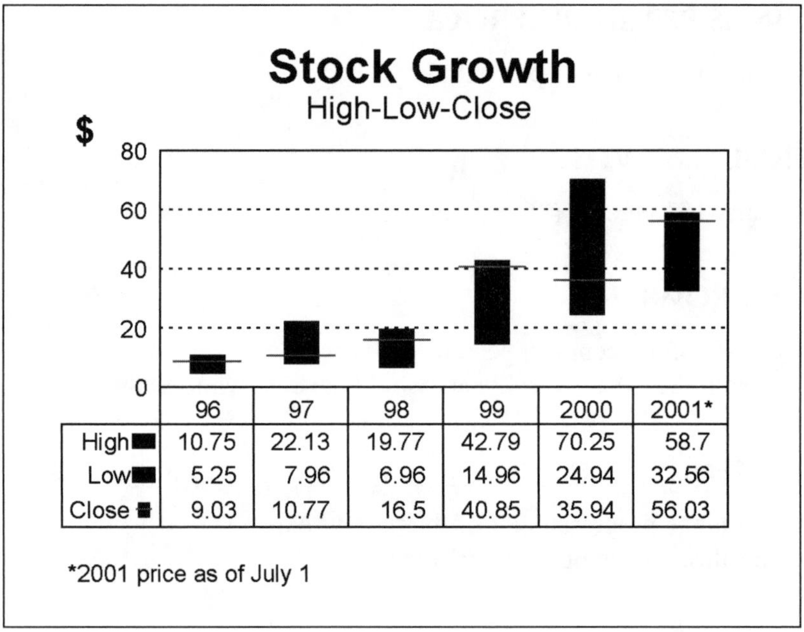

Stock Growth
High-Low-Close
$
80
60
40
20
0
96
97
98
99
2000
2001*
High
10.75
22.13
19.77
42.79
70.25
58.7
Low
5.25
7.96
6.96
14.96
24.94
32.56
Close
9.03
10.77
16.5
40.85
35.94
56.03
*2001 price as of July 1

81

Intel Corporation

2200 Mission College Boulevard
Santa Clara, CA 95052
408-765-8080
Nasdaq: INTC
www.intel.com

Chairman: Andrew S. Grove
President and CEO: Craig R. Barrett

Earnings Progression	★ ★ ★
Revenue Growth	★
Stock Growth	★ ★
Consistency	★ ★ ★
Total	**9 Points**

Microchips have been slowly taking over our lives—they're in our cars, our home appliances, and across the whole realm of technology. Intel is the world's leading manufacturer of microchips. Its line of Pentium chips has been installed in millions of computers, serving as the brains of the personal computer by processing data and controlling other devices in the system.

The more advanced the microprocessing chips, the faster and more powerful the computer. Intel's ability to develop ever-faster chips has kept it at the forefront of the computer revolution. With its Pentium 4 chips, Intel continues to be the dominant player in the worldwide microprocessor market.

Intel's computer microchips process system data and control input, output, and peripheral and memory devices in the PC. They are also used to control the operation of communications systems, automobile control applications, robotics, electronic instrumentation, keyboards, home video machines, and a wide range of other electronics products.

Microprocessor sales account for more than 80 percent of Intel's total revenue. Intel's computing enhancement group, including chipsets, embedded processors, microcontrollers, flash memory, and graphics products, accounts for about 15 percent of total revenue. Its network communications group, which makes network and Internet connectivity products, accounts for less than 5 percent of revenue.

Founded in 1968, the Santa Clara, California company has been the world leader in the microchip market since the mid-1980s, after designing the original microprocessor for the IBM PC. It has maintained its lead by first turning out its popular 286 chip, followed by the 386, then the 486, and finally the Pentium generation of chips. Worldwide, well over 100 million PCs are based on Intel architecture. Intel's primary customers are computer manufacturers who incorporate the chips into their computers.

Intel has about 70,000 employees and a market capitalization of $200 billion.

EARNINGS PER SHARE PROGRESSION ★ ★ ★

Past 4 years: 106 percent (20 percent per year)

REVENUE GROWTH ★

Past 4 years: 62 percent (13 percent per year)

STOCK GROWTH ★ ★

Past 4 years: 87 percent (17 percent per year)
Dollar growth: $10,000 over 4 years would have grown to $18,700.

CONSISTENCY ★ ★ ★

Increased earnings per share: 3 of the past 4 years
Increased sales: 4 consecutive years

Semiconductors

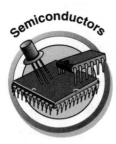

INTEL AT A GLANCE

Fiscal year ended: Dec. 31
Revenue and net income in $billions

	1996	1997	1998	1999	2000	4-Year Growth Avg. Annual (%)	4-Year Growth Total (%)
Revenue ($)	20.8	25.1	26.3	29.4	33.7	13	62
Net income ($)	5.16	6.94	6.07	7.31	10.5	20	103
Earnings/share ($)	0.73	0.97	0.86	1.05	1.50	20	106
PE range	8–24	16–26	19–36	23–42	19–50		

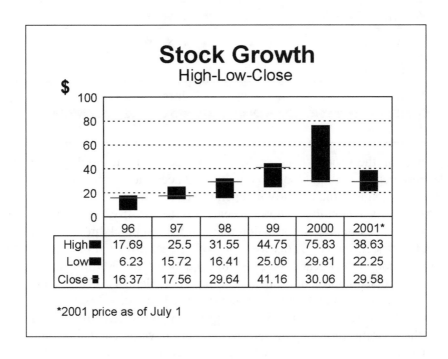

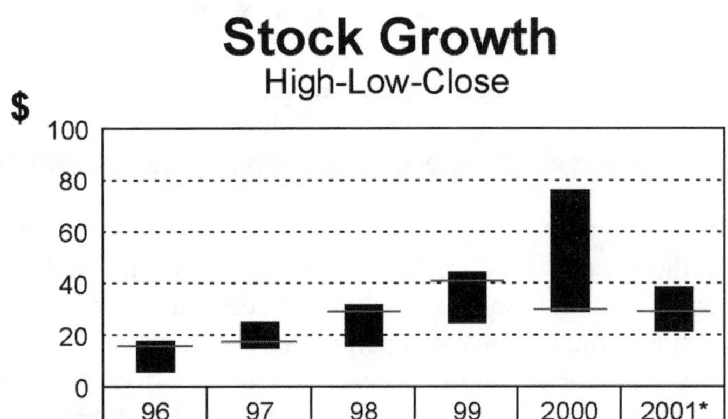

	96	97	98	99	2000	2001*
High	17.69	25.5	31.55	44.75	75.83	38.63
Low	6.23	15.72	16.41	25.06	29.81	22.25
Close	16.37	17.56	29.64	41.16	30.06	29.58

*2001 price as of July 1

Biotech and Medical

82

Affymetrix, Inc.

3380 Central Expressway
Santa Clara, CA 95051
408-731-5000
Nasdaq: AFFX
www.affymetrix.com

Chairman and CEO: Stephen P.A. Fodor
President: Susan E. Siegel

Earnings Progression	
Revenue Growth	★ ★ ★ ★
Stock Growth	★ ★ ★ ★
Consistency	★
Total	**9 Points**

A pioneer on the genetic frontier, Affymetrix GeneChip technology provides researchers with the tools to quickly and accurately process genetic data as they explore the recently mapped human genome.

Affymetrix technology allows researchers to identify, analyze, and manage complex genetic information that can lead to breakthrough treatments for cancer, infectious diseases, and other health-related problems.

Even though the decade-long task of sequencing the 3 billion sets of instructions that compose the human genome is complete, it will take many more decades to fully interpret the blueprint and generate life-saving and life-extending treatments. In addition to providing basic scientific knowledge, the genome project will help researchers develop safer and more effective drugs that will precisely target the cause of disease.

Stephen Fodor, chairman and CEO of Affymetrix, says that a major goal of genomics research is to find ways to help physicians use genetic information to customize treatment for individual patients, launching a new era of "personalized medicine." He says genotypying tests will be developed in the next decade allowing clinicians to diagnose disease with unprecedented precision.

Medical applications of genomic research, however, are only one facet of the coming Genetic Age. Genetic information will also be used to improve the nutritional quality of food and water. In addition, Affymetrix has established relationships with leading diagnostic companies to support the development and marketing of its products. With a company called bioMeriux, Affymetrix is investigating the use of its technology to improve water quality monitoring and bacterial and virological testing.

Affymetrix technology, which can measure the presence of dozens of organisms in a single test, is expected to reduce testing time from four days to four hours and decrease the costs of the tests tenfold.

The company markets its technology to more than 40 university research centers, to 11 of the 20 largest pharmaceutical companies, as well as to clinical laboratories and biotechnology companies. Founded in 1992, the company has about 500 employees and a market capitalization of about $3 billion.

EARNINGS PER SHARE PROGRESSION

The company is not yet profitable and has posted a series of slightly higher losses 3 of the past 4 years.

REVENUE GROWTH ★★★★

Past 4 years: 1,575 percent (102 percent per year)

STOCK GROWTH ★★★★

Past 4 years: 247 percent (36 percent per year)
Dollar growth: $10,000 over 4 years would have grown to about $35,000.

CONSISTENCY ★

Positive earnings progression: None
Increased sales: 4 consecutive years

AFFYMETRIX AT A GLANCE

Fiscal year ended: Dec. 31
Revenue and net income in $millions

	1996	1997	1998	1999	2000	4-Year Growth: Avg. Annual (%)	4-Year Growth: Total (%)
Revenue ($)	12.0	19.8	52.0	96.8	201	102	1,575
Net income ($)	–12.2	–22.5	–23.1	–23.1	–33.5	NA	NA
Earnings/share ($)	–0.30	–0.50	–0.55	–0.51	–0.61	NA	NA
PE range	NA	NA	NA	NA	NA		

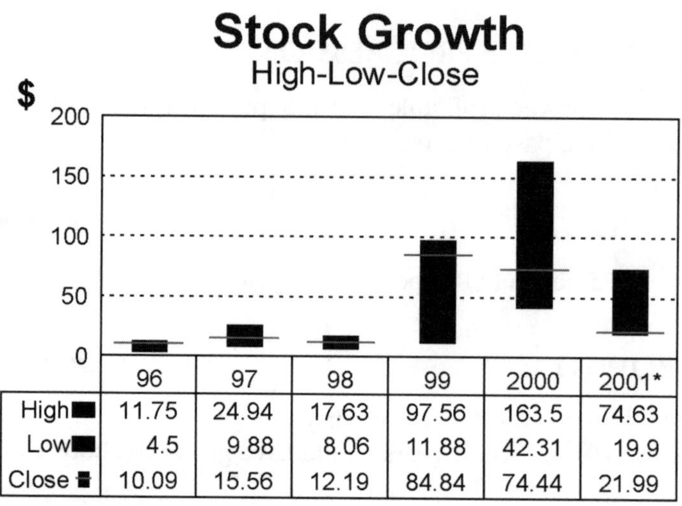

	96	97	98	99	2000	2001*
High	11.75	24.94	17.63	97.56	163.5	74.63
Low	4.5	9.88	8.06	11.88	42.31	19.9
Close	10.09	15.56	12.19	84.84	74.44	21.99

*2001 price as of July 1

83

Cypress Semiconductor

3901 North First Street
San Jose, CA 95134
408-943-2600
NYSE: CY
www.cypress.com

Chairman: Eric Benhamou
President and CEO: T.J. Rodgers

Earnings Progression	★ ★ ★ ★
Revenue Growth	★ ★ ★
Stock Growth	★
Consistency	★
Total	**9 Points**

Cypress Semiconductor makes a line of microchips for the telecommunications industry that helps enhance nearly every leg of the phone line infrastructure, from switches and routers to satellites and cellular base stations. The firm also makes chips for computers and instrumentation systems. In all, the San Jose, California operation manufactures more than 400 products.

The company has focused primarily on developing semiconductors and other products that address several key areas of the telecommunications market, including wireless terminals, wireless infrastructure, wide area networks, and storage networks. It sells to many of the leading companies in that industry, including Alcatel, Cisco, Ericsson, Motorola, and Nortel Networks. International sales account for about 50 percent of the company's total revenue.

Its leading product is the static random access memory chip, which is used for storage and retrieval of data in data communications, telecommunications, computers, and other electronic systems.

The firm also offers a broad range of nonmemory products that are also marketed to the telecommunications and computer markets, including:

- **HOTLink Transceivers.** The company's high-speed optical transceivers are used to move data at high rates and support a variety of applications and protocols, including fiber channel, enterprise system, connection, asynchronous transfer mode, digital video broadcast, and point-to-point applications.
- **Multi-port memories.** Its multi-port memory products are used for shared memory and switching applications, such as networking switches and routers, cellular base stations, mass storage devices, and telecommunications equipment.
- **Programmable clocks.** Cypress is the leader in the timing technology device market. These devices are used in personal computers, disk drives, modems, network routers and hubs, digital video disks, and home video games.

The company also makes Programmable Read-Only Memory chips (PROMs), Programmable System-on-a-chip microcontrollers, Programmable Logic Devices (PLDs), and Universal Serial Bus connections (USB).

Cypress was first incorporated in December 1982. It went public with its initial stock offering in 1986. The company has about 4,500 employees and a market capitalization of about $3 billion.

EARNINGS PER SHARE PROGRESSION ★★★★

Past 4 years: 244 percent (37 percent per year)

REVENUE GROWTH ★★★

Past 4 years: 144 percent (25 percent per year)

STOCK GROWTH ★

Past 4 years: 49 percent (10.5 percent per year)
Dollar growth: $10,000 over 4 years would have grown to $14,900.

CONSISTENCY ★

Increased earnings per share: 2 of the past 4 years
Increased sales: 3 of the past 4 years

CYPRESS AT A GLANCE

Fiscal year ended: Dec. 31
Revenue and net income in $millions

	1996	1997	1998	1999	2000	4-Year Growth Avg. Annual (%)	4-Year Growth Total (%)
Revenue ($)	528	598	555	705	1,288	25	144
Net income ($)	53	7.53	–105	91	277	51	423
Earnings/share ($)	0.59	0.07	–1.03	0.81	2.03	37	244
PE range	9–17	105–270	NA	NA	22–71		

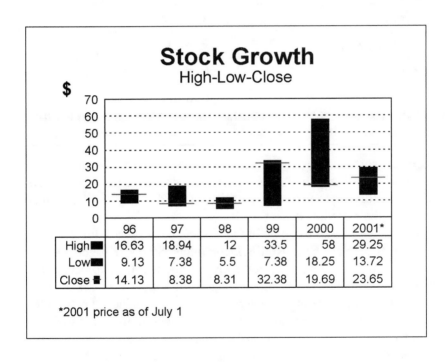

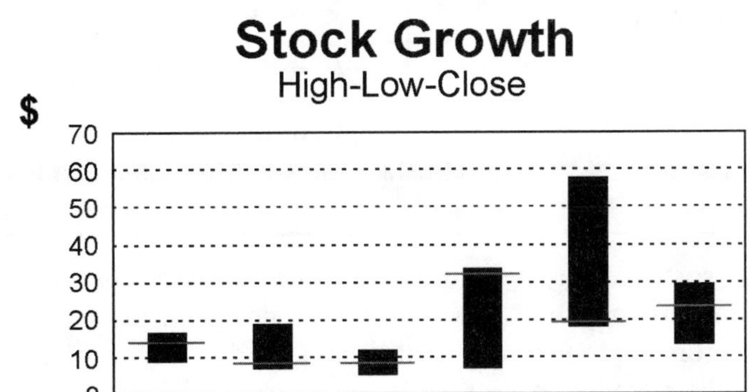

	96	97	98	99	2000	2001*
High	16.63	18.94	12	33.5	58	29.25
Low	9.13	7.38	5.5	7.38	18.25	13.72
Close	14.13	8.38	8.31	32.38	19.69	23.65

*2001 price as of July 1

84

Retek, Inc.

801 Nicollet Mall
Minneapolis, MN 55402
612-630-5700
Nasdaq: RETK
www.retek.com

Chairman and CEO: John Buchanan
President: Gordon Masson

Earnings Progression	
Revenue Growth	★ ★ ★ ★
Stock Growth	★ ★ ★
Consistency	★ ★
Total	**9 Points**

Retek makes software that helps retailers squeeze every possible penny out of the consuming public. The software is designed to help retailers manage inventory and customer relationships and effectively set prices and promote their products.

The software is used by some of the world's most successful retail operations, such as Best Buy, Kohl's Department Stores, Kroger, Family Dollar Stores, and The Gap. The company has about 150 customers in all.

Retek's customer relationship management software is designed to help stores build a profile of customers, and to give managers a better idea of exactly who the customers are, what they like, and how they respond to special promotions. The software also enables retailers to use the Internet to communicate and collaborate with suppliers, distributors, wholesalers, brokers, transportation companies, and manufacturers in the retail supply chain.

The company's software works by using advanced mathematical algorithms to develop accurate and effective plans and forecasts for retailers to price and stock items at optimal levels. The software also helps retailers increase sales, reduce inventory levels, and improve customer satisfaction.

The Minneapolis operation has been working with Accenture (formerly Andersen Consulting) to design its next generation of retailing software. Retek is using Accenture's retailing business research to produce a software application that will address both the demand and supply side functions of a retailer's business, including assortment and space optimization, pricing and advertising decisions, customer behavior, dynamic fulfillment, integrated planning, in-stock optimization, and vendor collaboration.

Retek has also forged a strategic alliance with IBM to sell its Internet retailing software. In exchange, Retek will use IBM hardware and software in its products.

Founded in 1985, Retek had been a subsidiary of HNC Software. HNC took Retek public with its initial stock offering in 1999, then spun off its remaining stake in Retek in 2000. Retek has about 700 employees and a market capitalization of about $2 billion.

EARNINGS PER SHARE PROGRESSION

The company has had losses the past 2 years.

REVENUE GROWTH ★★★★

Past 4 years: 586 percent (62 percent per year)

STOCK GROWTH ★★★

Past year: 61 percent
Dollar growth: $10,000 over the past year would have grown to about $16,000.

CONSISTENCY ★★

Positive earnings progression: 2 of the past 4 years
Increased sales: 4 consecutive years

RETEK AT A GLANCE

Fiscal year ended: Dec. 31
Revenue and net income in $millions

	1996	1997	1998	1999	2000	4-Year Growth Avg. Annual (%)	4-Year Growth Total (%)
Revenue ($)	13.4	30.9	55.0	69.1	91.9	62	586
Net income ($)	2.23	3.48	3.88	–5.37	–42.9	NA	NA
Earnings/share ($)	0.05	0.08	0.09	–0.13	–0.91	NA	NA
PE range	NA	NA	NA	NA	NA		

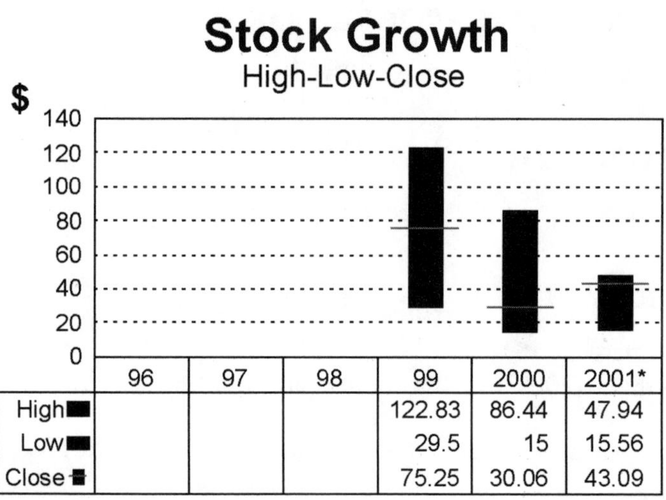

	96	97	98	99	2000	2001*
High				122.83	86.44	47.94
Low				29.5	15	15.56
Close				75.25	30.06	43.09

*2001 price as of July 1

85

Amazon.com, Inc.

1200 12th Avenue South, Suite 1200
Seattle, WA 98144
206-266-1000
Nasdaq: AMZN
www.amazon.com

Chairman and CEO: Jeffrey P. Bezos

Earnings Progression	
Revenue Growth	★★★★
Stock Growth	★★★★
Consistency	★
Total	**9 Points**

Will Amazon ever turn the corner? The online retailer of books, music, and a growing variety of other products has been the poster child of the Internet revolution. Its stock price blasted into the stratosphere—despite mounting losses—only to return to earth with a resounding thud along with the rest of the Internet retailers.

That collapse proved the company's harshest critics to be absolutely correct. They had long questioned how a company that had produced nothing but a string of losses could ever be a viable business model. The questions continue to haunt Amazon.com founder Jeff Bezos, who has adamantly defended his company's business plan. Bezos claims that profitability is just around the corner, and when that day comes, Amazon will rule the Web.

Shareholders hope that day will come before the company files for bankruptcy. If Amazon does succeed, it will be just about the only online retailer to survive. Other players in the market, such as Priceline.com and Value America, have long since crashed and burned.

Launched in 1995, the Seattle operation has spent hundreds of millions of dollars advertising its site, selling products at deep discounts, and building its order fulfillment infrastructure.

The company, which began as an online retailer of books, has steadily added new products to the mix. It is the leading Internet seller of books, music, and videos. In all, it lists about 28 million unique items at its site, including toys, electronics, cameras, software, games, hardware, lawn and patio items, and wireless products.

The company operates four international Web sites. It also operates "zShops," which allow any business or individual to sell virtually anything to Amazon's customers, and "Amazon Anywhere," which is a leader in mobile e-commerce, providing access from anywhere in the world to Amazon.com.

Amazon claims about 30 million customers worldwide.

Amazon.com went public with its initial stock offering in 1997. It has about 7,000 employees and a market capitalization of about $4 billion.

EARNINGS PER SHARE PROGRESSION

Past 4 years: The company has posted rising losses year after year.

REVENUE GROWTH ★ ★ ★ ★

Past 4 years: 17,492 percent (265 percent per year)

STOCK GROWTH ★ ★ ★ ★

Past 3 years: 219 percent (47 percent per year)
Dollar growth: $10,000 over 3 years would have grown to $31,900.

CONSISTENCY ★

Positive earnings progression: None
Increased sales: 4 consecutive years

AMAZON.COM AT A GLANCE

Fiscal year ended: Dec. 31
Revenue and net income in $millions

	1996	1997	1998	1999	2000	4-Year Growth	
						Avg. Annual (%)	Total (%)
Revenue ($)	15.7	148	610	1,640	2,762	265	17,492
Net income ($)	–6.25	–31	–121.6	–643.2	–1,107	NA	NA
Earnings/share ($)	–0.03	–0.12	–0.42	–2.20	–4.02	NA	NA
PE range	NA	NA	NA	NA	NA		

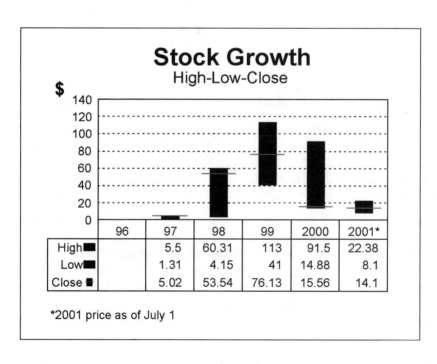

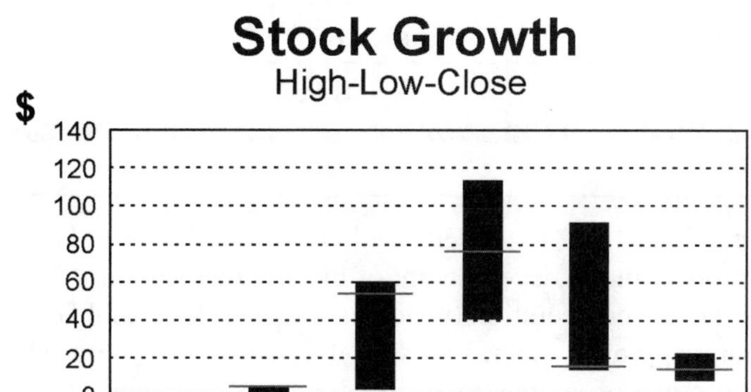

	96	97	98	99	2000	2001*
High		5.5	60.31	113	91.5	22.38
Low		1.31	4.15	41	14.88	8.1
Close		5.02	53.54	76.13	15.56	14.1

*2001 price as of July 1

86

Genentech, Inc.

One DNA Way
South San Francisco, CA 94080
650-225-1000
NYSE: DNA
www.gene.com

Chairman, President, and CEO: Arthur D. Levinson

Earnings Progression	
Revenue Growth	★ ★
Stock Growth	★ ★ ★
Consistency	★ ★ ★
Total	**8 Points**

Genentech put the "DNA" in modern medicine. The 25-year-old operation has been a pioneer in the development of biotech medications.

The San Francisco operation (which uses the stock symbol DNA) currently has nine approved medications on the market that are used to address a broad range of serious medical conditions and another 20 in the pipeline.

One new cancer treatment the company is developing uses "monoclonal" antibodies specially engineered from the body's own antibodies. These "biologics" are designed to track down cancer cells and initiate a process that eliminates them.

Genentech uses human genetic information to discover and develop pharmaceuticals. Its leading products include:

- **Herceptin.** This antibody is used to treat breast cancer and lung cancer.
- **Rituxan.** This antibody is used to treat non-Hodgkin's lymphoma.
- **Activase.** This "tissue plasminogen activator" is used for the treatment of heart attacks, strokes, and acute massive pulmonary embolism.

- **Nutropin.** This growth hormone is used for the treatment of hormone deficiency in children and adults and other growth failure conditions.
- **Protropin.** Protropin is used to treat growth problems in children.
- **Pulmozyme.** This inhalation solution is used to treat cystic fibrosis.

The company also receives royalties on a number of other medications it helped develop that are marketed by other drug companies. Among those products are Humatrope, a human growth hormone from Eli Lilly; Roferon-A, a recombinant interferon alpha from Hoffmann-LaRoche; Recombivax, a hepatitis B vaccine from Merck; and Posilac, a bovine growth hormone from Monsanto.

Genentech's future looks promising, with 20 additional products under development or awaiting regulatory approval. They include treatments for Hodgkin's lymphoma, acute heart failure, breast cancer, solid tumors, lung cancer, inflammatory bowel diseases, chronic bronchitis, transplant rejection, allergic asthma, cystic fibrosis, and age-related macular degeneration.

The company spends about $500 million a year on research and development.

Founded in 1976, Genentech went public with its initial stock offering in 1980. It has about 4,500 employees and a market capitalization of about $27 billion.

EARNINGS PER SHARE PROGRESSION

Past 4 years: None

REVENUE GROWTH ★ ★

Past 4 years: 79 percent (16 percent per year)

STOCK GROWTH ★ ★ ★

Past 4 years: 166 percent (27.5 percent per year) (Totals include a buyout of stock in June 1999 by Roche Corp. and a reissue of shares in July 1999.)
Dollar growth: $10,000 over 4 years would have grown to about $28,000.

CONSISTENCY ★ ★ ★

Increased earnings per share: 3 of the past 4 years
Increased sales: 4 consecutive years

GENENTECH AT A GLANCE

Fiscal year ended: Dec. 31
Revenue and net income in $millions

	1996	1997	1998	1999	2000	4-Year Growth Avg. Annual (%)	4-Year Growth Total (%)
Revenue ($)	969	1,017	1,151	1,421	1,736	16	79
Net income ($)	118	129	182	–1,144	–16.4	NA	NA
Earnings/share ($)	0.24	0.25	0.35	–2.23	–0.13	NA	NA
PE range	NA	NA	NA	NA	NA		

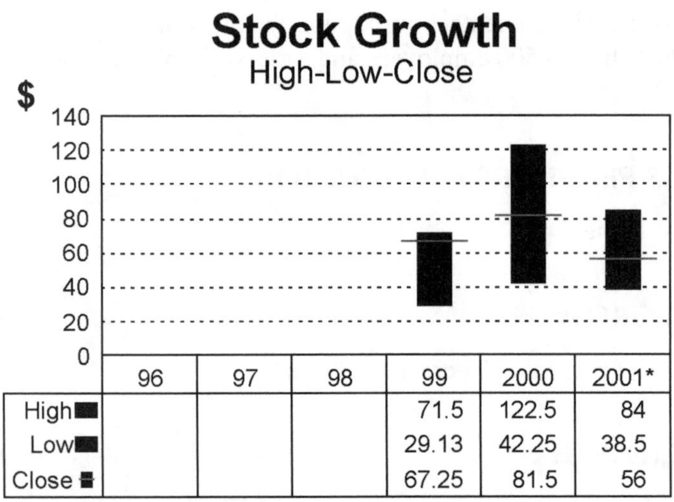

*2001 price as of July 1

87

Corning Inc.

One Riverfront Plaza
Corning, NY 14831
607-974-9000
NYSE: GLW
www.corning.com

Chairman: Roger Ackerman
President and CEO: John Loose

Earnings Progression	★
Revenue Growth	★ ★ ★
Stock Growth	★ ★
Consistency	★ ★
Total	**8 Points**

Corning used to live in a glass house. These days, the house is made largely of optical fiber.

The 150-year-old company, which had been known as Corning Glass Works until 1989, has remolded itself into a global technology corporation with expertise in telecommunications, advanced materials, and information displays such as liquid crystal display (LCD) glass.

Traditionally known for its kitchenware and lab products, Corning now generates about 60 percent of its revenues from its telecommunications unit, which makes optical fiber and cable, optical hardware, and photonic modules. The unit is well positioned to seize on the global crunch in communications bandwidth being driven by growing traffic on the World Wide Web and in e-commerce.

Corning, which pioneered optical fiber more than 30 years ago, remains the leading manufacturer in the category, producing 40 percent of the world's supply and twice as much as its nearest competitor. Its optical fiber and cable are critical for high-performance voice and data transmission. Corning's technologically advanced LEAF fiber has become the fiber of choice for large worldwide providers of networking services.

Corning reinforced its market-leading position with the recent acquisition of Siemens AG's worldwide optical cable and hardware business and the remaining 50 percent of Siecor Corporation, which had a strong presence in key European markets.

Although it no longer makes its famous line of cookware, Corning never abandoned its glass legacy. In fact, it's a rapidly growing segment of the Corning portfolio. Its Information Display Segment makes glass for LCD screens on computer desktops, for large LCD television sets, VCRs, for video lens assemblies, and for automotive applications. The company believes that demand for LCD glass by 2003 will triple what it was in 1999.

The company's Advanced Materials Segment makes emission control products, semiconductor materials, and lighting products. For its pharmaceutical customers, Corning has developed automated laboratory testing systems that reduce the time it takes to develop new drugs. Demand for its advanced life science products is expected to grow at a rate of 35 percent over the next five years.

The company has about 21,000 employees and a market capitalization of about $30 billion.

EARNINGS PER SHARE PROGRESSION ★

Past 4 years: 60 percent (12 percent per year)

REVENUE GROWTH ★ ★ ★

Past 4 years: 114 percent (22 percent per year)

STOCK GROWTH ★ ★

Past 4 years: 69 percent (15 percent per year)
Dollar growth: $10,000 over 4 years would have grown to about $17,000.

CONSISTENCY ★ ★

Increased earnings per share: 2 of the past 4 years
Increased sales: 4 consecutive years

CORNING AT A GLANCE

Fiscal year ended: Dec. 31
Revenue and net income in $millions

	1996	1997	1998	1999	2000	4-Year Growth Avg. Annual (%)	4-Year Growth Total (%)
Revenue ($)	3,327	3,831	3,832	4,741	7,127	22	114
Net income ($)	217	461	421	516	422	18	94
Earnings/share ($)	0.30	0.61	0.56	0.66	0.48	12	60
PE range	20–34	19–38	16–32	23–66	64–243		

Stock Growth
High-Low-Close

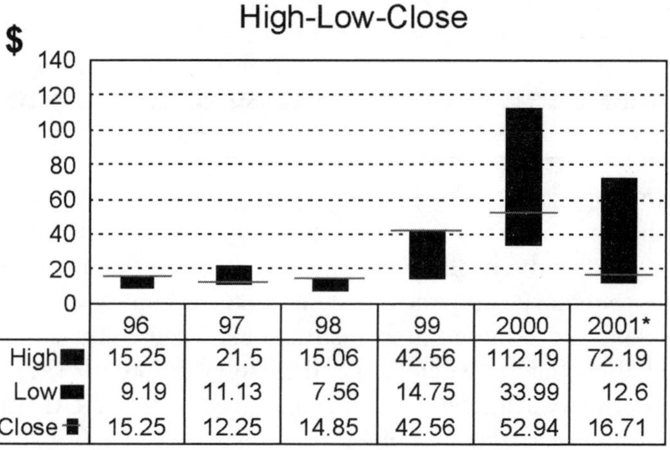

	96	97	98	99	2000	2001*
High	15.25	21.5	15.06	42.56	112.19	72.19
Low	9.19	11.13	7.56	14.75	33.99	12.6
Close	15.25	12.25	14.85	42.56	52.94	16.71

*2001 price as of July 1

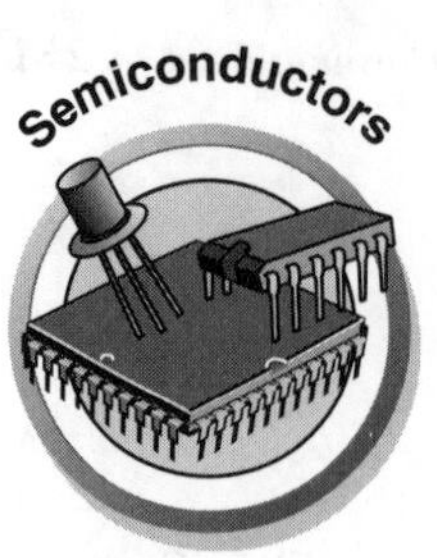

88

Micron Technology, Inc.

8000 S. Federal Way
P.O. Box 6
Boise, ID 83707
208-368-4000
NYSE: MU
www.micron.com

Chairman, President, and CEO: Steven R. Appleton

Earnings Progression	★ ★
Revenue Growth	★ ★
Stock Growth	★ ★ ★ ★
Consistency	
Total	**8 Points**

Micron Technology is in the business of making memory—not the kind to cherish but the kind that allows virtually every electronic device to operate.

Micron, which bills itself as "the future of memory," manufactures semiconductor memory components and modules. Memory chips temporarily store data and programming instructions. They run a computer's software and allow data to be created and changed before it's saved.

Micron's primary semiconductor memory product is a DRAM chip, or dynamic random access memory chip. Random access memory, or RAM, is sometimes called a personal computer's scratch pad. It temporarily stores the instructions or data for software programs when they are being used by the computer.

In addition to PCs, RAM is used in servers, workstations, computer games, servers, telecommunications equipment, personal digital assistants, and other memory-intensive systems. DRAM sales account for about 80 percent of the company's revenues.

Micron makes two other memory chips—static random access memory and Flash memory devices, which account for about 2 percent and 1 percent of sales, respectively.

The Micron brand is perhaps best known for its line of PCs, which the company was selling in 2001. The increasingly low-margin PC business generated about 14 percent of the company's revenues in 2000. In 1998, PC sales accounted for about half the company's sales, but it has been aggressively shifting focus to memory chips because of the bruising price battles in the PC sector.

Micron's Crucial Technology Division is the leading factory-direct memory upgrade supplier. It offers memory upgrades for consumers, corporations, governments, and educational institutions. It offers more than 40,000 memory upgrades for more than 10,000 different PCs, notebooks, servers, and printers. Micron Electronics is the company's Internet-based subsidiary that sells computer products and services, such as Web hosting and B2B e-commerce applications.

Founded in 1978, the company has about 18,000 employees and a market capitalization of about $22 billion.

EARNINGS PER SHARE PROGRESSION ★★

Past 4 years: 85 percent (17 percent per year)

REVENUE GROWTH ★★

Past 4 years: 101 percent (19 percent per year)

STOCK GROWTH ★★★★

Past 4 years: 188 percent (30 percent per year)
Dollar growth: $10,000 over 4 years would have grown to about $29,000.

CONSISTENCY

Positive earnings progression: 2 of the past 4 years
Increased sales: 2 of the past 4 years

MICRON TECHNOLOGY AT A GLANCE

Fiscal year ended: August 31
Revenue and net income in $billions

	1996	1997	1998	1999	2000	4-Year Growth Avg. Annual (%)	4-Year Growth Total (%)
Revenue ($)	3.65	3.52	3.02	3.76	7.34	19	101
Net income ($)	0.602	0.335	–0.230	–0.055	1.52	26	152
Earnings/share ($)	1.38	0.72	–0.57	–0.13	2.56	17	85
PE range	6–15	15–41	NA	NA	10–38		

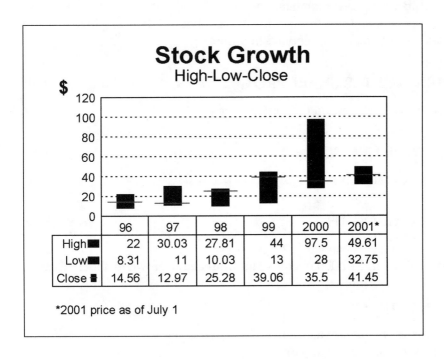

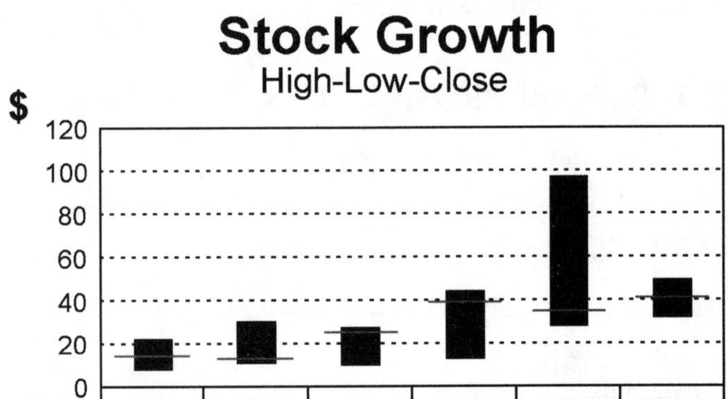

	96	97	98	99	2000	2001*
High	22	30.03	27.81	44	97.5	49.61
Low	8.31	11	10.03	13	28	32.75
Close	14.56	12.97	25.28	39.06	35.5	41.45

*2001 price as of July 1

89

Extreme Networks, Inc.

3585 Monroe Street
Santa Clara, CA 95051
408-579-2800
Nasdaq: EXTR
www.extremenetworks.com

Chairman, President, and CEO: Gordon Stitt

Earnings Progression	
Revenue Growth	★★★★
Stock Growth	★
Consistency	★★★
Total	**8 Points**

On the Internet, speed counts. Extreme Networks helps keep data moving across the Internet at an extreme pace with its line of high-speed switches.

The company manufactures Layer 3 switches—also known as hardware-based wire-speed routers—which have enabled local area network (LAN) traffic to be connected at higher speeds from end to end. Level 3 switches have replaced the traditional software-based routers. Extreme's Layer 3 switches not only provide higher speed, they are also less costly and less complex than traditional software-based routers. Extreme is the leading manufacturer of Layer 3 switches.

Extreme sells its switches to leading Internet service providers, applications service providers, Web content providers, e-commerce businesses, and large corporations. The company markets its products directly to end users as well as to large manufacturers, such as 3Com and Compaq, who resell Extreme products under private label.

The company's leading products include:

- **Summit access switches,** which connect personal computers, servers, and printers to LANs

- **Summit LAN switches,** which connect LANs together at 10 times the typical network speeds, allowing companies to create "local" area networks across entire metropolitan areas
- **BlackDiamond core switches,** which serve as the internal backbones that weave together traffic from many LANs and act as a gateway to the Internet
- **Summit Virtual Chassis,** which is a high-speed external backplane that interconnects multiple Extreme switches into one cohesive system
- **ExtremeWare,** which is networking software used by companies to configure and manage their internal networks

All of Extreme Networks's switches are built on a common architecture, which requires less maintenance and lower operating costs.

Founded in 1996, the Santa Clara, California operation introduced its first product in 1997 and went public with its initial stock offering in 1999. The company has about 700 employees and a market capitalization of about $2 billion.

EARNINGS PER SHARE PROGRESSION

The company showed a profit in 2000 after several years of losses, but was headed for a loss in 2001.

REVENUE GROWTH ★★★★

Past 3 years: 102,243 percent (902 percent per year)

STOCK GROWTH ★

Past 2 years: 30 percent (14 percent per year)
Dollar growth: $10,000 over 1 year would have diminished to $3,800.

CONSISTENCY ★★★

Positive earnings progression: 2 of the past 3 years
Increased sales: 3 consecutive years

EXTREME NETWORKS AT A GLANCE

Fiscal year ended: June 30
Revenue and net income in $millions

	1996	1997	1998	1999	2000	4-Year Growth Avg. Annual (%)	4-Year Growth Total (%)
Revenue ($)	NA	0.256	23.6	98	262	902	102,243
Net income ($)	NA	–7.9	–13.9	–1.6	20	NA	NA
Earnings/share ($)	NA	–0.12	–0.22	–0.02	0.18	NA	NA
PE range	NA	NA	NA	NA	117–715		

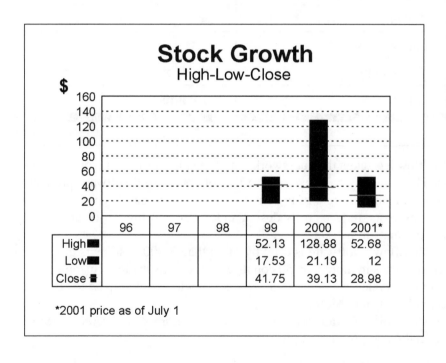

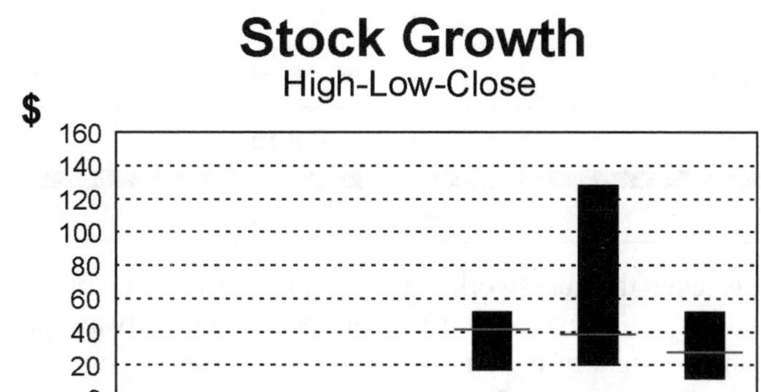

	96	97	98	99	2000	2001*
High				52.13	128.88	52.68
Low				17.53	21.19	12
Close				41.75	39.13	28.98

*2001 price as of July 1

90

Moldflow Corporation

430 Boston Post Road
Wayland, MA 01778
508-358-5848
Nasdaq: MFLO
www.moldflow.com

Chairman: Charles D. Yie
President and CEO: Marc J. L. Dulude

Earnings Progression	★ ★ ★
Revenue Growth	★ ★
Stock Growth	
Consistency	★ ★ ★
Total	**8 Points**

Moldflow has taken the guesswork out of the plastics manufacturing process. The company has developed a line of specialized software products that help manufacturers of injection-molded plastic parts decrease manufacturing costs, reduce costly design and manufacturing errors, and speed their products to market.

Moldflow's software is used by more than 3,000 customers at manufacturing sites in more than 50 countries. Among its leading customers are DaimlerChrysler, DuPont, Fuji, Xerox, Hewlett-Packard, Lego, Lucent Technologies, and Motorola.

Moldflow software helps plastics manufacturers in several stages of the design and production process:

- It assists part designers in the selection of plastic material based on their design criteria.
- It helps determine the strength and rigidity of a given part design.
- It evaluates the ease of manufacturing a given part design.
- It predicts the amount a part will shrink or warp during production.

- It determines the optimal locations in a mold to inject the plastic material.
- It selects the optimal machine temperatures, injection speeds, and cooling times for part production.
- It identifies and provides solutions for adverse variations during production.

Moldflow claims to be the world leader in plastic simulation software, a sector with strong growth potential. The company has identified about 750,000 injection molding machines that are currently operating *without* the benefit of integrated software.

The company markets its software through a direct sales staff with offices in nine countries and a network of distributors and value-added resellers. The firm has also established a Web site, <www.plasticszone.com>, that assists engineers with technical aspects of the software.

The Massachusetts operation was originally founded in Australia in 1980 and moved its headquarters to the U.S. in 1997. The company went public with its initial stock offering in March 2000. Moldflow has about 240 employees and a market capitalization of about $130 million.

EARNINGS PER SHARE PROGRESSION ★ ★ ★

Past 2 years: 1,725 percent

REVENUE GROWTH ★ ★

Past 4 years: 96 percent (18 percent per year)

STOCK GROWTH

Past 1 year (since its IPO): About even
Dollar growth: $10,000 over 1 year would have remained at about $10,000.

CONSISTENCY ★ ★ ★

Increased earnings per share: 3 of the past 4 years
Increased sales: 4 consecutive years

MOLDFLOW AT A GLANCE

Fiscal year ended: June 30
Revenue and net income in $millions

	1996	1997	1998	1999	2000	4-Year Growth Avg. Annual (%)	4-Year Growth Total (%)
Revenue ($)	14.0	14.8	16.4	20.2	27.4	18	96
Net income ($)	–4.2	–4.2	0.189	0.481	3.45	NA	1,725*
Earnings/share ($)	–0.91	–0.96	0.02	0.08	0.48	NA	2,300*
PE range	NA	NA	NA	NA	27–64		

*Net income and earnings per share growth figures are for 2 years.

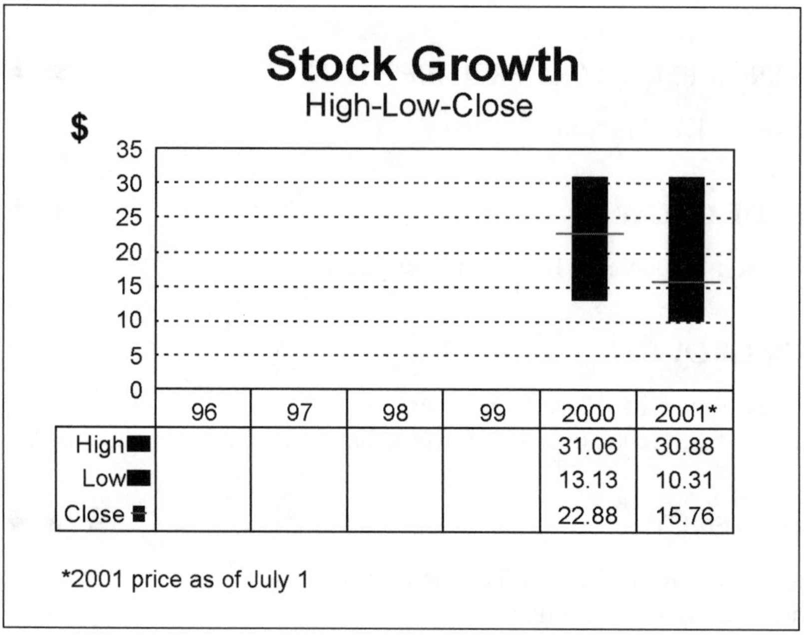

91

Palm, Inc.

5470 Great America Parkway
Santa Clara, CA 95052
408-326-9000
Nasdaq: PALM
www.palm.com

CEO: Carl J. Yankowski

Earnings Progression	★
Revenue Growth	★ ★ ★ ★
Stock Growth	
Consistency	★ ★ ★
Total	**8 Points**

What's on your Palm? These days, it can be just about anything, as the increasingly ubiquitous handheld computers have access to the Internet and corporate intranets.

Palm is playing a leading role in transforming the Internet into a useful, secure, and mobile medium for e-mail and messaging, news and information, commercial transactions, education, and entertainment.

Palm believes that more users will access the Internet wirelessly than through the more traditional wired connections. Naturally, Palm wants to be the device of choice. Sales of its Palm VII series handhelds exceeded all non-Palm platforms combined—solidifying its position as the best-selling handheld computer in the world.

Consumers and corporate customers alike have been taken with Palm's operating systems, which manage information simply and intuitively. To maintain its leadership position, Palm is working with more than 100,000 developers who have been drawn to its popular operating system.

Palm is an independent publicly traded company comprising 3Com's handheld computing business. Shares of the new company were initially offered to the public in March 2000. The Palm Pilot was introduced in

1996, and sales of Palm products have been soaring ever since, both in the United States and overseas, where 35 percent of the new freestanding company's sales are generated.

The company has introduced its subscription-based wireless access service, which allows Palm VII handheld users to access specialized content on the Internet. For example, subscribers to Palm.net can wirelessly access Fidelity.com or E*Trade to get real-time stock quotes, UPS to monitor package delivery, ESPN.com for the latest sports score, WSJ.com for business news, and Travelocity to check flights and delays.

Another Internet initiative is Palm.com, where customers can directly purchase Palm devices, accessories, and peripherals. Customers can also download Palm software and upgrades and link to third-party software. The site is also designed to help developers obtain software development tools and technical support.

The company has about 950 employees and a market capitalization of about $13 billion.

EARNINGS PER SHARE PROGRESSION ★

The company has gone from losses to positive earnings the past 4 years.

REVENUE GROWTH ★ ★ ★ ★

Past 4 years: 14,893 percent (248 percent per year)

STOCK GROWTH

Past year (since its IPO): –73 percent
Dollar growth: $10,000 over the past 1 year would have declined to about $2,300.

CONSISTENCY ★ ★ ★

Increased earnings per share: 3 of the past 4 years
Increased sales: 4 consecutive years

PALM AT A GLANCE

Fiscal year ended: May 31
Revenue and net income in $millions

	1996	1997	1998	1999	2000	3-Year Growth Avg. Annual (%)	3-Year Growth Total (%)
Revenue ($)	7.05	114	272	563	1,057	248	14,893
Net income ($)	–3.1	–7.8	4.2	29.6	45.9	NA	NA
Earnings/share ($)	–0.01	–0.01	0.01	0.06	0.08	NA	NA
PE range	NA	NA	NA	NA	233–1941		

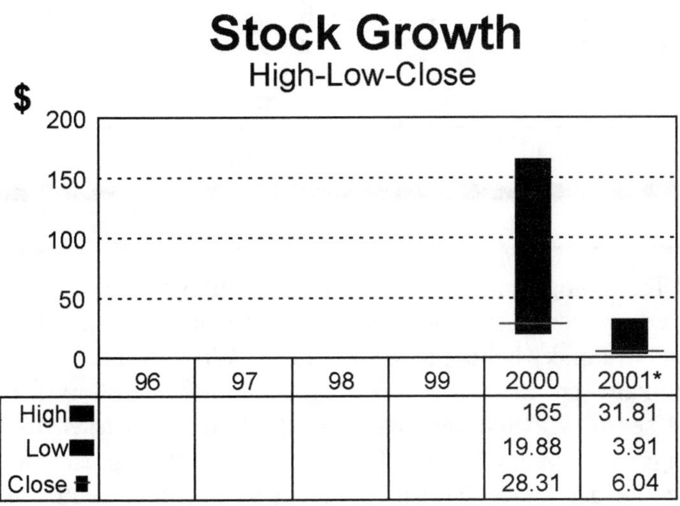

	96	97	98	99	2000	2001*
High					165	31.81
Low					19.88	3.91
Close					28.31	6.04

*2001 price as of July 1

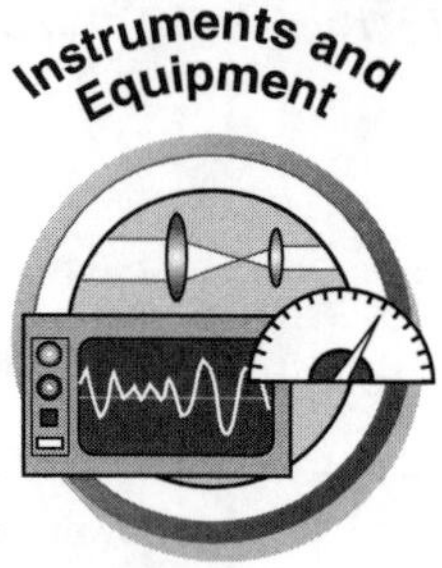

92

United Technologies

United Technologies Building
One Financial Plaza
Hartford, CT 06101
860-728-7000
NYSE: UTX
www.unitedtechnologies.com

Chairman and CEO: George David
President: Karl Krapek

Earnings Progression	★ ★
Revenue Growth	
Stock Growth	★ ★ ★
Consistency	★ ★
Total	**7 Points**

The United Technologies name may not ring a bell, but many of the products produced by its subsidiaries certainly do: Carrier air conditioners, Otis elevators, Sikorsky helicopters, and Pratt & Whitney aircraft engines.

The company produces a broad range of high-technology products and support services to the aerospace and building industries. In 2001, *Fortune* magazine ranked United Technologies as the "most admired" company in the aerospace industry, placing it ahead of such rivals as Boeing and Lockheed Martin.

The company's principal subsidiaries are:

- **Otis Elevator.** The world's largest elevator company does 77 percent of its business outside of the U.S. The commercial construction market drives Otis and construction in the U.S. and international markets has been steady, although U.S. commercial construction peaked in 1998.
- **Carrier.** Carrier is the world's largest manufacturer of commercial and residential heating, ventilation, and air conditioning (HVAC) systems

and equipment. It also makes refrigeration equipment for trucks and provides aftermarket service and components for the HVAC and trucking markets.

- **Pratt & Whitney.** Pratt & Whitney is a major supplier of commercial, general aviation, and military aircraft engines for both domestic and international aircraft manufacturers. Its engines have been selected for the Air Force's F-22 fighter aircraft and for the demonstration aircraft of the Joint Strike fighter program of the U.S. military and the United Kingdom's Royal Navy.
- **The Flight Systems.** This division produces commercial and military helicopters. Sikorsky supplies the U.S. military with the Blackhawk helicopter and is developing, with Boeing, the Comanche helicopter for the U.S. Army. The Hamilton Sunstrand unit provides aerospace and industrial products and aftermarket services for a broad range of industries.

Founded in 1934, the company has about 150,000 employees and a market capitalization of about $36 billion.

EARNINGS PER SHARE PROGRESSION ★ ★

Past 4 years: 104 percent (20 percent per year)

REVENUE GROWTH

Past 4 years: 16 percent (3 percent per year)

STOCK GROWTH ★ ★ ★

Past 4 years: 150 percent (26 percent per year)
Dollar growth: $10,000 over 4 years would have grown to $25,000.

CONSISTENCY ★ ★

Increased earnings per share: 3 of the past 4 years
Increased sales: 3 of the past 4 years

UNITED TECHNOLOGIES AT A GLANCE

Fiscal year ended: Dec. 31
Revenue and net income in $billions

	1996	1997	1998	1999	2000	4-Year Growth Avg. Annual (%)	4-Year Growth Total (%)
Revenue ($)	23.0	21.3	22.8	24.1	26.6	3	16
Net income ($)	1.0	1.06	1.24	0.932	1.9	17	90
Earnings/share ($)	1.74	1.89	2.33	1.65	3.55	20	104
PE range	13–20	17–23	13–24	31–46	13–22		

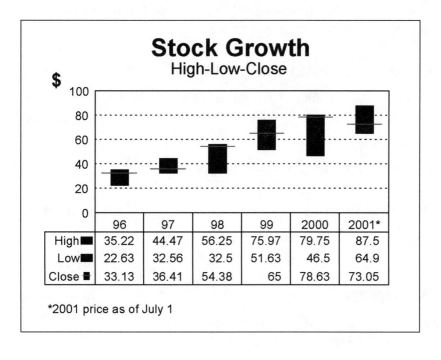

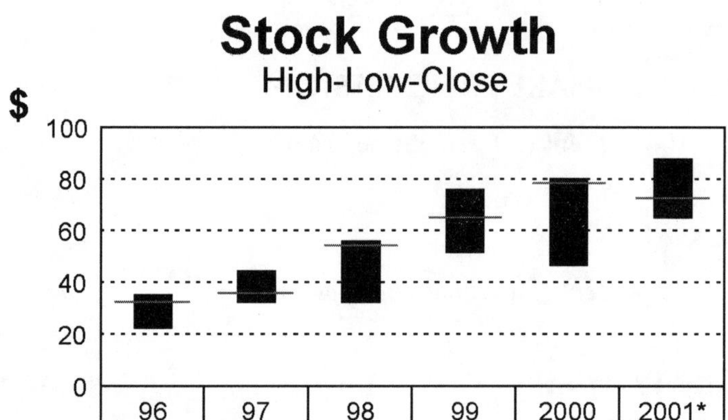

	96	97	98	99	2000	2001*
High	35.22	44.47	56.25	75.97	79.75	87.5
Low	22.63	32.56	32.5	51.63	46.5	64.9
Close	33.13	36.41	54.38	65	78.63	73.05

*2001 price as of July 1

93

IntraNet Solutions, Inc.

7777 Golden Triangle Drive
Eden Prairie, MN 55344
952-903-2000
Nasdaq: INRS
www.intranetsolutions.com

Chairman and CEO: Robert F. Olson
President: Vern Hanzlik

Earnings Progression	
Revenue Growth	★ ★
Stock Growth	★ ★ ★ ★
Consistency	★
Total	**7 Points**

Posting documents and information from a company computer onto the World Wide Web has been a source of constant frustration for corporations trying to establish a Web presence. IntraNet Solutions, a young Minnesota software company, has already helped hundreds of companies around the world solve that problem with its innovative Xpedio software.

Xpedio software converts documents of nearly any format into a Web-based format. It is used by companies in a broad range of industries, from government agencies and public utilities to technology companies, airlines, and large manufacturers. The company already has several high-profile clients, including Yahoo (which uses Xpedio to convert attachments in its e-mail program), Merrill Lynch, General Motors, Bristol-Myers Squibb, Toyota, IBM, Hewlett-Packard, and a growing number of other Fortune 500 companies. In all, IntraNet has about 1,500 corporate customers worldwide.

IntraNet's software makes it easier for companies to set up business-to-business (B2B) and business-to-employee (B2E) intranet and extranet applications. Xpedio gives every content contributor in an organization the ability to automatically Web-publish content to Hypertext Markup Language (HTML) and Extensible Markup Language (XML) Web formats from general desktop formats.

The company's Xpedio Web Content Management software, which can be deployed in as few as three to five days, is designed to provide rapid, secure access and publication of a variety of unstructured business data, such as documents, contracts, product catalogs, marketing materials, design specifications, CAD drawings, enterprise reports, and regulatory documentation.

The company's Xpedio Content Server features a Web-ready platform with an open Java server-based architecture to help customers build end-to-end enterprise-level, content-focused Web applications.

IntraNet also offers a number of other software modules, including Xpedio Content Publisher, an automated way to publish material directly to the Web; Xpedio WAM, a system for managing Web assets; and Xpedio Report Parser, a streamlined system for publishing enterprise reports in XML, HTML, PDF, or text.

The company has about 140 employees and a market capitalization of about $500 million.

EARNINGS PER SHARE PROGRESSION

The company has gone from losses to a gain in fiscal 2000, but was headed for a loss in 2001.

REVENUE GROWTH ★★

Past 4 years: 76 percent (15 percent per year)

STOCK GROWTH ★★★★

Past 4 years: 409 percent (50 percent per year)
Dollar growth: $10,000 over 4 years would have grown to about $50,000.

CONSISTENCY ★

Positive earnings progression: 2 consecutive years
Increased sales: 3 of the past 4 years

INTRANET SOLUTIONS AT A GLANCE

Fiscal year ended: March 31
Revenue and net income in $millions

	1996	1997	1998	1999	2000	4-Year Growth Avg. Annual (%)	4-Year Growth Total (%)
Revenue ($)	12.7	16.2	22.2	17.0	22.4	15	76
Net income ($)	–.049	–1.19	–2.09	–.838	.479	NA	NA
Earnings/share ($)	–0.04	–0.58	–0.67	–0.19	0.03	NA	NA
PE range	NA	NA	NA	NA	NA		

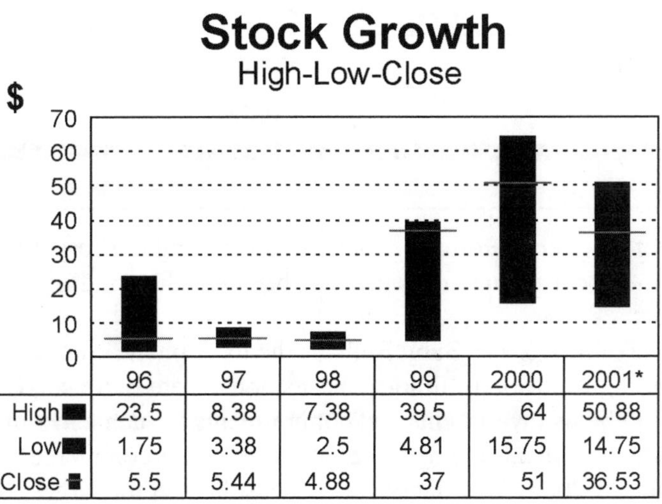

	96	97	98	99	2000	2001*
High	23.5	8.38	7.38	39.5	64	50.88
Low	1.75	3.38	2.5	4.81	15.75	14.75
Close	5.5	5.44	4.88	37	51	36.53

*2001 price as of July 1

94

SBC Communications Inc.

175 E. Houston
San Antonio, TX 78205
210-821-4105
NYSE: SBC
www.sbc.com

Chairman and CEO: E. E. Whitacre
President: R. S. Caldwell

Earnings Progression	
Revenue Growth	★ ★ ★
Stock Growth	★
Consistency	★ ★
Total	**6 Points**

With a raft of new service offerings across its far-flung territory, SBC, the nation's No. 2 local phone company, has been steadily ringing up sales and profits.

SBC, one of the former Baby Bells, is the local phone company in 12 states, including California, Illinois, and its home state of Teaxs. Driving its growth will be its investments and commitments to such telecommunications services as data, long distance, wireless, and e-commerce.

In the fall of 2000, SBC successfully consolidated the largest brands in the wireless industry under the Cingular Wireless name. It combines the wireless operations of BellSouth and SBC. SBC has 60 percent ownership of Cingular, which has the second-largest national customer base for wireless behind Verizon.

Cingular launched data and wireless information services in several major markets, including Chicago, St. Louis, and Baltimore. The services allow customers to send messages, access personal information such as address books and calendars, and receive personalized stock, news, sports, and weather reports.

SBC has begun moving into the long-distance market with the launch of service in Texas and plans to begin service in Kansas and Oklahoma. SBC is the only former Bell company to win federal approval to provide long-distance service in multiple states.

Other initiatives include the expansion of its Web hosting capabilities with the purchase of a controlling interest in Webhosting.com. SBC and Webhosting.com plan to launch new hosting and e-commerce services for small- and medium-sized businesses in 2001.

SBC's Project Pronto is building a high-speed broadband local network that will serve as a growth platform for DSL and other leading-edge telecommunication services. To strengthen its Internet service provider capabilities, SBC joined with Prodigy Communications to offer several new Internet services.

To enhance its Internet-based B2B services, SBC acquired Sterling Communications, which has more than 45,000 customer relationships, including nearly all of the Fortune 500.

SBC, the former Southwestern Bell, was created in the 1984 breakup of AT&T. It has about 215,000 employees and a market capitalization of about $168 billion.

EARNINGS PER SHARE PROGRESSION

Past 4 years: 35 percent (8 percent per year)

REVENUE GROWTH ★ ★ ★

Past 4 years: 104 percent (20 percent per year)

STOCK GROWTH ★

Past 4 years: 69 percent (14 percent per year, including dividends)
Dollar growth: $10,000 over 4 years would have grown to about $17,000.

CONSISTENCY ★ ★

Positive earnings progression: 2 of the past 4 years
Increased sales: 4 consecutive years

SBC COMMUNICATIONS AT A GLANCE

Fiscal year ended: Dec. 31
Revenue and net income in $billions

	1996	1997	1998	1999	2000	4-Year Growth Avg. Annual (%)	4-Year Growth Total (%)
Revenue ($)	25.2	43.1	46.2	49.5	51.5	20	104
Net income ($)	3.39	4.08	7.73	6.57	7.97	24	135
Earnings/share ($)	1.72	1.20	2.24	1.90	2.32	8	35
PE range	13–17	20–31	15–24	23–31	15–25		

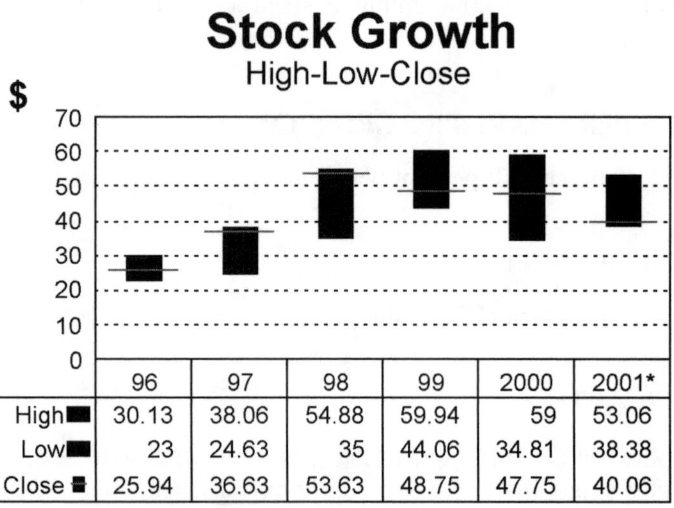

	96	97	98	99	2000	2001*
High	30.13	38.06	54.88	59.94	59	53.06
Low	23	24.63	35	44.06	34.81	38.38
Close	25.94	36.63	53.63	48.75	47.75	40.06

*2001 price as of July 1

95

Verizon Communications

1095 Avenue of the Americas, 36th Floor
New York, NY 10036
212-395-2121
NYSE: VZ
www.verizon.com

Chairman and Co-CEO: Charles R. Lee
President and Co-CEO: Ivan Seidenberg

Earnings Progression	★ ★
Revenue Growth	
Stock Growth	★ ★
Consistency	★ ★
Total	**6 Points**

What's on the horizon for Verizon? A larger presence in the fast-growing fields of data communications and wireless communications is a top priority for the telecommunications giant that was created by the 2000 merger of GTE and Bell Atlantic.

The company wants to be a key player in data communications, which is growing at a rate of 30 percent a year. The wireless market is expected to be just as buoyant, with more than a billion users worldwide by 2005.

The company has wasted no time in making its presence known since its creation in 2000. Verizon is already the nation's largest local telephone company with more than 67 million access lines in 31 states and the District of Columbia. Verizon Wireless is the largest wireless provider in the U.S. and offers service in 96 of the country's top 100 markets.

Verizon Wireless has been adding about 4 million customers a year, with a total customer base of nearly 30 million. British telecom powerhouse Vodaphone owns 45 percent of Verizon Wireless, which combines Vodaphone AirTouch, GTE's and Bell Atlantic's wireless business.

Verizon's other new ventures include the launch of long distance service in New York and the establishment of high-speed Internet access over digital subscriber lines, or DSL. On the international front, Verizon has operations in 19 countries with 4 million access lines and 8 billion wireless customers.

More than 40 percent of the company's revenues derive from wireless, data, international, and information services.

The company sees strong demand for its services in the coming years. It expects to expand the footprint of its long distance business as it muscles into the turf traditionally held by AT&T, WorldCom, and Sprint. DSL service will also drive future growth as both residential and commercial customers demand quicker Internet connections.

The company has about 260,000 employees and a market capitalization of about $132 billion.

EARNINGS PER SHARE PROGRESSION ★★

Past 4 years: 99 percent (19 percent per year)

REVENUE GROWTH

Past 4 years: 28 percent (6 percent per year)

STOCK GROWTH ★★

Past 4 years: 80 percent (16 percent per year, including dividends)
Dollar growth: $10,000 over 4 years would have grown to about $18,000.

CONSISTENCY ★★

Increased earnings per share: 2 consecutive years
Increased sales: 4 consecutive years

VERIZON COMMUNICATIONS AT A GLANCE

Fiscal year ended: Dec. 31
Revenue and net income in $billions

	1996	1997	1998	1999	2000	4-Year Growth Avg. Annual (%)	4-Year Growth Total (%)
Revenue ($)	50.5	53.5	57.1	58.2	64.7	6	28
Net income ($)	5.94	5.48	5.64	8.45	11.0	17	85
Earnings/share ($)	2.16	1.89	1.79	2.97	4.31	19	99
PE range	25–34	30–48	21–55	16–23	9–16		

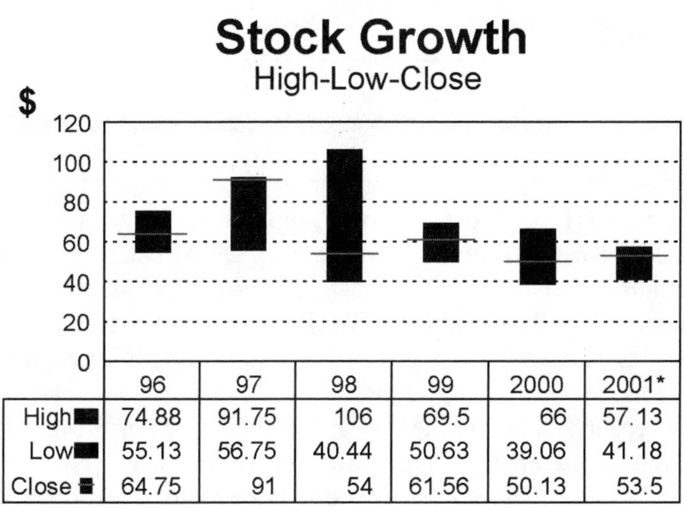

	96	97	98	99	2000	2001*
High	74.88	91.75	106	69.5	66	57.13
Low	55.13	56.75	40.44	50.63	39.06	41.18
Close	64.75	91	54	61.56	50.13	53.5

*2001 price as of July 1

96

Applied Biosystems Group

761 Main Avenue
Norwalk, CT 06859
203-762-1000
NYSE: ABI
www.appliedbiosystems.com

Chairman, President, and CEO: Tony L. White

Earnings Progression	
Revenue Growth	★ ★ ★
Stock Growth	★
Consistency	★ ★
Total	**6 Points**

In the complex world of biotechnology, Applied Biosystems makes the tools that scientists need to solve the mysteries of DNA. The Norwalk, Connecticut operation develops instrument-based systems, reagents, and software for biotechnology research. The firm's instrument systems are used for nucleic acid synthesis, Polymerase Chain Reaction DNA sequencing, genetic analysis, and cellular detection. These products and services are used in both research and commercial applications for purifying, analyzing, synthesizing, sequencing, and amplifying genetic material.

Applied Biosystems is one of two operating units of Applera Corp. (along with Celera Genomics Group). The two operating units function separately and trade on the New York Stock Exchange as separate "tracking" stocks.

Applied Biosystems offers products that fall into several specific categories, including:

- **Polymerase Chain Reaction (PCR) products.** The company makes PCR amplification products that help scientists duplicate or amplify a short strand of DNA so that it can be more readily detected and analyzed.

- **Genetic analysis.** The firm's products help researchers separate molecules based on their differential mobility in an electric field. The company's genetic analysis products generally perform both DNA sequencing and fragment analysis.
- **DNA synthesis.** The firm makes DNA synthesizers that are used to produce synthetic DNA for genetic analysis. The synthetic DNA is used for PCR and DNA sequencing primers and is also used in drug discovery applications.
- **Peptide nucleic acid (PNA).** Applied Biosystems has an exclusive license to manufacture and sell PNA for molecular biology research and various other applications. PNA is a synthetic copy of a DNA molecule with a modified uncharged peptidelike "backbone." The unique chemical structure of PNA enhances its affinity and specificity as a DNA or RNA probe.
- **Cellular detection systems.** The company is helping develop a fluorometric microvolume assay technology system, which uses proprietary scanning technology to detect and measure fluorescence associated with objects as small as a single cell.

Founded in 1981, the company has about 4,000 employees and a market capitalization of about $10 billion.

EARNINGS PER SHARE PROGRESSION

Past 3 years: 6 percent (1.5 percent per year)

REVENUE GROWTH ★ ★ ★

Past 3 years: 81 percent (21 percent per year)

STOCK GROWTH ★

Past 2 years: 30 percent (14 percent per year)
Dollar growth: $10,000 over the past 2 years would have grown to about $13,000.

CONSISTENCY ★ ★

Increased earnings per share: 1 of the past 3 years
Increased sales: 3 consecutive years

APPLIED BIOSYSTEMS AT A GLANCE

Fiscal year ended: June 30
Revenue and net income in $millions

	1996	1997	1998	1999	2000	4-Year Growth Avg. Annual (%)	4-Year Growth Total (%)
Revenue ($)	NA	767	940	1,222	1,388	21	81
Net income ($)	NA	133	29.6	162	186	12	40
Earnings/share ($)	NA	0.81	0.32	1.10	0.86	1.5	6
PE range	NA	NA	NA	34–87	49–186		

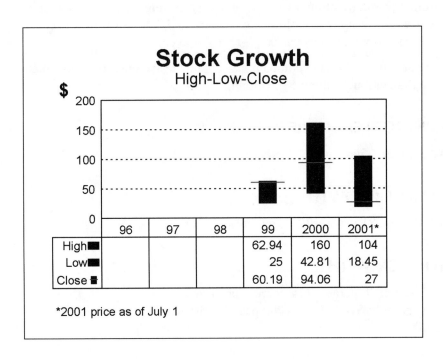

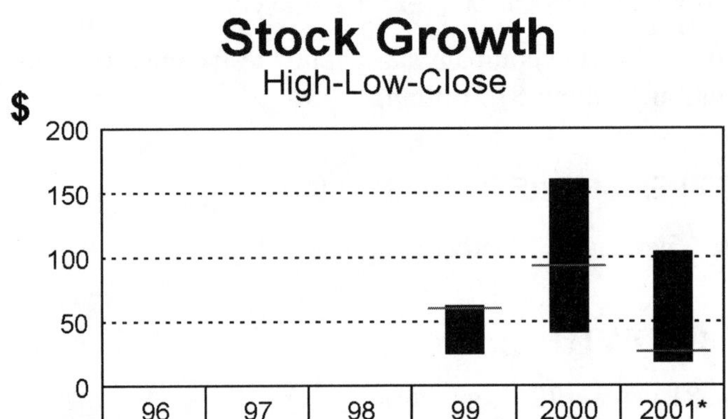

	96	97	98	99	2000	2001*
High				62.94	160	104
Low				25	42.81	18.45
Close				60.19	94.06	27

*2001 price as of July 1

97
Exodus Communications

2831 Mission College Boulevard
Santa Clara, CA 95054
408-346-2200
Nasdaq: EXDS
www.exodus.com

Chairman and CEO: Ellen M. Hancock
President: Don Casey

Earnings Progression	
Revenue Growth	★ ★ ★ ★
Stock Growth	★
Consistency	★
Total	**6 Points**

Behind the closely guarded walls of its 40 Internet Data Centers around the world, Exodus Communications powers some of the Internet's biggest Web sites. The Santa Clara, California operation is the world's leading Web hosting company, providing hosting services for Yahoo!, eBay, USA Today, British Airways, and about 5,000 other companies.

Exodus pioneered the concept of building data centers expressly to handle the demands of high-volume Web site operations. The company's customers don't have to worry about such things as security, maintenance, facilities, or staffing—Exodus handles everything.

Exodus's business model differs from most Web hosting services. Instead of renting time on computers it owns, it houses customer-owned computers in locked cages and operates them according to the customer's instructions. Exodus has earned a reputation for expertise in keeping large sites up and running fast. And in the security-conscious Internet world, Exodus runs a tight ship. Its 40 Internet Data Centers, which are connected by a high-speed data network, are all protected with motion sensors,

24-hour-a-day secured access, video surveillance cameras, and security breach alarms.

Exodus earns about 42 percent of its revenue from Web hosting services, 38 percent from managed and professional services, and 20 percent from Internet connectivity services. The company provides performance monitoring, site management reports, data backup, content delivery and management services, and security services. The firm also integrates best-of-breed technologies from leading vendors with its industry expertise and proprietary technology.

Although the growth of the Internet has slowed, Exodus is in a position to benefit from future expansion of the Web. Web server hosting is essential for any company that wants to go online, and Exodus is the worldwide leader in that market.

Founded in 1995, Exodus went public with its initial stock offering in 1998. It has about 1,700 employees and a market capitalization of about $6 billion.

EARNINGS PER SHARE PROGRESSION

The company has had a string of losses.

REVENUE GROWTH ★★★★

Past 4 years: 26,034 percent (129 percent per year)

STOCK GROWTH ★

Past 3 years: 32 percent (10 percent per year)
Dollar growth: $10,000 over 3 years would have grown to about $13,000.

CONSISTENCY ★

Positive earnings progression: 1 of the past 4 years
Increased sales: 4 consecutive years

EXODUS COMMUNICATIONS AT A GLANCE

Fiscal year ended: Dec. 31
Revenue and net income in $millions

	1996	1997	1998	1999	2000	3-Year Growth Avg. Annual (%)	3-Year Growth Total (%)
Revenue ($)	3.13	12.4	52.7	242	818	129	26,034
Net income ($)	–4.13	–25.3	–67.3	–130	–248	NA	NA
Earnings/share ($)	–0.13	–0.87	–0.28	–0.39	–0.63	NA	NA
PE range	NA	NA	NA	NA	NA		

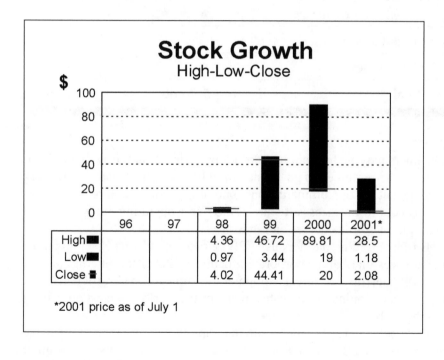

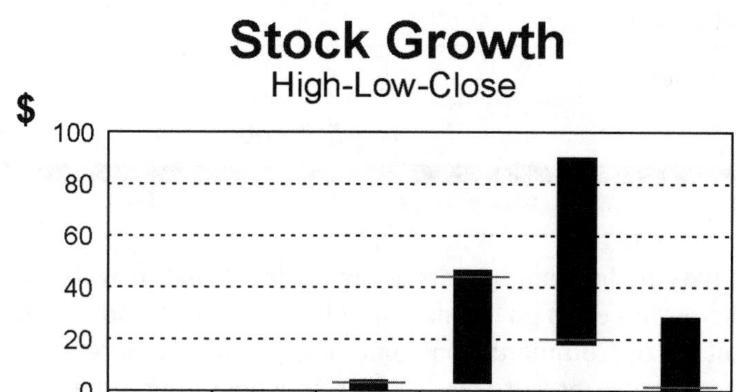

	96	97	98	99	2000	2001*
High			4.36	46.72	89.81	28.5
Low			0.97	3.44	19	1.18
Close			4.02	44.41	20	2.08

*2001 price as of July 1

98

Commerce One, Inc.

4440 Rosewood Drive
Pleasanton, CA 94588
925-520-6000
Nasdaq: CMRC
www.commerceone.com

Chairman and CEO: Mark B. Hoffman
President: Robert M. Kimmitt

Earnings Progression	
Revenue Growth	★★★★
Stock Growth	
Consistency	★
Total	**5 Points**

Consumers may be hesitant to start doing business on the Web, but businesses are being forced to go online or fall behind. That trend should work to the advantage of Commerce One, one of the world leaders in developing business-to-business software (B2B) and operating Internet digital marketplaces for businesses and industries.

Business trading partners use B2B software platforms to set up online marketplaces that handle corporate procurement over the Internet instead of via phone, fax, or direct computer file transfer. The efficiencies of doing business online have pushed many of the world's biggest operations onto the Web.

Commerce One has tapped into that rapidly growing market from two fronts. It sells B2B software products that businesses can use to set up or operate a B2B Web site, and it operates a number of specialized digital marketplaces for various businesses and industries, collecting a small commission on each sale made.

The Silicon Valley operation offers a number of products and services, including:

- **Global Trading Web.** This worldwide trading community comprises many vertical marketplaces and is operated by Commerce One using its own software. It also provides services including content management, order availability information, status tracking, and transaction support.
- **Public e-marketplace solution.** This integrated set of software products and services enables companies to build and run e-marketplace businesses focused on automating inter-company business processes. The firm also offers a private e-marketplace option for companies that want to build their own sites.
- **MarketSite operating environment.** This is the foundation for over 140 e-marketplaces as well as the Global Trading Web. Aspiring Internet market makers use this software package to set up digital marketplaces of their own. Customers can buy the software and run it themselves or let Commerce One host it for a fee.

Founded in 1994, Commerce One went public with its initial stock offering in 1999. The company has about 600 employees and a market capitalization of about $2 billion.

EARNINGS PER SHARE PROGRESSION

The company has posted a string of losses.

REVENUE GROWTH ★★★★

Past 4 years: 49,407 percent (371 percent per year)

STOCK GROWTH

Past 2 years (since IPO): Even
Dollar growth: $10,000 over 2 years would have stayed at about $10,000.

CONSISTENCY ★

Positive earnings progression: None
Increased sales: 4 consecutive years

COMMERCE ONE AT A GLANCE

Fiscal year ended: Dec. 31
Revenue and net income in $millions

	1996	1997	1998	1999	2000	4-Year Growth	
						Avg. Annual (%)	Total (%)
Revenue ($)	0.812	1.75	2.56	33.5	402	371	49,407
Net income ($)	–1.8	–11.2	–24.6	–63.3	–335	NA	NA
Earnings/share ($)	–0.11	–0.70	–1.37	–0.74	–2.05	NA	NA
PE range	NA	NA	NA	NA	NA		

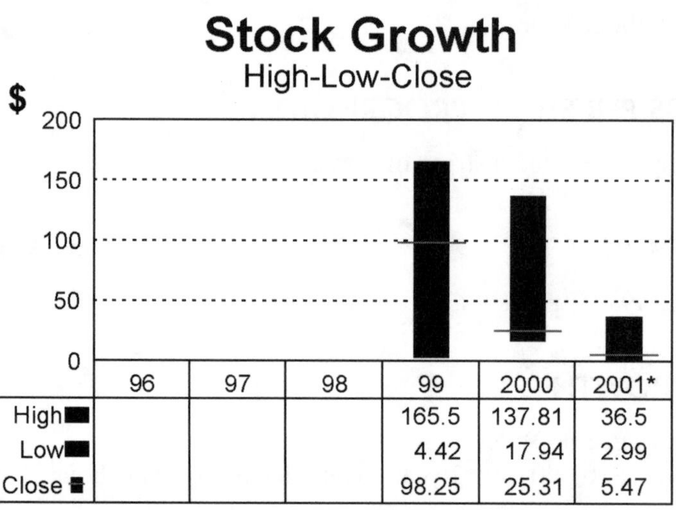

	96	97	98	99	2000	2001*
High				165.5	137.81	36.5
Low				4.42	17.94	2.99
Close				98.25	25.31	5.47

*2001 price as of July 1

99

DoubleClick, Inc.

450 West 33rd Street
New York, NY 10001
212-683-0001
Nasdaq: DCLK
www.doubleclick.com

Chairman: Kevin J. O'Connor
CEO: Kevin P. Ryan

Earnings Progression	
Revenue Growth	★ ★ ★ ★
Stock Growth	
Consistency	★
Total	**5 Points**

Like many of the nation's elite advertising agencies, DoubleClick has its headquarters on New York's Madison Avenue. But there is something very different about DoubleClick. The company focuses exclusively on online advertising.

DoubleClick is the leader of the online advertising market, helping Web publishers large and small attract advertisers to their sites. In the process, the company siphons off a full 30 to 50 percent of the ad revenue it collects before passing the balance onto the sites that run the ads.

Although the market for online advertising declined dramatically with the Internet meltdown of 2000, DoubleClick is well positioned to capitalize on the future growth of Web advertising. The company serves about 2,000 online advertisers worldwide, delivering more than 60 billion ad hits per month for its advertising clients.

The company uses a technology it terms "Dynamic Advertising, Reporting and Targeting" (DART), which tracks ad results and uses those results to identify the best targets for those specific ads. The company can also handle planning and execution of online media campaigns for its customers.

The company offers a range of specialized services for its customers, including DoubleClick Techsolutions and DoubleClick Media, which enable companies to advertise on the Web through various Web sites and through a special e-mail ad service. Its DoubleClick Publishers Service is geared to publishers who want to target their ads, and its Advertisers Service is geared to agencies who want to streamline and control their online ad campaigns.

DoubleClick also owns Abacus Direct, which manages the nation's largest database of consumer buying behavior information used for target marketing on the Internet and through direct mail.

DoubleClick is not involved in the creative end of the advertising market, leaving that to its advertising clients.

The company went public with its initial stock offering in 1998. DoubleClick has about 2,000 employees and a market capitalization of about $2 billion.

EARNINGS PER SHARE PROGRESSION

The company has had a string of increasing losses.

REVENUE GROWTH ★★★★

Past 4 years: 7,673 percent (196 percent per year)

STOCK GROWTH

Past 3 years: 18 percent (5 percent per year)
Dollar growth: $10,000 over 3 years would have grown to about $12,000.

CONSISTENCY ★

Positive earnings progression: None
Increased sales: 4 consecutive years

DOUBLECLICK AT A GLANCE

Fiscal year ended: Dec. 31
Revenue and net income in $millions

	1996	1997	1998	1999	2000	4-Year Growth Avg. Annual (%)	4-Year Growth Total (%)
Revenue ($)	6.51	67.9	139	258	506	196	7,673
Net income ($)	–3.19	–7.74	–18	–55.8	–157	NA	NA
Earnings/share ($)	–0.07	–0.16	–0.21	–0.51	–1.29	NA	NA
PE range	NA	NA	NA	NA	NA		

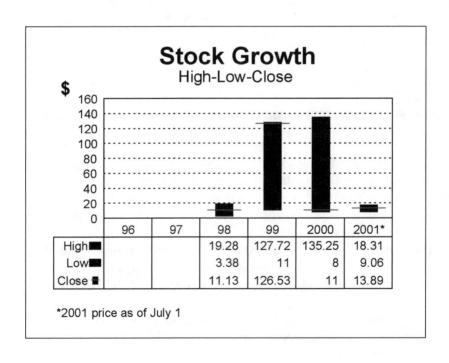

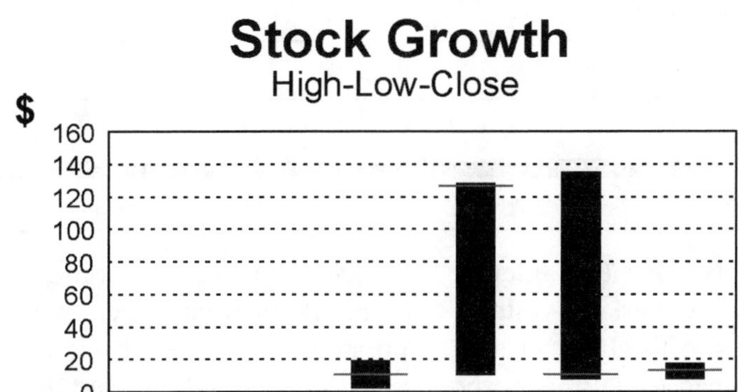

	96	97	98	99	2000	2001*
High			19.28	127.72	135.25	18.31
Low			3.38	11	8	9.06
Close			11.13	126.53	11	13.89

*2001 price as of July 1

100
Redback Networks, Inc.

1195 Borregas Avenue
Sunnyvale, CA 94089
408-571-5200
Nasdaq: RBAK
www.redback.com

Chairman: Pierre R. Lamond
President and CEO: Vivek Ragavan

Earnings Progression	
Revenue Growth	★ ★ ★ ★
Stock Growth	
Consistency	★
Total	**5 Points**

Redback Networks helps Internet and telecommunications companies set up advanced networking systems that provide their customers with high-speed access to the Internet and corporate networks. Redback's product line is designed to help its corporate customers rapidly create their own end-to-end broadband networks.

The company's line of advanced networking systems is being used by many of the world's largest telecommunications carriers and service providers, such as Bell South, Korea Telecom, Qwest, SBC, MCI World-com, and Verizon.

The Sunnyvale, California operation offers sophisticated data switching systems that combine networking hardware and software. The three key product lines include:

- **Subscriber management systems.** These systems connect and manage large numbers of subscribers across major high-speed access technologies. They are designed to bridge the operational gap between the devices used to gather together high-speed Internet users at one end of the network and the devices at the other end of the network, such as routers that are used to connect to the Internet.

- **SmartEdge.** The SmartEdge optical and multiservice networking products simplify the architecture of regional voice and data networks and improve their capacity and performance.
- **Service management products.** These software products allow service providers to publish, activate, and manage Internet Protocol services and allow their customers to subscribe to these services on demand.

The advantage of subscriber management systems over normal switches and routers is flexibility. Network managers can configure customer circuits without touching hardware. The ability to customize service offerings to fit customer needs is increasingly important to network providers as a way to hold onto customers and keep margins up in the face of rising competition.

Redback markets its products through a direct sales force, resellers, and distribution partners worldwide.

The company went public with its initial stock offering in 1999. Redback has about 1,200 employees and a market capitalization of about $3 billion.

EARNINGS PER SHARE PROGRESSION

The company has had a string of losses that continued into 2001.

REVENUE GROWTH ★ ★ ★ ★

Past 2 years: 2,922 percent (440 percent per year)

STOCK GROWTH

Past 2 years (since the IPO): Even
Dollar growth: $10,000 over 2 years would have remained at about $10,000.

CONSISTENCY ★

Positive earnings progression per share: None
Increased sales: 3 consecutive years

REDBACK NETWORKS AT A GLANCE

Fiscal year ended: Dec. 31
Revenue and net income in $millions

	1996	1997	1998	1999	2000	2-Year Growth Avg. Annual (%)	2-Year Growth Total (%)
Revenue ($)	NA	0.048	9.2	64.3	278	440	2,922
Net income ($)	NA	–4.4	–9.8	–7.9	–1,007	NA	NA
Earnings/share ($)	NA	–0.09	–0.19	–0.15	–8.68	NA	NA
PE range	NA	NA	NA	NA	NA		

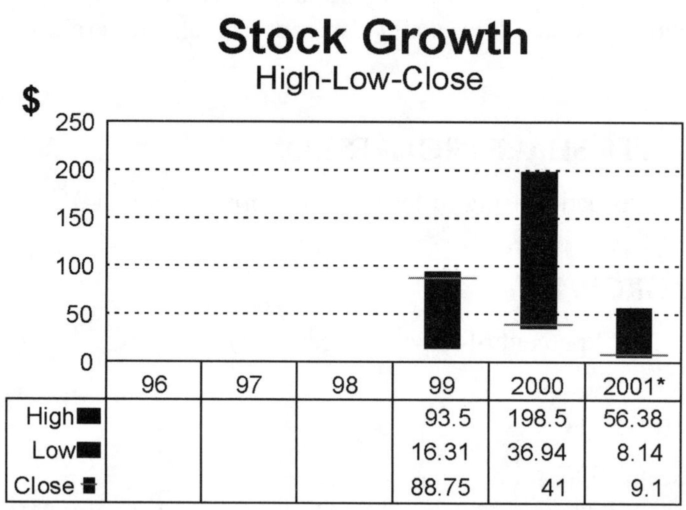

*2001 price as of July 1

The 100 Best Technology Stocks by Industry Sector

Industry Sector	Ranking
BIOTECH AND MEDICAL	
Affymetrix, Inc.	82
Amgen, Inc.	71
Applied Biosystems Group	96
Genentech, Inc.	86
Immunex Corp.	12
MedImmune, Inc.	30
Medtronic, Inc.	52
COMPUTERS AND PERIPHERALS	
Advanced Digital Information Corp.	17
Celestica, Inc.	45
Dell Computer Corp.	6
EMC Corp.	4
Extreme Networks, Inc.	89
International Business Machines	70
Mercury Computer Systems, Inc.	11
Network Appliance, Inc.	22
Palm, Inc.	91
Research In Motion, Ltd.	66
Tech Data Corp.	75
BUSINESS AND CONSUMER SERVICES	
Clear Channel Communications	33
The InterCept Group, Inc.	61
TeleTech Holdings, Inc.	78
Verizon Communications	95
ENERGY	
AstroPower, Inc.	31
INSTRUMENTS AND EQUIPMENT	
BEI Technologies, Inc.	54
Newport Corp.	34
United Technologies	92

Industry Sector	Ranking
INTERNET	
E-commerce	
Amazon.com, Inc.	85
AOL Time Warner Inc.	37
CheckFree Corp.	68
Commerce One, Inc.	98
DoubleClick, Inc.	99
eBay, Inc.	36
Yahoo! Inc.	35
Infrastructure	
Check Point Software Technology	3
Cisco Systems, Inc.	27
Exodus Communications	97
IntraNet Solutions, Inc.	93
Internet Security Systems	39
Juniper Networks, Inc.	7
Macromedia, Inc.	76
Mercury Interactive Corp.	1
VeriSign, Inc.	29
Verity, Inc.	50
NETWORKING	
Brocade Communications	10
Foundry Networks, Inc.	77
Sun Microsystems, Inc.	25
OUTSOURCING	
Celestica, Inc.	45
Flextronics International	5
Jabil Circuit, Inc.	14
Sanmina Corp.	15
SEMICONDUCTORS	
Advanced Micro Devices	67
Altera Corp.	21
Analog Devices, Inc.	49
Applied Materials	47
Broadcom Corp.	23

Industry Sector	Ranking
SEMICONDUCTORS, continued	
Cypress Semiconductor	83
Flextronics International	5
Intel Corp.	81
Jabil Circuit, Inc.	14
Linear Technology Corp.	46
Maxim Integrated Products	26
Microchip Technology, Inc.	63
Micron Technology, Inc.	88
Novellus Systems, Inc.	80
NVIDIA Corp.	32
PMC-Sierra, Inc.	53
Semtech Corp.	20
Texas Instruments	72
TriQuint Semiconductor, Inc.	19
Vishay Intertechnology, Inc.	38
Vitesse Semiconductor Corp.	60
Xilinx, Inc.	28
SOFTWARE	
Adobe Systems, Inc.	58
Avant! Corp.	73
BEA Systems, Inc.	55
Citrix Systems, Inc.	9
Electronic Arts, Inc.	51
i2 Technologies, Inc.	74
Micromuse, Inc.	69
Microsoft Corp.	8
Moldflow Corp.	90
Oracle Corp.	24
Rational Software Corp.	59
Retek, Inc.	84
Siebel Systems, Inc.	16
SunGard Data Systems, Inc.	41
Take-Two Interactive Software	43
Veritas Software Corp.	56

Industry Sector	Ranking
TELECOMMUNICATIONS	
ADC Telecommunications	62
Cable Design Technologies	64
China Mobile Limited	57
CIENA Corp.	40
Comverse Technology, Inc.	48
Corning, Inc.	87
Digital Lightwave, Inc.	44
JDS Uniphase Corp.	79
Nokia Corp.	2
Polycom, Inc.	18
Redback Networks, Inc.	100
SBC Communications, Inc.	94
Tellabs, Inc.	42
Vodafone Group PLC	65
ViaSat, Inc.	13

The 100 Best Technology Stocks by State/Country

State	Ranking
ARIZONA	
Microchip Technology, Inc. (Chandler)	63
CALIFORNIA	
Adobe Systems, Inc. (San Jose)	58
Advanced Micro Devices (Sunnyvale)	67
Affymetrix, Inc. (Santa Clara)	82
Altera Corp. (San Jose)	21
Amgen, Inc. (Thousand Oaks)	71
Applied Materials (Santa Clara)	47
Avant! Corp. (Fremont)	73
BEA Systems, Inc. (San Jose)	55
BEI Technologies, Inc. (San Francisco)	54
Broadcom Corp. (Irvine)	23
Brocade Communications (San Jose)	10
Cisco Systems, Inc. (San Jose)	27
Commerce One, Inc. (Pleasanton)	98
Cypress Semiconductor (San Jose)	83
eBay, Inc. (San Jose)	36
Electronic Arts, Inc. (Redwood City)	51
Exodus Communications (Santa Clara)	97
Extreme Networks, Inc. (Santa Clara)	89
Foundry Networks, Inc. (San Jose)	77
Genentech, Inc. (South San Francisco)	86
Intel Corp. (Santa Clara)	81
JDS Uniphase Corp. (San Jose)	79
Juniper Networks, Inc. (Sunnyvale)	7
Linear Technology Corp. (Milpitas)	46
Macromedia, Inc. (San Francisco)	76
Maxim Integrated Products (Sunnyvale)	26
Mercury Interactive Corp. (Sunnyvale)	1
Micromuse, Inc. (San Francisco)	69
Network Appliance, Inc. (Sunnyvale)	22
Newport Corp. (Irvine)	34
Novellus Systems, Inc. (San Jose)	80
NVIDIA Corp. (Santa Clara)	32

State	Ranking
CALIFORNIA, continued	
Oracle Corp. (Redwood Shores)	24
Palm, Inc. (Santa Clara)	91
PMC-Sierra, Inc. (Campbell)	53
Polycom, Inc. (Milpitas)	18
Rational Software Corp. (Cupertino)	59
Redback Networks, Inc. (Sunnyvale)	100
Sanmina Corp. (San Jose)	15
Semtech Corp. (Newbury Park)	20
Siebel Systems, Inc. (San Mateo)	16
Sun Microsystems, Inc. (Palo Alto)	25
VeriSign, Inc. (Mountain View)	29
Veritas Software Corp. (Mountain View)	56
Verity, Inc. (Sunnyvale)	50
ViaSat, Inc. (Carlsbad)	13
Vitesse Semiconductor Corp. (Camarillo)	60
Xilinx, Inc. (San Jose)	28
Yahoo! Inc. (Santa Clara)	35
COLORADO	
TeleTech Holdings, Inc. (Denver)	78
CONNECTICUT	
Applied Biosystems Group (Norwalk)	96
United Technologies (Hartford)	92
DELAWARE	
AstroPower, Inc. (Newark)	31
FLORIDA	
Citrix Systems, Inc. (Ft. Lauderdale)	9
Digital Lightwave, Inc. (Clearwater)	44
Jabil Circuit, Inc. (St. Petersburg)	14
Tech Data Corp. (Clearwater)	75
GEORGIA	
CheckFree Corp. (Norcross)	68
The InterCept Group, Inc. (Norcross)	61
Internet Security Systems (Atlanta)	39

State	Ranking
IDAHO	
Micron Technology, Inc. (Boise)	88
ILLINOIS	
Tellabs, Inc. (Lisle)	42
MARYLAND	
CIENA Corp. (Linthicum)	40
MedImmune, Inc. (Gaithersburg)	30
MASSACHUSETTS	
Analog Devices, Inc. (Norwood)	49
EMC Corp. (Hopkinton)	4
Mercury Computer Systems, Inc. (Chelmsford)	11
Moldflow Corp. (Wayland)	90
MINNESOTA	
ADC Telecommunications (Minnetonka)	62
IntraNet Solutions, Inc. (Eden Prairie)	93
Medtronic, Inc. (Minneapolis)	52
Retek, Inc. (Minneapolis)	84
NEW YORK	
Comverse Technology, Inc. (Woodbury)	48
Corning, Inc. (Corning)	87
DoubleClick, Inc.	99
International Business Machines (Armonk)	70
Take-Two Interactive Software (New York)	43
Verizon Communications (New York)	95
OREGON	
TriQuint Semiconductor (Hillsboro)	19
PENNSYLVANIA	
Cable Design Technologies (Pittsburgh)	64
SunGard Data Systems, Inc. (Wayne)	41
Vishay Intertechnology, Inc. (Malvern)	38

State	Ranking
TEXAS	
Clear Channel Communications (San Antonio)	33
Dell Computer Corp. (Round Rock)	6
i2 Technologies, Inc. (Dallas)	74
SBC Communications Inc. (San Antonio)	94
Texas Instruments (Dallas)	72
VIRGINIA	
AOL Time Warner Inc. (Dulles)	37
WASHINGTON	
Advanced Digital Information Corp. (Redmond)	17
Amazon.com, Inc. (Seattle)	85
Immunex Corp. (Seattle)	12
Microsoft Corp. (Redmond)	8

Country	Ranking
CANADA	
Celestica, Inc. (Toronto, Ontario)	45
Research In Motion, Ltd. (Waterloo, Ontario)	66
CHINA	
China Mobile Limited (Hong Kong)	57
FINLAND	
Nokia Corp. (Espoo)	2
ISRAEL	
Check Point Software Technology (Ramat-Gan)	3
SINGAPORE	
Flextronics International (Singapore)	5
UNITED KINGDOM	
Vodafone Group PLC (Newbury, Berkshire)	65

Index

L

M

N

W

X–Z